Esoteric Wisdom of
LALITA SAHASRANAMA
COSMIC SYMPHONY

Vinita Rashinkar

ISBN
Hardcase 979-8-89588-633-5
Paperback 979-8-89556-344-1

Devi Lalita Tripurasundari

Lopamudra Devi

To Puja, Amit and Snowy

Sri Matrye Namah

Contents

Preface 9

Chapter 1   Introduction 15

Chapter 2   Poorva Bhaga 89

Chapter 3   Dhyana, Nyasa and Panchopachara Puja 97

Chapter 4   Madhyama Bhaga 111

Chapter 5   Moola Grantha (52-111) 137

Chapter 6   Names 112 to 200 172

Chapter 7   Names 201 to 300 193

Chapter 8   Names 301 to 400 233

Chapter 9   Names 401 to 534 256

Chapter 10   Names 535 to 600 283

Chapter 11   Names 601 to 700 297

Chapter 12   Names 701 to 800 317

Chapter 13   Names 801 to 900 336

Chapter 14   Names 901 to 1000 352

Contents

Chapter 15   Uttara Bhaga – Phala Shruti 369

Chapter 16   Namavali 385

References 425
Also by this Author 431

Preface

The eighteen Puranas, foundational to the Hindu religious and cultural tradition, are a rich blend of myth, legend, history, and spiritual teachings. These texts, composed over centuries, are classified into three broad categories based on the three primary deities of the Hindu pantheon – Brahma, Vishnu, and Shiva – who represent the forces of creation, preservation, and dissolution respectively. This classification reflects the three gunas: Sattva (purity and harmony), Rajas (activity and passion), and Tamas (inertia and darkness).

The Sattva Puranas, associated with Vishnu, include the Vishnu Purana, Bhagavata Purana, Narada Purana, Garuda Purana, Padma Purana, and Varaha Purana. These texts emphasize the qualities of righteousness, devotion, and the protection of the universe, often extolling the virtues of bhakti and the worship of Vishnu in his various avatars.

The Rajas Puranas, linked to Brahma, are the Brahmanda Purana, Brahmavaivarta Purana, Markandeya Purana, Bhavishya Purana, Vamana Purana, and Brahma Purana. These texts often focus on the creation of the universe, the genealogy of gods and sages, and the duties and responsibilities of individuals in society. They also explore the role of ritual and sacrifice in maintaining cosmic order.

The Tamas Puranas, associated with Shiva, include the Shiva Purana, Linga Purana, Skanda Purana, Agni Purana, Kurma Purana, and Matsya Purana. These texts are replete with stories of destruction and regeneration, emphasizing the transformative power of Shiva. They delve into the esoteric practices, the significance of sacred spaces (tirthas), and the worship of Shiva and his consort, Parvati, along with other deities.

Among these, the Brahmanda Purana holds a unique place, especially for followers of the Shakta tradition. As one of the Rajas Puranas, it not only discusses cosmology and the genealogical details of the universe but also contains significant Shakta material, including the Lalita Sahasranama. This hymn, which extols the thousand names of Goddess Lalita, is a cornerstone of the Sri Vidya tradition, revered for its deep spiritual meanings and the potent vibrations it is believed to carry. The Lalita Sahasranama within the Brahmanda Purana is more than just a devotional chant; it is an intricate guide to understanding the nature of the cosmos, the dynamics of energy, and the path to self-realization through the worship of the Divine Mother.

Commentaries on the Lalita Sahasranama began to emerge as scholars sought to delve deeper into the esoteric meanings of the names and to guide practitioners in their devotional practices. These commentaries serve not only as interpretations of the text but also as manuals for spiritual practice, integrating philosophy, ritual, and meditation. These commentaries vary in their approach, ranging from purely devotional interpretations to highly philosophical exegeses grounded in Vedantic and Tantric traditions.

Bhaskaracharya, also known as Bhaskararaya, is one of the most authoritative commentators on the Lalita Sahasranama. His work, Saubhagya Bhaskara, is considered a cornerstone in understanding the deeper nuances of the text. Bhaskararaya was a scholar and a practitioner of the Sri Vidya tradition, and his commentary reflects a synthesis of Tantra, Vedanta, and Bhakti. He elaborates on each name with references to Vedic literature, the Upanishads, and Tantric texts, emphasizing the non-dualistic nature of the Divine Mother as both the immanent and transcendent reality. Bhaskararaya's work is meticulous in its philosophical rigor and is regarded as a comprehensive guide for both scholars and practitioners.

Lakshmidhara, a scholar from the medieval period, wrote a popular commentary on the Lalita Sahasranama. His work is often noted for its clarity and accessibility, making it popular among a broader audience. Lakshmidhara interprets the names in a manner that highlights the devotional aspects, encouraging the reader to cultivate a personal relationship with the Divine Mother. His commentary is also noted for its integration of poetic elements, making it a work of literary as well as spiritual significance.

Swami Chidbhavananda, a 20th-century monk and scholar, provided a modern commentary on the Lalita Sahasranama that appeals to contemporary readers. His interpretation combines traditional insights with practical advice for spiritual aspirants in the modern world. Chidbhavananda's commentary is devotional but also seeks to explain the metaphysical principles underlying the names, making it suitable for those interested in both bhakti and jnana.

Another significant commentary is the Anandalahari, attributed to Adi Shankaracharya, which is more mystical and poetic in nature, focusing on the experiential aspects of the Lalita Sahasranama. It is particularly favored in the Sri Vidya tradition for its emphasis on the inner spiritual journey and the transformative power of the Divine Mother's grace.

Although not a traditional commentary in prose form, the South Indian composer Muthuswami Dikshitar's musical compositions on the Lalita Sahasranama provide an interpretative layer through the medium of Carnatic music. Dikshitar, a devout follower of the Sri Vidya tradition, composed kritis (devotional songs) that align with the names in the Lalita Sahasranama, thereby creating a unique commentary that blends music, devotion, and philosophy.

The various commentaries on the Lalita Sahasranama reflect different interpretative strategies, each rooted in the commentator's philosophical orientation and spiritual practice. Key themes across these commentaries include: Non-Dualism (Advaita Vedanta), Devotional Mysticism (Bhakti), Tantric Symbolism, and Integration of Shakti and Shiva.

Non-Dualism (Advaita Vedanta): Many commentaries, particularly those in the Sri Vidya tradition, emphasize the non-dual nature of

Lalita as the ultimate reality (Brahman) that manifests as the universe. Bhaskararaya's work is a prime example of this, where he explains each name in the context of non-dual philosophy, often correlating it with Upanishadic teachings.

Devotional Mysticism (Bhakti): Commentators like Lakshmidhara and Chidbhavananda emphasize the devotional aspect, interpreting the names as expressions of divine love and grace. This approach encourages the practitioner to surrender to Lalita and experience her presence in every aspect of life.

Tantric Symbolism: The Lalita Sahasranama is deeply embedded in Tantric symbolism, and this is explored extensively in commentaries like Bhaskararaya's. The names are seen as mantras, each holding specific vibrations and powers. The commentary often provides insight into the ritualistic and meditative practices associated with the recitation of the names.

Integration of Shakti and Shiva: The commentaries also explore the concept of Lalita as the embodiment of Shakti (Divine Energy) and her inseparable union with Shiva (Pure Consciousness). This theme is central to the Tantric interpretation of the text, where Lalita is both the dynamic force of creation and the stillness of pure awareness.

This book does not aim to be a commentary on the Lalita Sahasranama. My endeavor is to bring to common knowledge the secret, inner meanings that all the above-mentioned commentators have discussed in their works. Every name in this stotra is rich with undertones and analogies that are not so commonly known. Surely, there are tremendous benefits that come with merely chanting the Lalita Sahasranama without making an effort to comprehend its deeper nuances. But can one even begin to fathom how much more potent these thousand names will be when they are chanted after their meaning has been understood? It is stated in the Upanishads that any vidya is better assimilated when the ritual is performed upon serious study and profound understanding of its meaning.

All vidya is sacred and transformative. True knowledge is not just intellectual but must be experienced and internalized. One of the ways to internalize this knowledge is through rituals (karma or kriya). However, the Upanishads caution that performing rituals without understanding their underlying significance can be futile or even misleading. The proper performance of a ritual, therefore, requires serious study and profound understanding which are to be undertaken with dedication, seeking guidance from a guru or any source when necessary. Understanding the symbolism, purpose, and spiritual underpinnings transforms the ritual from a mere set of actions into a conscious practice that aligns the sadhaka with the deeper truths of the universe. When these elements – serious study and profound understanding – are in place, the ritual becomes a dynamic expression of the vidya, helping the practitioner to fully assimilate the knowledge into their being. It moves beyond the physical or mental plane and reaches the spiritual level, creating an inner transformation that leads to true wisdom or self-realization.

Chapter 1

Introduction

Yani Namasahasrani Sadhya: Siddhipradani Vai
Tantreshu Lalita Deveeyasteshu Mukhyamidam Mune

The Tantra Shastras enumerate several Sahasranamas known for yielding immediate results, with the Lalita Sahasranama being the foremost among them.

In Hindu spirituality, which deeply values dharma, moksha, karma, and yoga, the Lalita Sahasranama stands out as a profound treasure from the Tantra and Sri Vidya traditions. This revered hymn, comprising a thousand names embedded in 365 lines, extols the divine qualities of Lalita Tripurasundari. She is the radiant and compassionate goddess from the Dasa Mahavidya lineage, presiding over the cosmic dance of creation, preservation, and dissolution. Each of the thousand names is a sacred mantra, reflecting the poetic brilliance and profound spiritual insights of ancient seers.

Chanting the name of the Ishta Devata (personal deity) holds significant importance and is a key aspect of the Bhakti tradition. This adoration takes two forms: Japa and Stotra. Japa involves silently repeating a single divine name or mantra, a lengthy formula, while Stotra consists of verses sung aloud to praise the Divine. Among all stotras, the Sahasranama is especially cherished and sacred. Rooted in Vedic tradition, the concept of a single manifesting sound (Shabda) representing the Supreme Being is embodied in the sacred syllable 'Om.' Just as 'Om' represents the divine attributes and qualities in various sound forms, the Sahasranama elaborates on this divine name in a beautiful and evocative manner.

Sahasranama means one thousand names in Sanskrit, although one must understand it as meaning countless or infinite rather than an exact thousand in number. It is a type of stotra literature where a deity is praised through a list of a thousand names, attributes, or epithets. These texts, such as the Vishnu Sahasranama or Shiva Sahasranama, are essentially compositions that explore the deity's attributes, functions, and stories, serving as a comprehensive guide to the deity. They align with the Bhakti tradition and function as a means of devotion and worship.

Sahasranamas can vary in length; while many have a thousand names, shorter versions with 108 names, known as ashtottara-shata-nama, also exist. They serve different purposes in Sanatana practices:

- Shravana: Listening to recitals of the deity's names and glories
- Nama-sankirtana: Reciting the deity's names, sometimes set to music
- Smarana: Retelling divine stories and teachings
- Archana: Ritualistic worship through the repetition of divine names

Some of the most revered Sahasranamas include:

- Vishnu Sahasranama: Found in the Mahabharata and related Puranas
- Shiva Sahasranama: Also in the Mahabharata, with eight different versions
- Ganesha Sahasranama: In the Ganesha Purana
- Hanuman Sahasranama: Attributed to Ramachandra and found in Valmiki's work

Each Sahasranama serves as a unique invocation to a specific deity, encapsulating philosophical, theological, and ritualistic doctrines through its verses. The composition typically includes six key elements: salutation, benediction, statement of doctrine, praise of the deity, detailed exploration of attributes, and a concluding prayer, offering a holistic exploration of the deity.

The Lalita Sahasranama Stotra is a part of the Lalitopakhyana, which can be found in the fourth pada of the Brahmanda Purana, which is the last of the 18 great Puranas. The Lalitopakhyana has several divisions, such as the Mantra Kanda, Pooja Kanda, Homa Kanda, etc. The Lalita Sahasranama forms a part of the Stotra Kanda along with the Shyamala and Varahi Sahasranamas.

The Lalita Sahasranama is a conversation between Hayagriva and Agastya. The total from the beginning to the end is 182.5 stanzas (each comprising of 2 lines). Thus, the total number of lines is 365, with each line standing for one day in a year. The hymn is divided into three parts:

1. Poorva Bhaga, which describes the origins of the hymn
2. Madhyama Bhaga, which contains the 1000 names
3. Uttara Bhaga, which is the Phala Shruti, defines the results obtained from chanting the names.

Hayagriva, an avatar of Vishnu and the deity of knowledge and wisdom, was worshipped by Agastya and his wife Lopamudra Devi. Instead of directly imparting Sri Vidya knowledge, Hayagriva manifested a sage named Hayagriva, who then initiated Agastya into the Lalita Sahasranama and Sri Vidya worship. This Sahasranama is unique as it was composed by the Vag Devatas under Lalita's direction. All these aspects are covered in the chapter titled Poorva Bhaga.

The Lalita Sahasranama is unique and set apart from other Sahasranamas for several reasons:

It is not merely a collection of names but a profound text that encapsulates the entire metaphysical and theological framework of the Shakta tradition, particularly the Sri Vidya school of thought. Lalita Tripurasundari is seen as the embodiment of the supreme reality, Parabrahman, and the text reflects her as the ultimate cause of the universe, both immanent and transcendent. She is called Lalita, which means "the playful one," indicating her dynamic aspect in creating, sustaining, and dissolving the universe. Tripura signifies her presence in the three states of consciousness (waking, dreaming, and deep sleep), and Sundari means the beautiful one, reflecting her transcendental and immanent beauty.

The Lalita Sahasranama is central to the practice of Sri Vidya, a tantric tradition that involves the worship of the Divine Mother as the ultimate reality and the source of all creation. The hymn reflects the esoteric teachings of Sri Vidya, particularly the significance of the Sri Chakra and the Mantra of Lalita.

It is unique in its structure and the way it is composed. Unlike other Sahasranamas, which list the names in a relatively straightforward manner, the Lalita Sahasranama is composed in the form of a dialogue format, which adds a narrative element to the text, setting it apart from the other Sahasranamas. The text begins with Sage Agastya seeking knowledge from Hayagriva about the Supreme Goddess, leading to the revelation of the thousand names of Lalita. This story is woven into the Sahasranama, giving it a rich narrative context that is absent in many other Sahasranamas.

The Lalita Sahasranama is embedded with esoteric meanings that are central to Tantric worship, particularly the worship of the Sri Chakra. Many of the names are coded references to various aspects of tantric practice, the chakras and the kundalini. It emphasises the worship of the Sri Chakra, which is considered the yantra of Lalita Tripurasundari. The Sri Chakra is a geometric representation of the universe and the body of the Goddess, and the Sahasranama is recited in conjunction with its worship.

The Lalita Sahasranama is not only a theological and philosophical text but also a powerful tool for spiritual practice. It is linked to the awakening of Kundalini energy, which is said to rise through the chakras during the recitation, leading to spiritual enlightenment. Many devotees recite the Lalita Sahasranama for protection against negative influences, to overcome obstacles, and for healing.

The Lalita Sahasranama has a profound influence not only in spiritual practice but also in the cultural and religious life of many Hindu communities. It is recited during festivals, special rituals, and personal devotional practices. The hymn is especially prominent during the Navaratri festival, a nine-night celebration dedicated to the Goddess. Reciting the Lalita Sahasranama during this period is considered highly auspicious. The text has been written about and revered by many saints, scholars, and poets throughout Indian history, adding to its cultural and spiritual richness.

The Lalita Sahasranama has three outstanding features:

1. There are exactly 1000 names, and no name is repeated.
2. There are no fillers such as Cha, Tu, Eva, Hi, Api, etc., which is a common feature that is seen in most compilations to fulfil the demands of the meter.
3. The entire 1000 names begin with 32 letters of the Sanskrit alphabet. The reason why 19 letters are not used by the Vag Devis is not known. Manblunder writes in his blog: "In the mantra initiation procedures of Devi, there are thirty-two types of diksha (types of initiation). Yet another interpretation is also possible. This Sahasranamam starts only with 32 letters out of the 51 alphabets in Sanskrit. This 32 represents Her teeth. This could also mean that the initiation into Sri Vidya is to be done verbally by Guru to his disciple."

Let us now look into the profound esoteric meanings of the Lalita Sahasranama, covering a range of topics, including an introduction to the ancient, mystical tradition of Sri Vidya, the concept of non-duality as expressed through the teachings on the Divine Consciousness as the substratum of the ever-changing world, and the principle of Neti Neti. We will also discuss Lalita's control over the five aspects of creation, the dynamic interplay between Vimarsha and Prakasha, and the paths of Nivrutti and Pravrutti. The chapter will illuminate the symbolism of Bhandasura, the secrets of Kundalini and Chakras, the various paths within Sri Vidya, the significance of the Sri Chakra, and the concept of Leela. By drawing parallels between Lalita Sahasranama and the Brahma Sutra, we can uncover the intricate layers of wisdom embedded within this sacred text, offering a deeper understanding of its spiritual significance. Lalita Sahasranama, through its intricate descriptions and symbolic language, leads the seeker on a journey from duality (the worship of forms) to non-duality (the realisation of the formless, absolute reality).

Why do we worship the Divine in its Manifest Form?

Worshipping the Divine in its manifest form is a practice deeply rooted in many spiritual traditions, particularly in Hinduism. This form of worship, also known as Saguna or Sakara Upasana, involves venerating the Divine through tangible representations such as idols, images, or symbols. The reasons for this practice are multifaceted:

1. **Accessibility and Relatability**: The human mind often finds it challenging to comprehend the formless, infinite aspect of the Divine (Nirguna Brahman). Manifest forms provide a more accessible and relatable way to connect with the Divine, allowing worshippers to develop a personal and emotional bond.

2. **Symbolism and Focus**: The manifest forms of the Divine are not merely physical objects but are imbued with deep symbolic meanings. They serve as focal points for concentration and meditation, helping devotees to channel their spiritual energies towards a higher purpose.

3. **Divine Presence**: In many traditions, it is believed that the Divine can and does manifest in these forms when invoked with devotion and proper rituals. This belief holds that the deity becomes present in the idol or image, allowing devotees to experience the Divine's presence more directly.

4. **Facilitating Inner Transformation**: Worshipping the Divine in a manifest form is often seen as a preparatory step for more advanced spiritual practices. It helps in cultivating virtues like devotion, humility, and surrender, which are essential for progressing towards the realization of the formless Divine.

5. **Cultural Continuity and Tradition**: Manifest forms of the Divine are often deeply embedded in cultural and spiritual traditions. Worshipping these forms connects devotees to a lineage of practices and teachings that have been passed down through generations, creating a sense of continuity and belonging.

In his book 'Kamakala Vilasa', Arthur Avalon (also known as Sir John Woodruffe) wrote: "God may have no inherent name or form, but when we seek to build a relationship with God, we must clothe Him in some name and form. Similarly, the Bhagavad Gita addresses the concept of contemplating the unmanifest form of the Divine, particularly in Chapter 12, verses 1-7, where Lord Krishna discusses the relative merits of worshiping the formless, unmanifest aspect of the Divine versus the personal, manifest form. In response to Arjuna's question about which path is superior, worshiping the formless, unmanifest Brahman or the personal form of God, Krishna explains that both paths can lead to the ultimate goal, but each has its own challenges and characteristics.

Krishna acknowledges that contemplating the unmanifest form is difficult for most people. In verse 12:5, he states:

Greater is the difficulty of those whose minds are set on the Unmanifest; for the goal of the Unmanifested is very hard for the embodied to reach.

This verse highlights the inherent challenge of focusing on the formless, all-pervading Brahman. The unmanifest form is beyond the senses, thoughts, and imagination, making it an abstract and intangible concept. For those who are embodied living in the physical world and bound by the limitations of the mind and senses this path can be arduous. It requires intense concentration, detachment, and a highly disciplined mind capable of transcending all forms and attributes.

Krishna contrasts the difficulty of worshiping the unmanifest with the relative ease of focusing on a personal form of God. In verses 12:2-4, he explains that those who worship the personal form of the Divine, with faith and single-minded devotion, find it easier to achieve spiritual progress.

The personal form provides a tangible focus for devotion, allowing the devotee to express love, surrender, and service more naturally. However, Krishna also affirms that those who are steadfast in their practice, free from attachment, and even-minded in all circumstances can eventually realize the unmanifest Brahman. This suggests that while the path of the unmanifest is difficult, it is not impossible for those with the necessary qualities and dedication.

In the broader context, the unmanifest form of the Divine represents the highest, most abstract reality, Brahman, which is without attributes, beyond time, space, and causation. This path aligns with Jnana Yoga, the path of knowledge, where the goal is to realize the oneness of the individual self with the formless Brahman. In the Lalita Sahasranama each name encapsulates a different aspect of the Divine Mother, highlighting how she manifests in various forms and functions within the cosmos.

Names like Nirguna (One who is beyond all attributes) and Saguna (One who possesses attributes) illustrate how the Divine Mother embodies both the formless, attribute-less reality and the manifest, attribute-filled reality. The Lalita Sahasranama recognizes the unity of these two aspects, emphasizing that the manifest form is a doorway to understanding the formless essence. Other names describe Lalita as the embodiment of various cosmic principles and elements, such as Pancha-Kritya-Parayana (One who is engaged in the five cosmic acts of creation, preservation, dissolution, veiling, and grace). Through these names, the text acknowledges that the Divine Mother's manifest form is not merely symbolic but is a dynamic presence actively involved in the governance of the universe.

Names such Divyavigraha (One who has a divine body) highlight the importance of the Divine Mother's physical form as an object of devotion. These names invite devotees to contemplate and worship her in her divine, beautiful, and accessible forms, thus facilitating a personal connection with the Divine.

The Lalita Sahasranama extensively describes the Divine Mother's qualities, like Sukharadhya (She who can be worshipped with pleasure), Shubhakari (She who makes everything auspicious), and Bhavani (She who is the source of existence). These qualities are not abstract; they are manifested in the Mother's form and actions, making her an approachable and relatable figure for worshippers. The text also integrates the worship of the manifest form with the realization of the formless essence. For instance, names like Chidagnikunda-Sambhuta (One who emerged from the fire of consciousness) suggest that the Divine form of Lalita is born out of pure consciousness itself, linking the worship of her form to the ultimate realization of the non-dual reality. Names such as Guru Mandala Roopini (She who is the form of a group pf teachers) and Muktida Muktiroopini (One who grants liberation) emphasize that the Divine Mother, in her manifest form, is an instrument of grace. Worshipping her form leads to spiritual progress and ultimately to liberation, reflecting the belief that the manifest form is a vital means to transcendence.

The Lalita Sahasranama also portrays Lalita as Vishwagarbha (The womb of the universe) and Parapara (One who transcends the universe). These names suggest that the entire cosmos is a manifestation of her divine form, and by worshipping her, devotees connect with the universal aspect of the Divine.

Non-duality is expressed in the Lalita Sahasranama

Non-duality, or Advaita (literally meaning "not two"), is a profound philosophical and metaphysical concept that forms the cornerstone of various spiritual traditions, particularly within Hinduism, Buddhism, and certain mystical branches of other religions. At its core, non-duality posits that the ultimate reality is one indivisible whole, devoid of any inherent distinctions or separations. This idea challenges the common perception of the world as a collection of separate, individual entities and instead suggests that all phenomena, including the self, are manifestations of a single, undivided reality.

Advaita Vedanta is one of the most systematic and influential expressions of non-duality. The school is traditionally attributed to the philosopher Adi Shankaracharya (8th century CE), who articulated the core tenets of Advaita through his commentaries on the Upanishads, the Bhagavad Gita, and the Brahma Sutras. According to Advaita Vedanta, the ultimate reality is Brahman, which is described as Nirguna (without attributes), Nirvikalpa (without distinctions), and Aparoksha (immediate, direct experience). Brahman is the singular, infinite, and formless essence that pervades everything. The apparent multiplicity of the world, including the individual self, is considered an illusion The essential teaching of Advaita is encapsulated in the phrase "Tat Tvam Asi" ("Thou art That"), which expresses the identity of the individual self with Brahman.

In this view, the perception of duality of subject and object, self and other, creator and creation are a result of ignorance. Liberation is achieved through the realization that these distinctions are illusory and that the true nature of the self is non-different from Brahman. This realization is not merely intellectual but an experiential awakening to the oneness of all existence.

Non-duality challenges the conventional metaphysical assumptions about the nature of reality, particularly the dichotomy between the material and the spiritual, the finite and the infinite, and the self and the other. In a non-dual framework, these dichotomies are seen as artificial constructs that arise from limited perception and understanding.

One of the central implications of non-duality is the assertion that separateness is an illusion. The sense of being a distinct, autonomous individual is considered a fundamental misunderstanding of reality. This illusion of separateness leads to a host of other dualities such as those between mind and body, spirit and matter, good and evil that obscure the true nature of existence. In non-dual traditions, the goal is to see through these illusions and to recognize the underlying unity of all things. This recognition is described as a shift in consciousness, where the boundaries between self and other, subject and object, dissolve, revealing the interconnectedness of all life.

Non-duality has profound implications for our understanding of perception and cognition. In a dualistic framework, perception is seen as the interaction between a subject (the perceiver) and an object (the perceived). However, in a non-dual perspective, this distinction collapses. Perception is no longer a process of a separate self-interacting with an external world; rather, it is the unfolding of a single, unified consciousness.

This leads to a reinterpretation of the relationship between the observer and the observed. In non-dual awareness, the observer and the observed are not two separate entities but are expressions of the same underlying reality. The act of perception itself is seen as a manifestation of this unity, where the distinctions between subject and object are seen as provisional rather than absolute.

One of the most striking ways in which non-duality is expressed in the Lalita Sahasranama is through the dual portrayal of the goddess as both immanent and transcendent. The names Sarva sakshini (She who is the witness to everything) and Sarvadhara (She who is the basis of everything) emphasize her immanence, indicating that the goddess permeates every aspect of the universe. On the other hand, names like Nirguna (She who is without attributes) and Nishkala (She who is part less) reflect her transcendent nature, pointing to her existence beyond all forms and qualities.

This duality of immanence and transcendence is not a contradiction but a reflection of the non-dual reality where the divine is simultaneously beyond creation and fully present within it. In this sense, Lalita is both the creator and the creation, the cause and the effect, and the seer and the seen.

The Lalita Sahasranama also delves into the concept of non-duality through its depiction of the Divine Mother as the ultimate consciousness that underlies all existence. Names like Chit-Shakti (She who is the power of consciousness) and Chidagni Kunda Sambhuta (She who is born from the fire of consciousness) highlight that the goddess is not separate from consciousness itself. Here, the distinction between the knower, the known, and the process of knowing is dissolved, reflecting the Advaitic notion that all is one undifferentiated consciousness.

The name Vishwa rupa (She who has the form of the universe) further reinforces this idea, suggesting that the universe itself is a manifestation of this single, non-dual consciousness. The multiplicity of forms is seen as a divine play (Leela), where the one consciousness appears as many, yet remains essentially one.

A central theme in the Sri Vidya tradition, and by extension the Lalita Sahasranama, is the union of Shiva and Shakti. This union is a metaphor for non-duality, where Shiva represents pure consciousness and Shakti represents the dynamic power of creation. Names like Shiva Shaktyaikya rupini (She who is the form of the union of Shiva and Shakti) illustrate this inseparable oneness.

In the Advaitic framework, this union is not merely symbolic but is the very essence of non-duality. It conveys the idea that the ultimate reality is beyond dualities, transcending the apparent distinctions between the static and the dynamic, the passive and the active, or the male and the female. This oneness of Shiva and Shakti is a direct pointer to the non-dual truth, where the Divine Mother is both the manifest and the unmanifest, the dynamic power, and the silent witness.

The Lalita Sahasranama also touches upon the identity between the individual self and the universal self-Brahman, a core teaching of Advaita. Names like Antar mukha samaradhya encourage the devotee to look within, where the non-dual reality is realized as the essence of one's own being. This inward journey, which the Sahasranama guides through its mantras, is the path to realizing that the self is not separate from the Divine.

Sri Vidya – an ancient, secret and sacred tradition

To successfully navigate the mystical terrain of Lalita Sahasranama, it is necessary to investigate the connection it shares with the revered tradition of Sri Vidya. Sri Vidya, referred to as the "science of auspicious wisdom," encompasses a comprehensive spiritual system that incorporates mantra, yantra, and tantra. At its heart lies the worship of Lalita Tripurasundari, as the ultimate reality, the embodiment of pure consciousness, and the source of all creation. The Sri Vidya tradition provides a systematic and transformative approach to spiritual evolution, guiding the seeker through various stages of meditation, ritual worship, and contemplation.

The Lalita Sahasranama serves as a key scripture in the Sri Vidya tradition, offering a profound synthesis of the fundamental principles of this sacred path. Each name in the thousand-fold hymn is not merely a poetic expression but a sacred bija mantra, a seed syllable carrying the vibrational essence of the Divine Mother. The recitation and meditation on these names are considered a potent means to invoke the grace of Lalita Tripurasundari and attain spiritual elevation.

> "Sri Sundari sevana tatparanam
> Bhogascha mokshascha karastaeva"

Those who practice Sri Vidya are assured of both worldly pleasures (bhoga) and eternal solace /liberation (moksha).

One of the foremost practitioners of Sri Vidya was a renowned philosopher and scholar named Bhaskaracharya who moved to a small town of Tamil Nadu to be close to his guru sometime during the 18th century. He never spoke about his sadhana except to state that he was a Sri Vidya upasaka. A wandering monk from the Advaita lineage was passing through the town where Bhaskaracharya lived and was intrigued by the comings and goings of the silent and devout sadhu. He noticed that unlike most other sadhus, Bhaskaracharya never greeted or prostrated before other holy men that he encountered. The monk made this a subject of discourse amongst the town dwellers and followers.

Bhaskaracharya heard about the monk's talk and cordially approached him with due humility. He addressed the monk to say: "Revered Swami, I shall prostrate before every passing holy man but first I would like to demonstrate something to you before I start this practice. Please place your kamandalu (the water pot), danda (walking stick) and turban before me so I may prostrate before them. You see what happens and if you still insist, I will prostrate before you a thousand times." The monk placed his personal items before Bhaskaracharya and he prostrated with utter respect. Instantaneously all the three items caught fire and were reduced to ashes.

The awe-struck monk gaped at Bhaskaracharya who calmly explained that it is not out of arrogance that he did not prostate before others but because no human can stand before the power of a genuine Sri Vidya sadhaka who attains such levels of energy and oneness with the Divine that he no longer identifies with either his own ego or needs to acknowledge others as separate beings for he has witnessed the oneness of all things in the Universe.

Swami Veda Bharati says that learning Sri Vidya is not like mastering any of the sciences, it is mastering one's own self. In Gifts from the Goddess, Sri Uma-Parvathinananda Natha Saraswathi writes: "Sri Vidya teaches us to live as embodied human beings and yet not be limited by our individual family and cultural histories; how to literally hold power and simultaneously by power all while remaining in our earthly bodies; how to confront a world in political ecological and humanitarian turmoil and still find meaning there without separation or elitism."

The practice of Sri Vidya, which is a gradual learning process spanning a lifetime (and beyond, possibly) will have a profound influence on the way you see life and will help you get ahead in both material and spiritual realms. Swami Amritananda Natha Saraswathi says that a comprehensive knowledge of the system is not a prerequisite for the benefitting from the practice. Begin your practice today in any way which feels right to you and it will help you, just as any other spiritual practice does to find clarity of thought, calmness, stability and the ability to manifest all desires while also liberating you from the limiting bounds of your ego and belief systems.

Sri Vidya is the knowledge of the Cosmic Mother who is the absolute reality, an embodiment of unsurpassed beauty and joy, the queen of the three worlds (sleeping, dreaming and waking). The entire Universe is her manifestation and the relationship she shares with the world is akin to that of the ocean and the waves that arise from it and subside in it.

In the Kubjika Tantram, Lord Shiva defines Sri Vidya as:

"Sridatri cha sada vidya Sri Vidya parikirtita"
The vidya that renders prosperity and abundance is called Sri Vidya

Our ancient texts and modern gurus are all in agreement on one aspect of Sri Vidya: in order for a person to practice this elegant and powerful discipline, one must have done thousands of years of sadhana in previous lives. It is said:

"Athava paschimam janma athava sankarah swayam"
This knowledge only becomes available to one who is in his/her final birth or is verily Shiva Himself.

Our seers point out that if a person who is not deserving of initiation into the practice but still is lucky enough to be exposed to this valuable knowledge based on some good karmas from the past, such a person may not reach Self Realisation in this lifetime but will surely enjoy a head start in his next life.

Sri Vidya is an ancient Shakta Tantra school of wisdom that is focused on the worship of Shakti, the feminine principle. Its ultimate goal is Self-Realization which is achieved through devotion to the primal force of Shakti which empowers Shiva who is otherwise in Samadhi (in fact this is very forcefully expressed as Shiva is merely "shava" or corpse until he unites with Shakti) and this union of Shakti and Shiva gives rise to all aspects of the Universe including creation, preservation and dissolution.

Scholars point out that Sri Vidya is not a philosophy like Advaita Vedanta or Sankhya. It can be termed as an "upasana paddhati" or a practice-related science. Most of the Sri Vidya texts are focused on the practical aspects of how to acquire this knowledge rather than about its philosophy. Swami Amritananda Natha Saraswati says Sri Vidya is advaita in action precisely because it stands at a point where soaring philosophical theory transforms into experience and outcomes.

Sri Vidya practice comprises of tantra (a technique or framework for worship) whose two main elements are mantra (sacred sound) and yantra (sacred geometry). Tantra can be described in simple terms as the utilisation of the mental faculty to pursue the objectives of worship using mantra and yantra. Mantra is the use of sound energy to bring about a oneness with the Divine while yantra is a geometric drawing which serves as a tool to reach the Divine.

Sri Vidya is a systematic, esoteric discipline combining elements of knowledge, devotion and ritual. In the Shakta tradition Srividyopasana (the pursuit of enlightenment via Sri Vidya) is considered to be the pinnacle of human achievement as it promises the practitioner an experience of union with the Ultimate Reality or Consciousness.

In the tradition of the Sri Vidya, the Self is worshipped as a deity and mantras are offered to the divinity (seen as the Yantra inside our body) that lies within us. Many scholars describe Sri Vidya as the embodiment of the tantric experience and see all forms of tantric practices as subsumed in its practice.

So, what is Sri Vidya?

Sri Vidya is the sacred knowledge of Lalita Tripurasundari who is Adi Mahavidya or the primordial Wisdom Goddess. She is conceptualized as the supreme deity, a beautiful and auspicious manifestation of Mahadevi, the Great Goddess. The knowledge of the ritual worship of Lalita Tripurasundari using mantras such as the Panchadashi and Shodashi along with meditation on her yantra (the Sri Chakra Yantra) all come together to form Sri Vidya.

Vidya means knowledge ("vid" means "to know"), learning, discipline and a system of thought, and when the word Sri is prefixed to it, it becomes knowledge which is auspicious, beneficial and conducive to prosperity. Sri is also the name given to the Mother Goddess who rules over the universe (tvam sris tvam isvari). She is called the mother because all living beings depend on her for the fulfilment of their destiny.

Swami Veda Bharati writes in an article titled "What is Sri Vidya":

"Sri was a title originally reserved in ancient times for those who were initiated into Sri Vidya – they in whom God's glory of the universe has made a home, those who are endowed with knowledge, empowered with the energy and the intuition of mother Sri. The basic text of Sri Vidya says: one who knows mother Sri can never be orphaned. In the rituals and ceremonies in the Indian tradition, when one sips the holy water they say, Mayi Shrih Shrayatam: may Sri dwell in me. The word for refuge is Ashraya: to be one as Sri. "May many come taking refuge in me, may I seek refuge in none" – is the prayer of those who wish to have this capacity to give refuge. This capacity is Sri. One might translate Sri Vidya as the science of capacities, the science of potentialities."

Shakti is the source of all the principles and energies of the universe. The immense diversity of the manifestations of Shakti are seen in nature – in all cosmic bodies, forces, nature, all of life's creations and human beings. These are all expressions of Shakti's vidya. Therefore, the symbols of these energies and their expressions are regarded with immense awe, wonder and reverence and known as "Maha" (great) Vidya.

Devi Puranas and Bhagavata expound the glory of Shakti as the upholder of the cosmic order. The Mahavidya tradition restricts itself to only dealing with the diverse forms of Shakti that pervade all aspects of reality. Even though Her vidya is infinite and all-pervasive, it is classified into ten Mahavidya for the purpose of simplifying the sadhana for the seeker.

The tantric texts speak of ten wisdom goddesses (Dasa Mahavidya) whose worship brings about health, happiness and wealth in this life and liberation from the cycle of death and rebirth thereafter. The origin of Mahavidya as a group is quite unclear. Historians are of the view that

Mahavidya as a cluster of ten is of comparatively recent origin, possibly between the 12th and 14th centuries. It is entirely plausible that it began as a revolt against notions of purity and differentiation (much like Shaktism had at an earlier point in time). A cursory study of Mahavidya shows a definite urge to return to more primitive and indigenous faith as it is based more on human experience and draws from aspects of humdrum existence.

Devadutta Kali writes in the Power of Consciousness that "the highest spiritual truth is that reality is One. That reality, when personified as the Divine Mother, expresses itself in countless ways. The ten Mahavidya, or Wisdom Goddesses, represent distinct aspects of divinity intent on guiding the spiritual seeker toward liberation. For the devotionally-minded seeker, these forms can be approached in a spirit of reverence, love and increasing intimacy. For a knowledge-oriented seeker, these same forms can represent various states of inner awakening along the path to enlightenment."

The Mahavidyas represent ten different aspects of the One Truth, where the Divine Mother is revered and approached as ten distinct cosmic personalities. According to a story from the Shakta-Maha-Bhagavatha-Purana, the origin of the Dasa Mahavidyas is deeply connected to Sati, the daughter of Daksha Prajapati. Sati, madly in love with Shiva, marries him against her father's wishes. In retaliation, Daksha organizes a grand yagna and invites all the gods except Shiva. Insulted by this exclusion of her husband, Sati is determined to attend the yagna despite Shiva's refusal to permit her. Shiva warns that the fruit of the yagna would remain inauspicious if she went, but Sati, angered by what she perceives as an affront to her intelligence, resolves to show Shiva her own power.

In her divine wrath, Sati assumes the form of the Divine Mother in all her might. Shiva, fearful of her power, attempts to escape, but Sati manifests herself in ten different forms, guarding the ten directions. These ten forms, later known as the Mahavidyas, jointly subdue Shiva's resistance, allowing Sati to attend the yagna. Each of these forms of the Divine Mother has its own name, story, qualities, and mantras.

Kali, the first in the series of the Wisdom Goddesses, represents the power of consciousness in its highest form. As Adi Mahavidya, or the primary vidya, Kali is beyond time and space, known as the Devourer of Time and worshipped as the very essence of Brahman. She embodies the supreme power and ultimate reality, demonstrating the tantric tenet that consciousness and its power are one and the same. Kali, the transcendent cosmic power, dispels all darkness and fills us with the light of wisdom, symbolizing Jnana Shakti, the power of transformation. The rest of the Mahavidyas emanate from Kali, reflecting her virtues, powers, and nature in varying shades.

Tara is variously understood as a star, beautiful yet perpetually self-combusting. She is a guide and protector who helps her devotees cross the ocean of worldly existence. Tara symbolizes the absolute, unquenchable hunger that propels all life, representing the gracious liberator who leads us to transcend the ego and removes mistaken notions of our identities.

Lalita Tripurasundari is known as the most beautiful in the three worlds. These three worlds may represent the states of consciousness (sleeping, waking, and dreaming), aspects of humanity (physical, causal, and astral bodies), the universe (matter, energy, and thought), or energy (Iccha Shakti, Jnana Shakti, and Kriya Shakti). Also called Lalita, or the one who plays, she symbolizes creation as a beautiful, charming game of the Divine Mother. With four arms holding five arrows of flowers, a goad, a noose, and a sugarcane bow, she symbolizes our senses, repulsion, attachment, and the mind. Lalita represents the need to purify awareness and cleanse the mind of unworthy thoughts, and she symbolizes wealth. Her three manifestations – Sthula (physical), Sukshma (subtle), and Para (transcendent) are embodied in the Sri Chakra Yantra.

Bhuvaneshwari is known as the World Mother. Bhuvana means "this living world" and "Isvari" means "ruler." She embodies the entire cosmos, with the universe as her body and all beings as ornaments of her infinite being. Bhuvaneshwari represents the power of openness and infinite expansion, encouraging us to cultivate an attitude of universality, equanimity, and profound peace.

Bhairavi is a fierce and terrifying aspect of Devi, also known as Shubhamkari. She is both a good mother to the virtuous and terrible to the wicked. Seated on a headless corpse in a cremation ground, Bhairavi holds a sword of knowledge and a demon's head, while her other two hands are shown in mudras – one signifying fearlessness and the other granting boons. She symbolizes the maternal instinct to protect offspring, destroy ignorance, and help overcome internal negative forces while manifesting material desires.

Chinnamasta is known as the self-decapitated Goddess. According to the Panchatantra Grantha, Parvati once went to bathe in the Mandakini River with two friends. As the day progressed, the friends grew hungry and begged for food. Parvati laughingly decapitated herself, and blood spurted in three directions, nourishing both her friends and herself. Her severed head symbolizes liberation and the courage needed for ultimate sacrifice. The blood represents prana (cosmic life force), sustaining all beings in the universe. Chinnamasta also symbolizes the awakening of kundalini, as we transcend limitations that hinder spiritual progress.

Dhumavati is made of smoke – dark, polluting, and concealing the truth. She embodies the worst facets of humanity, including poverty, hunger, thirst, and anger. As the corrosive power of time, Dhumavati teaches us the transient nature of life, revealing ultimate knowledge and the necessity of detachment from sensory experiences.

Bagalamukhi paralyzes enemies and destroys misconceptions and delusions that hinder spiritual growth. In Tantra Shastra, she is depicted sitting on a golden throne in an ocean, sometimes with the head of a crane. Bagalamukhi ceases all motion at the appropriate time, silencing the mind and granting supernatural powers (siddhi and riddhi) to those who seek her through sadhana.

Matangi is the tantric form of Goddess Saraswati. Described in the Brhat Tantrasastra as seated on a corpse, adorned in red garments and jewelry, Matangi holds a skull and a sword. She helps devotees transcend sensory pollution, control enemies, attract people, and master the arts, ultimately leading to worldly success and spiritual salvation.

Kamala is the Lotus Goddess, also known as the Tantric Lakshmi. She symbolizes wealth, prosperity, and well-being, holding a lotus in two hands and bestowing blessings with the other two. The lotus, a recurrent symbol in Hinduism, represents the manifest universe and the potential to rise above worldly pollution to emerge as Divine Consciousness. Kamala teaches us to see beauty in all things and to understand that true wealth is achieved through selfless sharing with others.

Undoubtedly, the Mahavidya, as a group with its individual deities, depicts some of the most unusual, fierce, strange and vivid gods ever portrayed in any major world religion or culture. The forms are radically different from the benign and beautiful gods worshipped in the "cultured" society. They challenge accepted norms of social order with their outlandish behaviour, grotesque bodies, ugly faces and bizarre habits. These outrageous manifestations are meant to shock us and compel us to look beyond our comfort zones. The disturbing and distressing aspects force us to look deeper into our own selves to identify our shortcomings and show us for what we are, not what we are meant to be.

By rejecting and subverting conventionally accepted norms, the Mahavidya seeks to expand awareness to liberate the mind from inhibitions and prejudices.

An interesting aspect of the Mahavidya is that even though they are all about the power of the feminine principle, the deities are not shown as wives (although spouses are named in a few forms) or as mothers.

It is natural to wonder about the reason why our ancient seers divided all the great knowledge into ten diverse aspects. Scholars have indicated that it was an effort to drive home certain important points:

1. The Divine Mother is Absolute, ineffable and immutable and is beyond time and space.
2. In the act of creation, she subjects herself to constraints of time and space.

   Time is an aspect of prakruthi (Nature) and one of the 36 tattvas or principles of creation. However, as a concept, it is a creation of our intellect based on our sensory perception. It is a part of "Maya" or illusory state in which we all exist. For the Divine Consciousness, there is no division of time – there is only the present moment, a continuous and undivided state of existence.

Space is vast and beyond our comprehension. It is infinite, without a beginning or an end. To simplify matters, we divide it into ten cardinal directions – East, West, North, South, South-east, South-west, North-east, North-west, above and below.

3. Knowledge is one but is understood in ten different ways based on our five sense organs and five organs of action – skin, eye, ear, nose, tongue, mouth, foot, hand, anus and genitalia.
4. Truth is one but we perceive it in various facets, shapes, forms and meanings.

S. Shankaranarayanan says in his article on "The Ten Great Cosmic Powers":

"Each has a particular Cosmic function and leads to a special realization of the One Reality. The might of Kali, the sound-force of Tara, the beauty and bliss of Sundari, the vast vision of Bhuvaneshwari, the effulgent charm of Bhairavi, the striking force of Chinnamasta, the silent inertness of Dhumavati, the paralyzing power of Bhagalamukhi, the expressive play of Matangi and the concord and harmony of Kamala are the various characteristics, the distinct manifestations of the Supreme Consciousness that have made this creation possible. The Tantra says that the Supreme can be realized at these various points."

Each one of the Mahavidya holds individual significance as Brahmavidya and together as a group they contain all the wisdom of the universe – of past, present and the future and all the potential that ever existed or will exist. A true learner, who seeks with devotion, will be guided and inspired to find the spiritual strength and capability lying dormant within him to have his dreams manifested through a study of these great systems of knowledge.

Bhairavi, Bhuvaneshwari and Chinnamasta are called Vidya; Dhumavathi, Bagalamukhi, Matangi and Kamala are called Siddhi Vidya; The forms of Kali and Tara are considered to be Mahavidya. Tripurasundari is called Sri Vidya. Tripurasundari is the foremost of the Mahavidyas and is seen as the highest aspect of Adi Parashakti. The Tripura Upanishad mentions her as the ultimate Shakti, giving energy and power to the universe. She is described as the supreme consciousness, with her position higher than that of Shiva, Vishnu and Brahma. The text is one of the important works of the Shakta tradition and notable for its theory of Tripura (literally "three cities") symbolizing the three roads of work, worship and wisdom.

The Sanskrit word 'Tripura' is a combination of two Sanskrit words; "Tri" meaning "trayas (three)" and "pura" meaning a city or citadel, understood as referring to the three states of consciousness (waking, dreaming and sleeping). Therefore, "Tripura Sundari" literally means "She who is beautiful in the three states of consciousness".

In the waking state, consciousness is turned outward to the external world as we perceive the world through our senses and experience the gross objects of the physical world around us. In this second state which is the dreaming state, consciousness is turned towards the inner world. In the third state also known as Sushupti in Sanskrit, the senses are not operating either looking at external objects or focused on the internal state. In deep sleep, all experiences have receded into a realm of undifferentiated consciousness.

David Kinsley, describes Lalita Tripurasundari in his book Tantric Visions of the Divine Feminine: The Ten Mahavidyas "She is called Tripura because she is identical with the triangle (trikona) that symbolizes the yoni and that forms her chakra. She is also called Tripura because her mantra has three clusters of syllables. Here Tripura is identified with the alphabet, from which all sounds and words proceed and which is understood to occupy a primordial place in tantric cosmology. She is three-fold, furthermore, because she expresses herself in Brahma, Vishnu, and Shiva in her roles as creator, maintainer, and destroyer of the universe. She is threefold also because she represents the subject (maul), instrument (mina), and object (meya) of all things. Here again, she is identified with reality expressed in terms of speech, which involves a speaker, what is said, and objects to which the words refer."

Another unique feature of Sri Vidya which many scholars have pointed out is that the name of the Vidya/ Goddess/ Yantra are synonymous with Sri and there is no other name ascribed to the manifestations. For example, the Vidya is not called Lalita Vidya or Tripurasundari Vidya. Similarly, the Yantra is not called Lalita Yantra (notice how all other yantras carry the names of the deities such as Ganesha Yantra, Kali Yantra, Kubera Yantra). This points to the fact that Sri Vidya is so powerful and all-encompassing that it does not need another name.

In the Rig Veda, Sri Vidya is found as Sri Suktam. While in the Brahmanda Purana there is a comprehensive description of Sri Vidya, its method and philosophy, it also finds mention in the Bhavanopanishad, Shiva Sutras and Sri Vijjana Bhairava. The Bhavanopanishad is a major Sri Vidya text that postulates the symbolism of the Sri Chakra and outlines how this yantra is to be worshipped. The Saundarya Lahiri, composed by Adi Shankaracharya, is a hymn consisting of one hundred verses expounding the virtues of Lalita Tripurasundari. It is considered the most beautiful and profound explanation of Sri Vidya.

It is said that Brahma, Vishnu, Shiva and the seven great rishis (Saptarishis) of the Hindu tradition have all been Sri Vidya Upasakas. Adi Shankaracharya was a greatest exponent of Sri Vidya and was instrumental in spreading this knowledge across India. Bhaskararaya, a renowned spiritual scholar who later took up sanyasa was one of the foremost promoters of Sri Vidya in the 18th century. Sri Ramakrishna Paramahamsa and Swami Vivekananda are also known to be Sri Vidya upasakas who helped lend credibility and greater awareness to this school of worship. In modern times, Swami Amritananda, Om Swami, Swami Karunamaya and Sri M have been great exponents of Sri Vidya. I am sure there are many more enlightened Upasakas whom I have not heard of but the names I have mentioned above are people I have learnt a great deal from their talks and writings on the subject.

Swami Veda Bharati writes that "Sri Vidya begins where the current understanding of quantum physics ends. It is the science of sciences, the mega science and the art of arts, the mega art. Wherever we study configurations, charts and graphs it is a part of Sri Vidya. Wherever we study forms as fields of energy it is Sri Vidya. Wherever we study Marmas in Ayurveda, this too is a part of Sri Vidya. But it is experienced only in the assimilation of these principles into our consciousness not in an intellectual process but in our very being in our very essence so that our essence is not seen apart from the ever expanding and contracting universe."

The concept of Neti Neti

Neti Neti is a profound concept within the Vedantic tradition. The phrase translates to "not this, not this," or more simply, "neither this, nor that." It is a method of negation used to describe the indescribable nature of Brahman. The concept of Neti Neti is most notably found in the Upanishads. The Brihadaranyaka Upanishad is one of the primary texts where this method is discussed. The Upanishad presents Neti Neti as a process of understanding Brahman by systematically negating all attributes and forms that do not define it.

Brihadaranyaka Upanishad 2.3.6: "Now, therefore, the description [of Brahman]: 'Not this, not this.' Because there is no other and more appropriate description than this 'Not this.' Now the designation of Brahman: 'The Truth of truth.' The vital breath is truth, and It (Brahman) is the truth of that."

Here, the scripture suggests that Brahman cannot be fully comprehended through language, thought, or sensory perception. By negating all finite characteristics (name, form, attributes), one is left with the understanding that Brahman transcends all that is manifest and definable.

Neti Neti is closely associated with the Advaita Vedanta philosophy, which emphasizes the non-dual nature of reality where the Brahman is beyond all dualistic distinctions, including existence and non-existence, form and formlessness, subject and object.

- **Method of Negation**: Neti Neti is a meditative practice and a philosophical method that guides the seeker in peeling away the layers of Maya that obscure the Atman. By affirming "not this, not that" to every conceivable concept or object, the practitioner is encouraged to recognize the limits of intellectual knowledge and sense experience.
- **Transcendence of Attributes**: The process of negation in Neti Neti serves to highlight that Brahman cannot be categorized or limited by any qualities. It is beyond all forms of description (Nirguna Brahman – Brahman without attributes). This approach is a means to understand that the absolute reality is not something that can be directly apprehended but is instead beyond all perceptual and conceptual frameworks.

In practical terms, Neti Neti is employed as a technique of self-inquiry (Atma Vichara), a spiritual practice where one continuously negates all that is not the true self. The practice involves an introspective questioning of one's identity and experiences, leading to the realization that the true self is not the body, mind, or ego but is instead the infinite and unchanging consciousness, identical with Brahman.

Neti Neti is a pivotal concept in Hindu philosophy that offers a unique approach to understanding the nature of the ultimate reality, Brahman. By systematically negating all finite forms and concepts, it leads the seeker toward a realization of the infinite, unmanifest, and absolute nature of existence. This method underscores the limitations of human perception and the transcendent nature of the divine, which is beyond all categories of thought and language. In essence, Neti Neti serves as both a philosophical guide and a spiritual practice, leading to the realization of the oneness of Atman and Brahman, the non-dual reality that underlies all existence.

The method adopted by the Vedas and Vedanta to describe Brahman which is indescribable, is by denying all possible attributes is covered in the Lalita Sahasranama from stanzas 132 to 187.

The divine consciousness is seen as the substratum of the apparent and ever-changing world

Mitya jagadadisthana is a name attributed to Lalita in this Sahasranama. In the Vedanta tradition, the concept of Divine Consciousness as the substratum of the apparent and ever-changing world is a central and profound idea. This notion reflects the metaphysical framework in which the Brahman underlies and pervades all of existence, while the phenomenal world (Jagat) is seen as an appearance or manifestation of that reality.

Brahman is described as the infinite, unchanging, and eternal reality that is the source, support, and essence of everything. In Advaita Vedanta, Brahman is referred to as Nirguna Brahman (Brahman without attributes) when it is understood as pure, undifferentiated consciousness. This Brahman is described as Sat-Chit-Ananda (Existence-Consciousness-Bliss), encapsulating its nature as the foundation of all that exists, its consciousness as the ultimate reality, and its inherent bliss.

The apparent world (Jagat) is characterized as Maya, a term that denotes illusion or the power that creates the illusion of multiplicity and change. According to this view, the world we experience through our senses is not the ultimate reality; it is a transient and mutable manifestation of the underlying divine consciousness. The world appears to be diverse and dynamic, but this diversity is a superficial phenomenon like waves on the ocean while the ocean itself represents the unchanging reality, Brahman.

Chandogya Upanishad (6.2.1): "Sarvam khalvidam Brahma" (All this is indeed Brahman). This statement says that everything in the universe, despite appearing separate and distinct, is fundamentally Brahman.

In Vedantic thought, Brahman is understood as the substratum (Adhishthana) of the entire cosmos. This means that Brahman is the underlying reality that supports the apparent world, much like a screen supports images projected onto it.

Taittiriya Upanishad (2.1.1): "Brahman is the reality (Satyam), consciousness (Jnanam), and infinite (Anantam)." This verse indicates that Brahman is the foundational essence that pervades everything. The world, though ever-changing, rests upon this unchanging consciousness.

A classical Vedantic analogy to explain this concept is the rope-snake illusion (Rajju-Sarpa Nyaya). In dim light, a rope may be mistaken for a snake, leading to fear and confusion. However, when light is shed upon the rope, the illusion of the snake vanishes, revealing the rope as it truly is. In this metaphor:

- The rope represents Brahman, the underlying reality.
- The snake represents the world, which is perceived as real due to ignorance (Avidya).
- The light represents knowledge (Jnana), which dispels the illusion and reveals the truth of Brahman.

This metaphor illustrates that the world (like the snake) is a superimposition upon Brahman (like the rope), and through knowledge, one can realize that what appears as the world is, in fact, nothing but Brahman.

In Advaita Vedanta, Brahman is also considered both the material cause (Upadana Karana) and the efficient cause (Nimitta Karana) of the universe. This means that Brahman is not only the source from which the world arises but also the intelligence that governs its functioning.

Chandogya Upanishad (6.1.4-6): The famous "Tat Tvam Asi" ("That Thou Art") teaching asserts that the individual self (Atman) is identical with Brahman, reinforcing the idea that the self and the world are ultimately non-different from the divine consciousness.

The world is perceived as ever-changing due to the play of Maya, which creates the illusion of diversity and transformation. However, these changes are apparent and not real in the ultimate sense. Brahman, as the substratum, remains constant and unchanged. The appearance of change is akin to the changing patterns on the surface of an ocean, where the water itself remains the same.

Mandukya Upanishad (7) discusses the concept of Turiya, the fourth state of consciousness beyond waking, dreaming, and deep sleep. Turiya is identified with Brahman, the unchanging reality behind the changing experiences of life.

Avidya or ignorance is what veils the true nature of Brahman, making the world appear as separate and distinct. Through the practice of Jnana Yoga (the path of knowledge), one can overcome this ignorance and realize that the world is not separate from Brahman but is a manifestation of it. The realization that "All this is Brahman" leads to the dissolution of the apparent duality and the recognition of the oneness of all existence.

The ultimate goal in Vedantic practice is to achieve Moksha or liberation, which is the realization of the self's identity with Brahman. When one recognizes that the self is not different from the Brahman, one transcends the illusions of Maya and the cycle of birth and death. This realization leads to a state of blissful awareness of the non-dual reality.

While the world appears to be full of diversity and change, it is ultimately an expression of the one, unchanging Brahman. Through the process of negation, inquiry, and realization, one can see through the illusions of Maya and recognize that all forms, names, and phenomena are rooted in and sustained by the infinite, undifferentiated Divine Consciousness. This understanding forms the cornerstone of Advaita Vedanta and is essential to the pursuit of spiritual liberation in Hindu thought.

Lalita Sahasranama outlines how Lalita controls the five aspects of creation

The five aspects of creation – Shrusthi (Creation), Stithi (Sustenance), Laya (Dissolution), Thirodhana (Concealment), and Anugraha

(Grace) are central to Hindu cosmology and theology, particularly within the Shaiva and Shakta traditions. These aspects describe the cyclical process through which the universe is brought into existence, maintained, dissolved, obscured, and ultimately liberated. Each aspect is associated with a specific function of the Divine and finds expression in various scriptural narratives.

1. Shrusthi (Creation)

Shrusthi refers to the process of creation, where the Divine manifests the universe and all beings within it. This aspect is associated with the creative energy of the Divine, symbolized by deities such as Brahma or the Goddess in her creative form. The process of creation is described in texts like the Puranas, where the Divine, in its desire to manifest, projects the cosmos out of itself.

An example from the scriptures is found in the Nasadiya Sukta of the Rigveda, which explores the mystery of creation, contemplating the moment before the universe came into being and how the One, through a will to create, brought forth the cosmos. Similarly, in the Devi Bhagavata Purana, the Goddess creates the world out of her own body, demonstrating that creation is an act of self-projection.

2. Stithi (Sustenance)

Stithi is the aspect of sustenance or maintenance, where the Divine preserves and upholds the order of the universe. This function is attributed to Vishnu or the Goddess in her sustaining aspect. The universe, once created, requires balance and order, which is maintained through the principle of dharma (cosmic law).

An example can be found in the Bhagavad Gita, where Krishna, an avatar of Vishnu, declares that whenever dharma declines and adharma (unrighteousness) rises, he incarnates to restore order. This cyclical process of maintaining cosmic balance is central to the concept of stithi, ensuring that creation continues to exist harmoniously.

3. Laya (Dissolution)

Laya refers to the dissolution or destruction of the universe, a necessary process that makes way for renewal and regeneration. This aspect is associated with deities like Shiva, who, as the destroyer, brings the cosmic cycle to an end, allowing for the next cycle of creation. Laya is not merely annihilation but a transformation where the manifest returns to the unmanifest state.

The concept of laya is vividly depicted in the Shiva Purana, where Shiva performs the Tandava, the cosmic dance of destruction, symbolizing the dissolution of the universe. Similarly, in the Bhagavata Purana, the great deluge or pralaya occurs at the end of a cosmic cycle, where all creation is submerged in the primordial waters, waiting to be recreated.

4. Thirodhana (Concealment)

Thirodhana, or concealment, refers to the Divine's power to obscure the true nature of reality, veiling the ultimate truth from beings. This aspect is crucial in the play of maya where the Divine hides the oneness of all existence behind the diversity of the material world. This concealment is what allows beings to experience individuality and engage in the world of duality.

An example from the Mundaka Upanishad describes the process where the Supreme Reality is concealed by the veiling power of maya, leading beings to perceive the world as separate from the Divine. This concealment is also a means for the soul's journey through samsara (the cycle of birth and death), as it navigates the illusions of the material world.

5. Anugraha (Grace)

Anugraha is the aspect of grace or divine benevolence, through which the Divine bestows liberation (moksha) on beings. After creation, maintenance, dissolution, and concealment, the Divine, in its infinite compassion, reveals itself to the soul, dispelling the veil of maya and granting liberation. This aspect is associated with the Goddess in her form as Lalita Tripurasundari or with Shiva in his auspicious aspect as the liberator.

The Vishnu Purana provides an example where Vishnu, out of compassion, incarnates as various avatars to save devotees and guide them toward liberation. In the Tripura Rahasya, the Goddess bestows her grace on the devotee, revealing the true nature of reality and lifting the soul out of the cycle of samsara.

The five aspects of creation constitute the cyclical process through which the universe is continually brought into existence, sustained, dissolved, obscured, and ultimately liberated. These aspects illustrate the dynamic interplay between creation and destruction, illusion and enlightenment, within Hindu cosmology. They are not only metaphysical concepts but also integral to understanding the Divine's role in the universe and the soul's journey towards liberation.

The Lalita Sahasranama intricately weaves together these five aspects of creation, portraying Lalita as the all-encompassing Divine Mother who creates, sustains, dissolves, conceals, and liberates the universe. Each of these functions is reflected in the names and attributes of Lalita, offering devotees a comprehensive understanding of her cosmic role. Through these names, the Lalita Sahasranama not only glorifies the Divine Mother but also serves as a guide for spiritual practice, reminding devotees of the various ways in which Lalita interacts with the world and leads them towards ultimate liberation through her boundless grace.

Lalita is described in the Lalita Sahasranama as the source of all creation. Names such as "Viyadadhi Jagatprasuh" (She who created earth and sky) and "Aneka Koti Brahmanda Janani" (Mother of All Worlds) reflect her role as the origin of the cosmos. Through her will, she manifests the universe from her own being. In this context, Lalita is not only the creator but also the material cause of creation, meaning that the entire universe is an extension of her own divine essence.

The name "Vishwa Garbha" (She who is the womb of the universe) signifies that Lalita embodies the cosmos itself, highlighting her inseparability from her creation. This aspect aligns with the concept of Shrusthi, where the Divine Mother brings forth the universe and all living beings from her own creative energy.

Lalita's role in sustaining the universe is captured in names like "Vishwasakshini" (Witness of the Universe) and "Sarva Antaryamini" (She who is within everything). These names illustrate how Lalita, in her sustaining aspect, upholds the cosmic order and nurtures all beings within it. She is the force that ensures the continuity and harmony of the universe, preserving the balance between creation and dissolution.

Another name, "Maheshwari" (Great Goddess), emphasizes her supreme power in maintaining the universe. Lalita, as Maheshwari, is the ultimate source of dharma and the guiding force that ensures the proper functioning of the cosmos. This sustenance is not passive; it is a dynamic process where Lalita actively engages with her creation, ensuring its well-being.

The Lalita Sahasranama also acknowledges Lalita's role in the dissolution of the universe through names like "Mahapralaya Sakshini " (She who witnesses the dissolution) and "Mahagrasa" (She who swallows everything). These names describe Lalita as the power that dissolves the universe back into its primal state, preparing it for a new cycle of creation.

The name "Rudrani" (Consort of Rudra/Shiva) associates Lalita with Shiva, the destroyer, indicating that she shares in his function of bringing about the end of the cosmic cycle. In this role, Lalita is seen as the force that withdraws the universe into herself, returning all forms to their unmanifest origin. This aspect of dissolution is essential for the renewal and regeneration of the cosmos.

Thirodhana is represented in the Lalita Sahasranama through names like "Mahamaya" (The Great Illusion) and "Vimohini" (The Deluder).

Lalita, as Mahamaya, is the power that veils the ultimate truth, allowing beings to experience the world of duality and illusion. This concealment is not seen as negative but as a necessary aspect of the cosmic play (Leela) that enables the soul's journey through samsara.

The name "Maha Maya" particularly emphasizes Lalita's role in creating and maintaining the illusion that separates the individual soul from the Divine. By concealing the oneness of reality, Lalita allows the soul to engage in the world, learn, and evolve. This aspect is crucial in understanding the nature of human existence and the challenges on the path to spiritual liberation.

Anugraha, or divine grace, is one of the most celebrated aspects of Lalita in the Lalita Sahasranama. Names such as "Sarvartha Dhatri" (Bestower of abundance) and "Sukhaprada" (Bestower of joy) highlight her role as the compassionate mother who grants liberation and spiritual awakening to her devotees. Lalita's grace is the ultimate means through which the soul can transcend the cycle of birth and death. The name "Lalita" itself, meaning "She Who is Playful and Gracious," encapsulates her nature as the benevolent deity who, out of love and compassion, reveals the truth to her devotees. Another name, "Tripura Sundari" (Beautiful Goddess of the Three Worlds), signifies her role as the ultimate source of beauty, love, and grace, guiding souls towards the realization of their oneness with the Divine.

Order of Creation

Lalita extended Herself into both male and female forms to continue the process of creation.

A. From Her left eye, which embodied the essence of Soma (the moon), emerged Brahma and Lakshmi Devi.

B. From Her right eye, representing Soorya (the sun), came Vishnu and Parvati.

C. From Her third eye, symbolizing Agni (fire), arose Rudra and Sarasvati.

D. Brahma paired with Sarasvati, Vishnu with Lakshmi, and Shiva with Parvati, forming divine couples.

E. Lalita instructed these couples to continue the creation process.

Lalita then proceeded to create certain elements herself:

i. From Her long hair, She created darkness.

ii. From Her eyes, She brought forth the sun, the moon, and fire.

iii. The stars were created from the pendant hanging in front of Her forehead.

iv. The nine planets emerged from the chain above Her forehead.

v. From Her eyebrows, She established the laws and regulations.

vi. The Vedas were born from Her breath.

vii. From Her speech, She created poetry and plays.

viii. The Vedangas (limbs of the Vedas) were formed from Her chin.

ix. From the three lines on Her neck, She generated various Shaastras (scriptures).

x. Mountains were formed from Her breasts.

xi. She created the power of bliss from Her mind.

xii. The ten incarnations of Vishnu emerged from Her fingernails.

xiii. From Her palms, She brought forth the Sandhyas (twilight periods).

xiv. She created other entities as described in the Purusha Sookta.

xv. Bala Devi was created from Her heart.

xvi. From Her intellect, Shyamala Devi was brought forth.

xvii. Varahi Devi emerged from Her ego.

xviii. From Her smile, She created Vighneshwara.

xix. Sampatkari Devi was formed from Her Ankusha (a special hook).

xx. From Her noose, Ashwaa Roodha Devi was created.

xxi. Nakuleshvari Devi emerged from Her cheeks.

xxii. From Her Kundalini Shakti, She created Gayatri.

xxiii. The eight wheels of the Chakra Raja chariot gave rise to eight Devatas.

xxiv. At the ninth landing, in the Bindu Peetha, Lalita seated Herself.

xxv. Subsequently, She created the Devatas to protect the Chakra Raja chariot.

After completing this grand creation, Lalita requested Her consort, Shiva Kama Sundara, to create the Shiva Chakra.

Lalita Sahasranama throws light on the concepts of Vimarsha and Prakasha

In the context of the non-dualistic traditions of Kashmir Shaivism and Sri Vidya, the concepts of Vimarsha and Prakasha are central to understanding the nature of the Divine and its manifestation. These two terms describe the dynamic interplay between the static and dynamic aspects of consciousness, personified as Shiva (Prakasha) and Shakti (Vimarsha). Together, they form the basis of the universe and all its phenomena, highlighting the inseparability of the Divine from its creative power.

Prakasha is translated as light or illumination and refers to the pure, undifferentiated consciousness that is the essence of the Divine. In the context of Shakti worship, Prakasha represents Shiva, the transcendent, formless aspect of the Divine that exists beyond all creation. It is the self-luminous, ever-present awareness that underlies all reality. Shiva, as Prakasha, is the passive, witnessing consciousness that does not engage in activity but simply "is."

This concept is akin to the idea of the unchanging and eternal Brahman in Advaita Vedanta. Prakasha is the source of all light and knowledge, the fundamental reality that makes all experience possible. However, Prakasha alone, without interaction, remains in a state of pure potentiality. It is only through its dynamic counterpart, Vimarsha, that the universe comes into being.

Vimarsha is the reflective or self-referential aspect of consciousness. It represents Shakti, the dynamic, creative energy of the Divine that activates and manifests the potential of Prakasha. Vimarsha is translated as reflection or awareness and it signifies the aspect of consciousness that turns inward to recognize itself. This self-recognition is the first movement of creation, where the Divine becomes aware of its own existence and power.

In Shakti worship, Vimarsha is seen as the essential nature of the Goddess, who embodies the creative force that brings the universe into being. While Prakasha is the light of consciousness, Vimarsha is the power that causes this light to manifest as the diverse forms of the world. It is through Vimarsha that the Divine expresses itself as the multiplicity of the cosmos, while still remaining one with its source.

The relationship between Prakasha and Vimarsha is described as a dance or a play (Leela) between Shiva and Shakti. In this dynamic interplay, Prakasha provides the foundation of existence, while Vimarsha animates and diversifies it. They are not separate entities but two aspects of the same reality, inseparable and interdependent. Prakasha without Vimarsha would be inert, pure potentiality with no expression. Conversely, Vimarsha without Prakasha would have no foundation, no light in which to manifest.

In the worship of Shakti, this interplay is deeply significant. The Goddess, as Shakti, is revered not only as the source of all power and creation but also as the dynamic aspect of the Divine that allows the static consciousness of Shiva to express itself. This relationship is symbolized in the Sri Yantra, where the upward and downward triangles represent the union of Shiva and Shakti, or Prakasha and Vimarsha. The center point of the Sri Yantra (Bindu) represents their ultimate unity, where all dualities dissolve into the non-dual reality.

The concepts of Prakasha and Vimarsha have profound implications for both philosophy and spiritual practice in Shakti worship. Philosophically, they provide a framework for understanding how the One becomes many and how the unmanifest Divine gives rise to the manifest world. This understanding is central to non-dualistic traditions like Kashmir Shaivism, where the universe is seen as a reflection of the Divine's own self-awareness, rather than as something separate or illusory.

In spiritual practice, the recognition of Prakasha and Vimarsha is essential for realizing the non-dual nature of reality. Worship of the Goddess in her various forms is not merely the veneration of a higher power but a recognition of the dynamic force that is inherent within one's own consciousness.

In Sri Vidya, the union of Prakasha and Vimarsha is essential, symbolizing the non-dual reality where the Divine Mother is simultaneously the unmanifested consciousness and its manifested reflection. The Lalita Sahasranama expresses this unity through names like "Kameshvara Prananadi" (the life force of Kameshvara, who represents Shiva or pure consciousness) and "Kameshvara Mukhaloka Kalpita Shri Ganeshvara" (She who gave rise to Lord Ganesha by just a glance from Kameshvara). These names emphasize that the creation, preservation, and dissolution of the universe are all acts of the Divine Mother as she manifests consciousness (Prakasha) into form (Vimarsha) and reabsorbs it back into herself.

In the Lalita Sahasranama, names such as "Chidagni Kunda Sambhuta" (born from the fire of consciousness) and "Chaitanyarghya Samaradhya" (offered as oblation to pure consciousness) highlight this aspect of the Divine Mother as the embodiment of Prakasha. Here, Lalita is seen as the pure, unchanging light that underlies all existence. Names like "Sharvani" (She who is the essence of everything) and "Loka Yatra Vidhayani" (She who sets the universe in motion) illustrate how Lalita embodies Vimarsha, manifesting the cosmos from her own consciousness. This reflection of consciousness as the universe is a key concept in Sri Vidya, where the Divine Mother is both the source (Prakasha) and the manifestation (Vimarsha). The Lalita Sahasranama reveals the interplay between Prakasha and Vimarsha, portraying the Divine Mother as the ultimate reality, where consciousness and its reflective power are inseparable, giving rise to the entire cosmos.

Lalita Sahasranama defines the Nivrutti and Pravrutti paths

In Shaktism, as in other Hindu philosophical traditions, the concepts of Nivrutti and Pravrutti represent two fundamental paths or approaches to life and spiritual practice. These paths are not mutually exclusive but rather complementary, offering a balanced understanding of the relationship between worldly engagement and spiritual renunciation. In the context of Shaktism, where the Goddess or Shakti is revered as the ultimate reality and the dynamic force behind all creation, these paths take on specific nuances that align with the worship of the Divine Feminine.

Pravrutti refers to the path of active engagement in the world, where the practitioner participates fully in the duties, responsibilities, and experiences of life. It is the path of action (karma) and is associated with the creative and sustaining aspects of Shakti. In Shaktism, Pravrutti is seen as a legitimate and necessary path for those who are involved in worldly life, family, society, and the maintenance of dharma.

Shaktism celebrates life and the material world as expressions of the Divine Mother. The Goddess is worshiped not only as the transcendent reality but also as the immanent force that pervades every aspect of existence. Pravrutti in Shaktism involves recognizing the sacredness in all life's activities whether in work, relationships, or the pursuit of knowledge. By engaging in the world with awareness and devotion, practitioners can experience the Divine in every action.

The path of Pravrutti emphasizes fulfilling one's duties according to dharma. In the context of Shaktism, this involves the worship of the Goddess in her various forms, each of which presides over different aspects of life, such as wealth (Lakshmi), learning (Saraswati), or power (Durga). By honoring these deities and following the path of righteousness, adherents maintain harmony in the world while progressing spiritually.

The practice of Karma Yoga performing actions without attachment to their outcomes is integral to Pravrutti. In Shaktism, actions are offered to the Goddess as a form of worship, transforming everyday duties into spiritual practices. This approach aligns with the understanding that Shakti is the doer of all actions, and by aligning one's will with the Divine will, a practitioner can transcend ego and achieve spiritual growth even while remaining active in the world.

Nivrutti, on the other hand, represents the path of renunciation, where the practitioner withdraws from worldly engagements to focus on the inner spiritual journey. It is the path of knowledge and meditation, leading towards liberation. In Shaktism, Nivrutti is associated with the dissolution aspect of Shakti, where the individual seeks to transcend the material world and realize the ultimate, formless reality of the Divine.

In the Nivrutti path, the practitioner renounces worldly desires and attachments to focus on the inward journey toward self-realization. This path is pursued by ascetics, sages, and those who seek to experience the transcendent aspect of Shakti, beyond her manifest forms. It involves intense meditation, contemplation, and practices such as Kundalini Yoga to awaken the inner energy and unite with the formless Divine. The goal of Nivrutti is to understand and experience Shakti as the unmanifest, pure consciousness. While Pravrutti involves worshiping Shakti in her manifest forms, Nivrutti leads the practitioner to the realization that these forms are ultimately expressions of the same, non-dual reality. The dissolution of the individual ego and merging with the cosmic consciousness (Shiva) is the culmination of this path.

In Shaktism, Nivrutti is not about rejecting the world as illusory or evil but rather about transcending duality. The practitioner sees the world as the play (Lila) of the Goddess and understands that true liberation comes from seeing through this play to the underlying unity of all existence. By renouncing the fruits of actions and the attachments to worldly life, one attains the state of Kaivalya the realization of oneness with the Divine.

While Pravrutti and Nivrutti are seen as distinct paths, Shaktism encourages the integration of both. The Goddess is both immanent and transcendent, and her devotees are encouraged to recognize her presence in all aspects of life while also striving for spiritual liberation. The Lalita Sahasranama celebrates the Goddess as both the creator and the ultimate reality, embodying the balance of Pravrutti and Nivrutti.

In practical terms, this integration can be seen in the lives of householders who maintain their worldly responsibilities while cultivating spiritual practices that lead to inner detachment and eventual liberation. The Bhagavad Gita supports this integration, where Krishna advises Arjuna to perform his duties without attachment, blending the paths of action and renunciation.

Lalita is described as "Nirguna" (beyond the three gunas). This name reflects the essence of the Nivrutti path, where the seeker transcends the material qualities of sattva, rajas, and tamas to realize the unmanifested, pure consciousness. "Manonmani" refers to Lalita as the highest state of meditation, where the mind is completely still. It symbolizes the ultimate goal of the Nivrutti path, which is to attain a state of union with the Divine through deep meditation and self-realization.

"Shrishti-Karti" describes Lalita as "the creator of the universe." This name highlights her active role in the process of creation, symbolizing the Pravrutti path, where one engages in worldly activities with the understanding that they are a form of divine expression. "Maheshwari" depicts Lalita as "the great ruler." This name underscores her dynamic aspect as the one who governs the universe, guiding devotees on the Pravrutti path to act with righteousness and devotion while fulfilling their worldly roles.

The Lalita Sahasranama teaches that both paths are essential and complementary. While Nivrutti leads to self-realization and liberation, Pravrutti ensures that one fulfills their duties in the world, contributing to the welfare of society and the cosmos. "Yogini" shows Lalita is the embodiment of yoga, which is the union of both paths. Yoga represents the balance between renunciation (Nivrutti) and action (Pravrutti), showing that a spiritual life can be lived in harmony with worldly responsibilities. In essence, the Lalita Sahasranama guides devotees to understand and integrate both paths in their spiritual journey, realizing that the Divine Mother embodies and harmonizes the energies of both Nivrutti and Pravrutti.

Lalita Sahasranama describes the symbolism of Bhandasura

The story of Bhandasura's defeat by an army of goddesses led by Lalita Tripurasundari, as depicted in the Lalita Mahatmya and other Shakta texts, carries profound symbolic and esoteric meanings. The narrative, on a surface level, describes the battle between the demon Bhandasura and the divine feminine forces. However, beneath this mythological story lies rich spiritual and psychological symbolism that conveys deeper truths about the nature of the self, the power of the divine feminine, and the journey towards spiritual liberation.

Bhandasura represents the ego, ignorance, and the negative tendencies that bind the soul to the material world and the cycle of birth and death. His very creation is linked to negative energies born from the ashes of Manmatha after being incinerated by Shiva's third eye. This connection symbolizes the dominance of desires and attachments that cloud the true nature of the self, leading to ignorance and delusion. Bhandasura's reign signifies the condition of a soul trapped by ignorance, driven by desires, and bound by the illusion of separateness from the Divine. His arrogance and power are metaphors for the inflated ego, which assumes control over the individual, leading to spiritual stagnation and suffering.

The army of goddesses led by Lalita Tripurasundari represents the various aspects of Shakti that embodies wisdom, compassion, and transformative power. Each goddess in the army symbolizes a specific spiritual force or quality necessary for overcoming the ego and ignorance. For instance:

- Mantrini represents the power of mantra and sound, which purifies and elevates consciousness.
- Dandanatha embodies discipline and control, which are essential for overcoming lower tendencies.
- Mahakali, Mahalakshmi, and Mahasaraswati signify the three primary energies of destruction, sustenance, and creation, respectively, which together dismantle ignorance and restore cosmic order.

The army of goddesses can be seen as the collective forces of divine wisdom, spiritual practices, and virtues that lead the soul from ignorance to enlightenment. Their role in the narrative emphasizes that the path to liberation is guided and supported by divine grace, which manifests in various forms to aid the seeker.

Lalita Tripurasundari, as the commander of the divine army, symbolizes the ultimate reality and the supreme consciousness. She is the embodiment of Para Shakti the highest, unmanifested power that is both transcendent and immanent. Her beauty and grace represent the all-attractive nature of the Divine, which draws the soul towards liberation. Lalita's role in the defeat of Bhandasura signifies the victory of the highest wisdom and divine grace over ignorance and ego. It is through her intervention that the forces of ignorance are ultimately destroyed, emphasizing that spiritual liberation is achieved through the grace of the Divine Feminine.

Some of the names that describe this battle between good and evil are "Bhandasura Vadodyukta Shakti Sena Samanvita", "Mantrinyambha Virachita Vishanga Vadhatoshita", "Vishukra Prana Harana Varahi Viryanandita" and "Karanguli Nakhotpanna Narayana Dashaakrutih". The defeat of Bhandasura by the army of goddesses symbolizes the triumph of divine wisdom, inner strength, and spiritual practices over the forces of ignorance, ego, and attachment. This victory represents the dissolution of the ego and the realization of the self's true nature, which is one with the Divine. From a psychological perspective, this narrative can be seen as the process of self-transformation, where the lower tendencies and ignorance that dominate the mind are overcome through the awakening of higher consciousness, guided by divine grace. The battle is not external but internal, taking place within the individual as they progress on the spiritual path.

Lalita Sahasranama reveals many secrets of Kundalini and Chakras

Virtually all human cultures have some kind of concept of mind, spirit and soul as distinct from the physical body. While it is a common notion to associate the Chakras with the Indian traditions, in reality all cultures and religions have their own interpretations on similar lines of energy systems in the body. References can be found in ancient Egyptian, Chinese and Japanese philosophies while the Kabbala, Celtic and Sufi traditions also contain information about bodily energies. Renee Skuban writes, "The Chakras, when viewed collectively, reflect unified consciousness, or soul. When viewed individually, they reflect different aspects of consciousness, including body, instinct, vital energy, emotions, communication and connection to the Divine."

There is a single energy that pervades the entire Cosmos. This universal energy – found in everything from the tiniest grain of sand to the mightiest planet – is responsible for the creation and sustenance of life and forms the basis of all existence. Seen at its most fundamental level, matter is merely energy in a state of vibration. We perceive ourselves and the world around us to be made up of physical matter. In fact, it is very difficult for us to conceive that we (and everything around us) are not matter but pure energy. We find it hard to accept this view because we can see, touch and feel objects and so our reasoning mind asks – how can all of this be mere energy?

Matter is made up of atoms at its most fundamental level. Atoms are further made up of protons, neutrons and electrons. Looking deep into the atomic structure shows that everything inside an atom is in the form of waves or vibration. In short, studies in Quantum Physics clearly establish the fact that there is no matter inside of an atom; it is 99.9% empty space and energy is all there is. If the most basic element of creation is made up of only energy, then it stands to reason that everything in the Universe is just that – energy.

How then do we perceive differences in all forms of life? How do we differentiate between a solid object such as a rock, a liquid such as flowing water and gas such as the breeze that we undeniably can feel? The atoms in every form vibrate at a different speed and it is this speed or frequency that determines whether we perceive the energy as solid, liquid or gas. Atoms which vibrate at a slow speed are perceived as dense and tangible (such as the rock), those at a higher frequency are seen as liquid and at the highest speed, we perceive only the intangible such as light or the breeze.

The cells in our body also emit different energies based on where they are located and what functions they perform. These energies are called "prana" in Ayurveda and "chi" in Chinese medicine. In Ayurveda philosophy, prana is the Sanskrit word for "life-force" or vital principle that permeates all objects – animate and inanimate. Prana flows through several channels, criss-crossing the entire body through energy channels called Nadis. As it flows through the Nadis, prana collects in vortices at particular points in the body which are known as the Chakras. These key points operate like balls of energy interpenetrating the body.

We can use the analogy of a house to explain the Chakras better. Every house has several electrical connections and wires running throughout the building. Switches located at some key points help operate the electrical equipment and can be turned on or off at will. Similarly, we can see the Chakras as these switches that govern the energy systems in the body. Jayaram V writes, "The main function of the Chakras is to draw in the prana by spinning around their own axes and hold it in their respective sphere to maintain and balance the spiritual, mental, emotional and physical well-being of the mind and body."

The Tantra texts suggest that the complex network of Nadis is made up of as many as 72,000 channels through which prana circulates in the body. "Nadi" means "stream" in Sanskrit and according to the Shiva Samhita, there are fourteen main Nadis that are spread throughout our subtle body. Out of these, the three most important Nadis are:

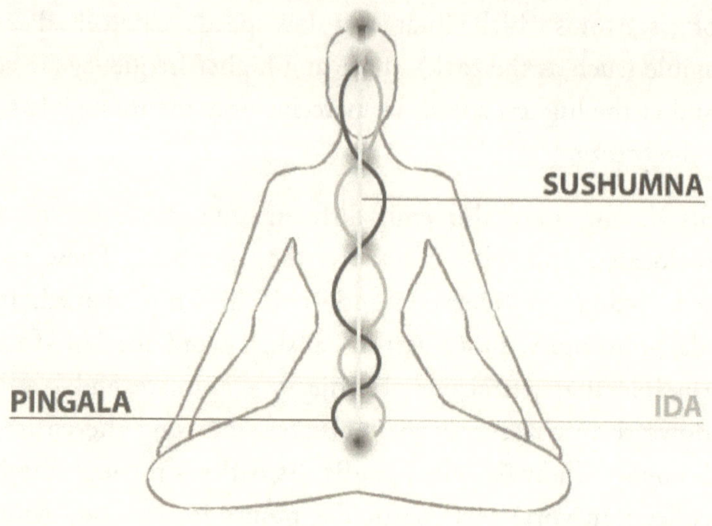

- **Sushumna** – the central channel made up of three subtle channels: Vajra, Chitrini and Brahma, through which energy moves upwards from the Muladhara Chakra to Sahasrara Chakra and controls the central nervous system.
- **Ida** – the feminine Nadi that is cooling in nature and is associated with the colour white and represents the moon. It journeys from the Muladhara Chakra to the left nostril and controls the parasympathetic nervous system.
- **Pingala** – masculine in its characteristics, hot by nature and associated with the colour red and represents the sun. It journeys from the Muladhara Chakra to the right nostril and controls the sympathetic nervous system.

Most experts agree that the study of the three main Nadis and seven main Chakras gives a fairly clear idea of the entire energy system in the body. Ancient Indian scholars suggest that there are 114 Chakras (out of which two lie just above the head) in total, but the seven main Chakras lying between the base of the spine and the crown of the head following the curvature of the spine are the most vital. They are:

- Muladhara or Root Chakra
- Swadisthana or Sacral Chakra
- Manipura or Navel Chakra
- Anahata Chakra or the Heart Chakra
- Vishuddha or Throat Chakra
- Ajna Chakra or the Mid-eyebrow Chakra
- Sahasrara Chakra or the Crown Chakra

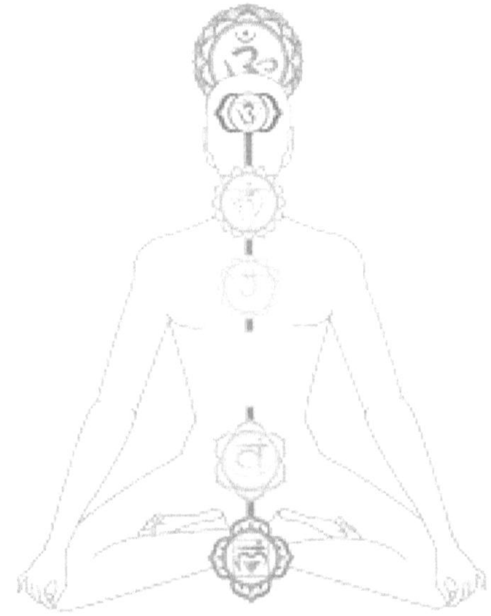

The Nadis and Chakras are not physical attributes. They exist in the subtle body or the Sukshma Sharira. In the Hindu tradition, a living being is made up of mind, body and spirit. The Sharira Tatva (Doctrine of Three Bodies) describes the human body as consisting of three aspects and five sheaths.

The three aspects are:

- Sthula Sharira or the gross physical body
- Sukshma Sharira or the subtle body
- Karana Sharira or the causal body

The Sthula Sharira is the gross physical body through which life or "jiva" is experienced. The main features of this body include birth, ageing and death. It is related to the waking state.

The Sukshma Sharira is the subtle body that houses the mind and vital energies (prana). The subtle body is said to be composed of the five elements (air, fire, water, earth and space) and is made up of the five sense organs (ear, eye, nose, tongue and skin), five organs of action (hand, foot, mouth, anus and genitalia) and the five-fold vital breath (respiration, elimination, circulation, digestion and actions such as sneezing, crying, etc.) along with Manas (mind) and Buddhi (intellect). The dream state is the distinct state of this Sharira. It is in this Sharira that the Chakras can be discerned.

The Karana Sharira is the causal body that merely contains the seed of the Sthula and Sukshma Sharira and it has no other function of its own. It is the most complex of the three bodies and is thought to be the portal to enter higher consciousness. It is identified with the deep sleeping state.

The gross body ceases to exist when death occurs and it then becomes one with Nature. The subtle body disintegrates when it is time to take a new birth, allowing us to develop a new personality in the new life. The causal body incarnates again and again with each rebirth and carries the imprints of the Karmas of our previous lives (samskaras), and disintegrates only at the time of moksha or liberation.

Each body has a dimension or a layer called a sheath or a kosha as it separates the body from the Atman. Each sheath is made up of increasingly finer shades of energy, beginning from the outermost layer of the skin to the innermost spiritual core of our being. There are five such sheaths (described in detail in nama 428 "Panchakoshantarashitha") and it is in the Pranamaya Kosha that the Chakras operate.

The 5 Koshas

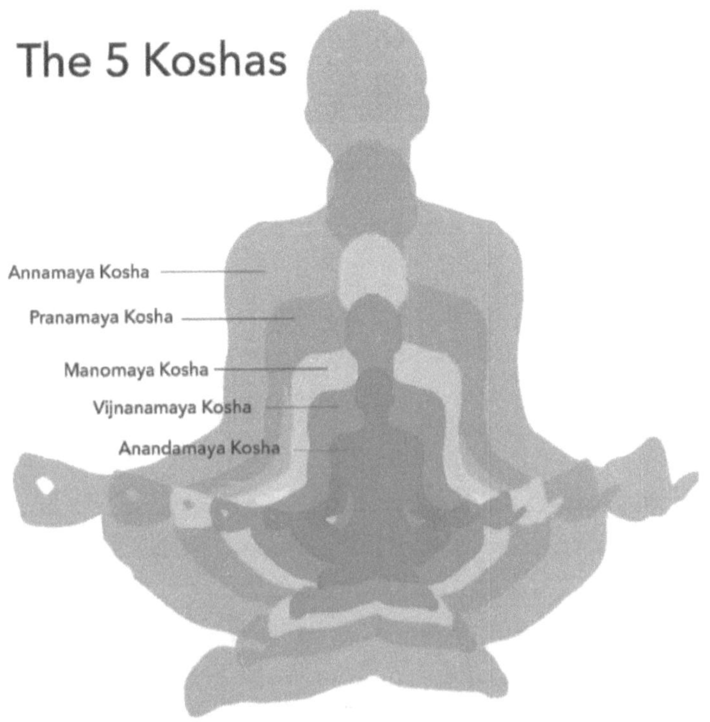

To understand the development of the process by which energy condenses from the unmanifest to the gross physical form of the human body, we can think of the Anandamaya Kosha as ether or space, Vijnanamaya Kosha as air, Manomaya Kosha as steam, Pranamaya Kosha as water and Annamaya Kosha as ice. Just as it is more difficult to give shape to ice than to water (as ice is solid and water as a liquid takes on the shape of its container more easily than ice), the various sheaths become more ephemeral as we move towards the higher realms.

All across Vedic literature, it is reiterated that the human body is a microcosm of the Universe. Whatever exists in the Universe is seen in the human body and vice versa. The human body is seen as comprising two portions – the top half beginning at the crown of the head and ending at the tailbone in the spine; the second half beginning at the tailbone and ending at the feet. The spine is the axis on which the body rests just as the Meru is the axis of the Universe. It is for this reason that the spine is called Meru-danda. We find that five of the Chakras lie along this Meru-danda and the final two at the top of the head. The inward journey of a practitioner begins at the base of the spine and moves upward till it reaches a point above the crown of the head.

There are many Chakras located along the hands and feet but these are minor in terms of the role that they play in the overall energy body. Some of the hand Chakras are located in the palms and are seen as an extension of the Anahata or Heart Chakra while some of the foot Chakras are found in the arch of the feet and are governed by the Muladhara or Root Chakra.

The Chakras, even though they are located in the subtle body, have a profound influence on our physical being. Each Chakra's location corresponds to and is associated with organs that lie in its vicinity and with the plexus – a specific group of nerves. Each Chakra is also associated with a major endocrine gland – the gonads correspond to the Muladhara Chakra, the pancreas to the Swadisthana, adrenals to the Manipura, thymus to the Anahata, thyroid and parathyroid to the Vishuddha, the pineal and pituitary to the Ajna and the entire cerebrospinal region to the master Chakra – the Sahasrara.

The Chakras not only govern aspects of the physical body but they are also deeply and intrinsically connected to the conscious experience of life itself. All senses, perceptions and states of awareness can be separated in seven categories, which in turn are related to a specific Chakra. When we feel fear, for example, we feel a sensation in the sacral region along with an urge to urinate or defecate. When we feel hurt in relationships, we feel it as a pain or discomfort in the heart region. When we feel unable to communicate, we feel the tightness in our throat Chakra and when we feel stress, it invariably leads to a headache in the Third Eye Chakra. Any discomfort perceived by the sense organs is immediately relayed to the Chakras by way of the nerve plexus connecting the brain to that specific Chakra. Extended discomfort, pain, stress and fear have a way of lodging themselves deeply in the cellular memory of the Chakra, thereby giving rise to blockages, which then lead to illness and disease.

Kundalini comes from the word "serpent" as this energy is shown as lying dormant like a coiled-up snake ready to spring into action. The goal of Kundalini is to open up all the Chakras of the body, thereby allowing the ascent of the energy from the Muladhara to the Sahasrara, traversing through the various Chakras. When the energy finally reaches the top of the head, it is said to bring about enlightenment and liberation of the soul. Vedic texts explain that from the Muladhara Chakra, Ida and Pingala alternate from the right to left sides at each Chakra until they reach Ajna Chakra where they meet again with Sushumna. The rising of the Kundalini is seen as the process of the awakening of spiritual consciousness and brings about liberation from illusion and ignorance, leading to the development of wisdom and ultimately a union with the Universal Consciousness.

"Like flowers, Chakras can be open or closed, dying or budding, depending on the state of consciousness within," says Tiffany Luptak. Why do we need to work on them to ensure that they are open, active and effervescent at all times? All our life experiences, possibly even those from our previous lifetimes, influence our Chakras. We are told by Vedic seers that the state of our Chakras depends on our vasanas, Karma and samskaras. Our negative experiences, feelings and emotions and the low-frequency energy associated with them can bring about a blockage in any one of the energy centres. Blockage of energy leads to a stagnation, which then has a cumulative effect on all the other Chakras. An underactive Chakra may push the adjacent Chakra into excessive energy, thereby causing imbalances across the entire Chakra system. The reason why we need to bring about a balance of the Chakras is to enable us to clear old blocks and move into higher states of frequency, leading to the evolution of our higher consciousness. This again is in keeping with the philosophy of the Kundalini Shakti.

Like every other aspect of life, the Chakras continuously move from a state of balance to imbalance and vice versa. Disease and ill health are an outcome of an energy blockage as prana cannot flow freely, thereby affecting the optimal functioning of the body part in question. Imbalances in the Chakras can occur as a result of poor diet, unhealthy lifestyle, lack of exercise, inadequate sleep, bad habits, performance pressure, physical and emotional trauma, stress, unfulfilled and purposeless life, and inability to maintain harmonious relationships with others.

Joy Gardner explains in Vibrational Healing through the Chakras, "As we journey through life, we respond to various events by opening up or closing down physically, emotionally, spiritually. Theoretically, a person who is fully enlightened is fully open at all the Chakras and is not susceptible to these kinds of fluctuations."

The Chakras in the Indian tradition correspond to the five elements – Muladhara represents the Earth element, Swadisthana is the Water element, Manipura is the Fire element, Anahata is the Air element and Ajna is the Space element. The progression is from the grossest to the most subtle element, and this ascent can be understood as a spiritual pilgrimage undertaken, starting at the point of the gross self to culminating in the merging of this self with the Universal Consciousness.

In Tantric texts, each of the seven Chakras has a unique symbol represented by a mandala. The circular design symbolises the belief that the cycle of life and death is never ending and that everything in the Universe is connected, and even more profoundly that everything is derived from a single source.

The lotus is a common motif that is used to depict the seven Chakras. Each Chakra contains a specific number of lotus petals (starting from four petals in the Muladhara and ending with the glorious thousand-petalled lotus of the Sahasrara), with the unfolding of the petals seen as an expression of the expansion of the soul. Even though a lotus is rooted in muddy waters, the flower itself blooms above the water. The mud said to be symbolic of our own personal attachments and desires and how we are blinded by "maya", while the flower stands as a shining example of beauty, emerging unaffected from an undesirable environment. "Just as the Lotus has its roots in the bottom of the lake, the world is the fertile soil from which we live and grow. But our consciousness is destined to raise itself above the clouded sphere of delusion to the clarity and freedom of Divine vision. The opening lotus blossom symbolises the unfolding of the consciousness and the awakening of wisdom within us. In Yoga literature the Chakras are also referred to as lotuses, for example the Muladhara Chakra is known as the Mula Kamala, the Manipura as Nabhi Kamala, the Vishudda as Kantha Kamala," says Paramahans Swami Maheshwarananda.

Recent studies have been undertaken to understand the Vagus nerve and its connection to the seven Chakras. The Vagus nerve is the 10th cranial ventricle, extending from the base of the spine to the brain. Its function is to gather information from the autonomous organs and glands of the body, such as the heart, intestines, thymus and thyroid, and bring this information to the brain for deduction. The Vagus nerve is the longest nerve in the human body and is called the communication highway of the body. It does not transmit the chemicals but only the electrical signals to the brain. Yoga and Tantra experts state that there is a distinct possibility that Vagus Nerve could very well be what the sages of old saw "lit up" in deep Samadhi as the fiery serpent running up the spine to the brain. Here are some of the similarities between the Vagus nerve and the Kundalini:

- It runs from the base of the spine to the brain
- The Vagus Nerve is two nerves recognised as one, just as the Kundalini is seen as the intermingling of Ida and Pingala coming together as one in the Sushumna Nadi.
- Both run through the spinal cord.
- Both touch and interact with the organs and glands along the spine.

For those seeking proof that the Chakras exist on a physical level, the similarities between the Kundalini Shakti, as described by Patanjali in the Yoga Sutras, and the Vagus nerve point to the possibility that the Vagus nerve is a physical manifestation of the primordial energy system outlined in the ancient Indian texts.

Swami Tadatmananda describes that whether we believe the Chakras exist or not is actually not a relevant matter to the practice of trying to bring our Chakras to a state of balance. The whole idea behind this wonderful concept is to bring attention and focus to all important parts of our body and meditate upon our feelings that arise there. Just as the goal of a pilgrimage is to get the blessings of a deity residing in a special place, the Chakras must be seen as divinity residing inside our own body which can be visited through a pilgrimage. This inner pilgrimage is a meditation practice in which we deliberately imagine sacred places within our body.

The Lalita Sahasranama has several names that list Devi's connection to Kundalini. In name 110, Lalita is identified as Kundalini Shakti. She is also called Muladharaika Nilaya, Ajna Chakra Antara Sthita and Sahasrara Ambuja Rudha. Her names that relate to the Chakras include Tatillata Samaruchi (She who shines like a streak of lightning), Chakra Raja Niketana, Nityaklinna (associated with the Svadhisthana chakra, which governs creative and reproductive fluids, emphasizing the flow of energy within the chakra) and Kaulini which refers to Lalita's power in the esoteric Kaula tradition, which involves the awakening and ascent of Kundalini through the chakras.

Lalita Sahasranama describes the various paths of Sri Vidya

Within Sri Vidya, there are three primary paths – Kaulachara, Mishrachar, and Samayachara. Each of these paths represents a different level of practice, catering to various levels of spiritual maturity and temperament. The differences lie in the methods of worship, the symbolism employed, and the degree of external versus internal focus.

Kaulachara is the most esoteric and secretive path within the Sri Vidya tradition, associated with the worship of the Goddess in her most powerful and sometimes fierce forms. The term Kaula comes from "Kula," which means "family" or "group," and in this context, it refers to the community of practitioners who follow this path. Kaulachara is also closely linked to the left-hand path (Vamachara) of Tantra, which involves practices that can be seen as unconventional or transgressive, particularly in orthodox Hindu contexts.

Key Features:

- **External Rituals:** Kaulachara involves elaborate rituals, performed in secret and sometimes using substances like wine and meat, which are traditionally taboo in Hindu rituals. These rituals are symbolic acts meant to transcend dualities and break down societal and psychological barriers that separate the practitioner from the Divine.
- **Sexual Rituals:** Some branches of Kaulachara involve sexual rites, known as maithuna, which are used as a means of awakening and channeling Kundalini energy. These practices are highly symbolic and are conducted with strict discipline and reverence.
- **Body and Universe as the Temple:** The body is seen as a microcosm of the universe, and therefore, practices involve the worship of the body and its energies. This path emphasizes the unity of the physical and spiritual realms, where the Divine is both immanent and transcendent

The Kularnava Tantra is one of the key texts of the Kaulachara tradition. It states, "In the left-hand path, the wise consider everything pure and there is nothing impure. The adept should transcend the dualities of pure and impure, and consider everything as the play of the Goddess."

Mishrachar (also spelled Mishraachara) represents a synthesis of the external rituals of Kaulachara and the internalized meditative practices of Samayachara. It is considered a middle path that balances ritualistic worship with inner contemplation and spiritual discipline. This path is adopted by practitioners who seek to transition from the external focus of Kaulachara to the more refined and internalized practices of Samayachara.

Key Features:

- **Combination of External and Internal Worship:** In Mishrachar, rituals and offerings are still performed, but there is a greater emphasis on internal visualization and meditation. The focus begins to shift from the external symbols to their inner meanings.
- **Mantra and Yantra:** The use of mantra (sacred sounds) and yantra (sacred geometric diagrams) is prominent in Mishrachar. The Sri Yantra is especially central, with practices involving its worship as a symbol of the entire cosmos and the body of the Goddess.
- **Balance of Dualities:** Mishrachar teaches the balance between the worldly life and spiritual aspirations. Practitioners engage in rituals that honor both the material and the spiritual, recognizing that both are expressions of the Divine.

The Rudra Yamala Tantra discusses the importance of this balanced approach, stating, "The middle path is the path of the wise, who know the essence of both external and internal worship. The Goddess, who is both immanent and transcendent, is pleased by this balanced devotion."

3. Samayachara: The Path of Internal Worship

Samayachara is the most refined and internalized form of worship within Sri Vidya, emphasizing the inner experience of the Divine over external rituals. The term Samaya means "inward" or "secret," and this path is characterized by its focus on internal meditation, the subtle aspects of consciousness, and the realization of the non-dual nature of the self and the Divine.

Key Features:

- **Internalized Practices:** In Samayachara, the focus is entirely on internal worship, where the rituals, offerings, and even the temple are envisioned within the practitioner's own body and mind. This path involves deep meditation, where the Goddess is visualized in the heart, and the Sri Yantra is meditated upon as existing within the subtle body.

- **Emphasis on Non-Dualism:** Samayachara aligns closely with the philosophy of Advaita (non-dualism), where the practitioner seeks to dissolve the ego and realize the unity of the individual self (Atman) with the Supreme Consciousness (Brahman). The worship is directed towards recognizing the Goddess as the ultimate reality, beyond all forms and attributes.
- **No External Rituals:** Unlike Kaulachara and Mishrachar, Samayachara avoids external rituals entirely, viewing them as unnecessary for those who have advanced to a level where internalized worship is sufficient for spiritual progress.

The Tripura Rahasya, a key text in the Sri Vidya tradition, extols the virtues of Samayachara, stating, "The supreme worship is that which is done in the secret cave of the heart, where the Goddess dwells. Those who realize her within need no external offerings, for their very being is an offering to the Divine."

The three paths of Sri Vidya represent a progression from external, ritualistic worship to the most internalized and subtle forms of spiritual practice. Each path is suited to different levels of spiritual development and temperament, allowing practitioners to engage with the Divine in a manner that aligns with their individual nature and spiritual maturity. The ultimate goal in all three paths is the realization of the Divine Feminine as both immanent and transcendent, leading to spiritual liberation.

Lalita Sahasranama describes the Sri Chakra

Thoughts and words cannot exist in the spiritual dimension since they are a construct of the intellect and mind. Sacred geometry arises from this fact that many philosophical truths cannot be expressed with words. The world around us is filled with geometrical designs and shapes. Hinduism is full of ancient and sacred geometric symbols – Om, swastika, the linga, vaastu purusha to name a few. They all hold the keys to unravelling the secrets of the cosmos.

Three words are commonly used in Hindu symbolism: Mandala, Chakra and Yantra.

The term mandala appears in the Rig Veda and is used generically to stand for any drawing, diagram or geometric pattern that represents the cosmos symbolically or metaphysically.

One of the chief symbolic purposes of the mandala is to represent the different layers of the universe – the spiritual realm, the lived environment, the inner experience of man – and how each of these layers can flow into and out of the next. Therefore, the mandala is perhaps the most essential tool when practitioners seek enlightenment or spiritual connection.

The Sanskrit word "chakra" essentially denotes a spinning vortex or wheel. In the "The Tantra of Sri Chakra Bhavanopanishat by Prof: S.K.Ramachandra Rao, he writes:

The etymology of the word would suggest that by which anything is done (kriyate aneana). The wheel of the cart, the wheel of the potter, the wheel like weapon that is flung against the enemy are all called 'chakras'. In its extended meaning, chakra also signifies a kingdom and because the wheels of the King's chariot can roll on there without hindrance. The King of the land is thus described as 'chakravartin'. The word also signifies arrangement of the army (charka vyuha) in order to fortify its position and secure victory. Sanskrit poets are found to employ characteristically circular patterns of letter of words (chakra bandha) to convey the meaning more forcefully (if also more tortuously) than usual. Whatever the sense in which the word is employed, it invariably means a 'power field', an arrangement of parts so as to accomplish the desired end. The circular form which the chakra usually brings to mind denotes both comprehension and facility. It comprehends all the parts, units and details in a compact and effective manner, so that the whole form is unitary and functional. But the form need not necessarily be circular. The idea of comprehension may be metaphorical, as in expressions like 'rituchakra' (the round of the seasons) 'nakshatra chakra' (the collection of stars) and 'nadi chakra' (the arrangement of the arteries).

The most common form of mandala is the powerful, mystical, esoteric and compelling "Yantra".

It is said that Lord Shiva created 64 yantras and gave them to mankind to help them progress materially and spiritually. Yantras are considered be the residence of its personal deity (ishta-devata) and therefore there are yantras named for specific desires and specifics Gods and Goddesses and are a representation of the energies they signify and embody. For example:

Ganesha Yantra – to clear obstacles and succeed in fresh ventures

Kali Yantra – to strengthen the feminine energy and become fearless

Lakshmi Yantra – to acquire material wealth

Dhanvantari Yantra – for healing diseases and getting good health

Navagraha Yantra – for general prosperity and to balance the chakras

Each yantra is a mantra (sacred phoneme) by means of which the individual mind calls the cosmic energy through the three bodies: causal, subtle and material. In addition, the yantras are complemented with mantras, since they combine the power of the practitioner with the of the yantra, which, in turn, vibrates with the infinite power of the universe. In meditation, both instruments are used simultaneously. A properly energized yantra contains the same energy of divinity and is the essence of the divinity. (Juan Carlos Ramchandani)

The word is derived from the root verb "Yantr" meaning to restrain or control. It can be understood as a machine or a device that controls human effort in performing a task (thereby providing assistance). A mantra uses sound energy to bring about a balance in the mind and body while a yantra uses the visual medium to bring about a state of equilibrium. Every yantra has to conform to three basic principles:

Akriti-rupa or Form

Kriya-rupa or Function

Shakti-rupa or Power

The geometric symmetry that lies within a yantra is a reflection of the unity of the individual with the universe and this pattern of repetition of seeing the microcosm in the macrocosm and vice versa is said to bring about a balance in the two hemispheres of the brain.

Recent studies have shown that merely looking at certain geometric patterns can alter brain waves and open gateways to higher states of consciousness. The reason why this can happen is because the geometric patterns bring about an alignment of the left and right aspects of the brain. The left hemisphere of the brain is involved in verbal, analytical and logic related activities while the right side performs more intuitive, creative and holistic thinking tasks. Visualising or meditating upon a yantra has been shown to bring about greater balance in the left brain-right brain activity.

One of the most powerful, auspicious and important Yantras in the Tantra tradition is the Sri Chakra Yantra. Tantric texts state that worship of any deity can be undertaken in the Sri Chakra as it is the foundation of all Yantras. Adi Shankaracharya was a great believer in the power of the Sri Chakra and he had it installed in all the temples he visited.

The Vedas suggest that while Shiva created 64 yantras and their corresponding mantras for the welfare of humanity, he gave the knowledge of the Sri Chakra Yantra to his wife along with its highly secret Shodasi mantra.

The deity that Sri Chakra Yantra represents is Lalita Tripurasundari but it is not called the Lalita Chakra or Tripurasundari Chakra to denote its auspiciousness and overriding power and authority.

In the tantric tradition, all symbols have three aspects:

The Gross aspect depicting an image of the body, face, weapons, etc., of the diety

The Subtle form which is shown in a yantra

The Causal form which is depicted by the mantra

The Vamakeshvara Tantra describes her thus:

"The Dear One, Tripura is the ultimate, primordial Shakti, the light of manifestation. She, the pile of letters of the alphabet, gave birth to the three worlds. At dissolution, She is the abode of all tattvas, still remaining Herself."

Lalita means "the playful one" reflecting the Vedic philosophy which sees all of creation as a mere game or play of the Divine Consciousness.

Tripurasundari means "beauty of the three worlds" where the three worlds can signify:

Three locations: Heaven, Hell and Earth

The three states of being: Sleeping, dreaming and waking

The three gunas: Tamas, Rajas and Sattva

The triad of human experience: intellect, feelings and physical sensation

The goddess is seen as residing in her physical and visible form in the bindu at the centre of the yantra while permeating the entire Universe at the same time.

"The Sri Chakra Yantra to give it the correct name, is regarded as the Supreme Yantra. Any other Yantra is but a part or fraction of the Sri Yantra; it both includes and transcends all Yantras ever made, and no existing Yantra can not be found in the Sri Yantra. The benefits of all Yantras are, therefore, to be found individually and collectively in the Sri Yantra. It is also considered to be the greatest achievement in the abstract, symbolic representation of the Divine. The Sri Yantra is traditionally held to have been divinely revealed rather than invented, a concept that is easily understood when one realizes the immense complexity of the Yantra."

Rohit Arya, Symbolism of the Sri Yantra

The Sri Yantra appears deceptively simple in its construction but is one of the most geometrical patterns in recorded history. Many accomplished mathematicians have wondered how Hindu sages were able to draw such complicated geometric patterns without any aids even as they struggle to achieve the same with all resources at hand. The Sri Yantra is precisely constructed to match the proportions of the Golden Ratio.

The Golden Ratio is called the blueprint of all creations. We see it all around us in nature (Genome, DNA, flowers, seashells) art (Da Vinci's Mona Lisa and Michelangelo's art on the ceiling of the Sistine Chapel), architecture (Egyptian Pyramids, Parthenon), branding (Pepsi and Nike logos). Even our faces and bodies follow this Golden Ratio and our perception of beauty is actually defined by this ratio. A person is seen as attractive because his/her proportions are closer to the Golden ratio. Our brain is hard wired to prefer objects and images that are close to this ratio.

The Golden Ratio in Nature

The Sri Chakra also contains several similarities with the Flower of Life which is seen as a blueprint for creation of sound, matter and consciousness. This pattern is seen repeated through nature. In the image below, we can see how a human embryo also replicates the pattern of the Flower of Life.

The study of visible sound is called Cymatics, and it reveals some fascinating truths about our universe that go unseen by the naked eye. Sounds actually have a distinct geometry, much like crystals and flowers and nautilus shells.

When picked up by a special apparatus, such as the sand-covered plate called a tonoscope these vibrations reveal incredible geometric shapes that are as unique and beautiful as a flurry of snowflakes.

The holy syllable Aum when sounded through a tonoscope (an instrument used to create patterns corresponding to different sounds) a geometric pattern very similar to that of Sri Yantra is created. Dr Hans Jenny (a pioneer in the field of cymatics) first established the correlation between sounds and their vibrational patterns. Our ancient sages had the knowledge to reverse engineer the sacred sound of Aum to a geometrical form! Just as the number 108 is believed to be the numeric representation of Aum, the Sri Yantra is its the visual representation.

A study conducted in Moscow University used an EEG machine to observe the brainwaves of test subjects who were asked to stare into a Sri Yantra. Within a few minutes of mild concentration on the geometric pattern, it was found that there was a change in the brain activities of the subject as the brain waves slowed down considerably and reached an Alpha level, a state of mind associated with heightened intuition, greater creativity and deeper relaxation. (Source: Biology Faculty of Moscow University, October 1987)

Itagi Ravi Kumar and Jang Jungyun conducted an experiment using the Sri Yantra to see if it had any effects on the germination of green gram. Two types of Sri Yantra made of copper were used. One was a two-dimensional Bhuprasthana yantra and the other was a Maha Meru yantra. It was discovered that samples treated with both the yantras showed a marked increase in percentage of germination, radical length and fresh and oven dry weight of germinated seeds when compared to the control sample seeds. The two-dimensional Bhuprasthana yantra showed a more positive effect than the three-dimensional meru yantra. (Source: International Journal of Geology, Agriculture and Environmental Sciences (Vol 5, Issue 2 April 2017)

R.K.Sennaya Swamy Muthukrishnan, an Indian Egyptologist travelled to the Pyramids of Giza to prove that the base triangles of the great pyramids are equal in angular measurements to those found in the Sri Chakra Yantra. In his book "The Egyptian Code: The Secret Code used by Pharaohs that can turn small businesses into empires" he writes that far from being the tombs of Pharaohs, the pyramids served as a recuperation and resting place for important persons among the Egyptian elite. The bio-energy found inside a pyramid helps cure ailments and restore vitality and good health. Recent deciphering of Egyptian hieroglyphics lends credence to Muthukrishnan's theories. (Source: The Hindustan Times Oct, 28 1997 – Pyramidal Facts)

An award-winning American artist called Bill Witherspoon has written extensively about his experiment with a diagram of the Sri Chakra Yantra on a dry lake in Oregon. He states that after the sacred drawing was dissolved by natural causes, there were many changes recorded in the area with an increase noted in soil fertility, plant nutrients and yield. (Source: John Hopkins University – Project MUSE digital library)

The well-known American physicist Dr. Patrick Flanagan calls the Sri Yantra "the king of power diagrams", and describes its energetic effect as seventy times greater than that of a pyramid construction. (Source: Research paper by Marcus Schmieke featuring Dr. Flanagan's findings)

The Sri Yantra can be seen in three forms – plane, pyramidical and spherical. In its plane two-dimensional form, it is also called the Bhuprasthana and is typically presented as engravings on copper, silver or gold. In its three-dimensional form, it is called a Maha Meru, the mythological cosmic mountain said to be at the center of the universe. The Meru in plan is the same as in the plane Sri Chakra but the triangles surrounding the innermost triangle are piled one on top of another in different planes to arrive at a whole which is shaped like a pyramid. The bindu is at the top most part of the structure. In yet another complex three-dimensional form, the Sri Yantra is presented in a spherical shape called the Kurma (as it resembles a tortoise's shell) thereby becoming phenomenally more complex in structure and construction.

Worship can be of two kinds – external worship (baahya pooja) in which the worshipper sees himself as disparate from the object of his devotion or internal worship (antah pooja) in which the worshipper identifies completely with the object of his devotion. The Sri Chakra Yantra is a device which is used in both forms of worship as a guide to ultimately fulfilling the desires of the worshipper.

Meditation on any of the forms are acceptable and there is no need to go out and buy an expensive Maha Meru or Kurma Sri Yantra. An accurate drawing on paper will work just as well as the most intricately carved

Maha Meru. However, if you intend to become a serious practitioner, I would advise you to buy a two-dimensional Bhuprasthana Sri Yantra engraved on copper after due research and checking if it indeed it is an accurate representation of the sacred geometry.

Each of the nine Avaranas is a distinct level of the Sri Yantra, symbolizing both the external universe and the internal journey of the practitioner towards ultimate unity with the Divine. The journey through these Avaranas is a symbolic path from the outermost aspects of the material world to the innermost core of spiritual realization, culminating in the experience of non-dual consciousness represented by the Bindu.

1. The Outer Square (Bhupura) – The Earth Realm

- **Description:** The outermost enclosure of the Sri Yantra is a square with four gates, known as the Bhupura, which symbolizes the material world and the foundational elements of creation. It is the realm of physical existence, representing the earth element (Prithvi Tattva).
- **Deities:** The four gates are guarded by the Chatur Ayudhas (four weapons) and the Chaturashiti Yoginis (84 Yoginis), symbolizing the protective forces of the divine.
- **Symbolism:** The Bhupura represents the physical body and the world of form, the starting point of the spiritual journey. It serves as the boundary between the mundane and the sacred, reminding the practitioner of the need to transcend material attachments.

2. The Sixteen-Petaled Lotus (Shodasha-Dala)

- **Description:** The second Avarana is a lotus with sixteen petals, each associated with a specific energy center or Tattva. It corresponds to the vital energy (Prana) that sustains life and the senses.
- **Deities:** The sixteen petals are associated with the Shodashi Nityas, the sixteen aspects of the Goddess Lalita, representing different stages of lunar energy.

- **Symbolism:** This Avarana represents the subtle body and the senses, where the practitioner begins to withdraw from external distractions and focus on internal purification.

3. The Eight-Petaled Lotus (Ashta-Dala)

- **Description:** The third Avarana is an eight-petaled lotus, symbolizing the higher aspects of the mind and intellect (Buddhi). It is associated with the eight forms of wealth (Ashta Lakshmis) and the eight divine qualities.
- **Deities:** The eight petals are home to the Vasini Devis, representing speech and communication, which govern the power of words and their manifestation in the world.
- **Symbolism:** This layer represents the purification of the intellect and the control of speech, encouraging the practitioner to cultivate wisdom and discernment.

4. The Fourteen Triangles (Chaturdasha-Kona)

- **Description:** The fourth Avarana is composed of fourteen triangles, symbolizing the fourteen channels of energy (Nadis) in the subtle body. These channels correspond to different aspects of life and consciousness.
- **Deities:** The triangles are associated with the Kulotteerna Nityas, deities who preside over the subtle elements of the body and mind, helping to integrate and balance the energies within.
- **Symbolism:** This layer represents the mastery over the mind and emotions, signifying the alignment of internal energies with the divine will.

5. The Ten Triangles (Bahirdasara)

- **Description:** The fifth Avarana consists of ten outer triangles, representing the ten vital breaths (Pranas) and the ten aspects of the cosmic law (Dharma).

- **Deities:** The ten triangles are inhabited by the Dasara Mudra Devatas, deities associated with the sacred hand gestures (Mudras) used in ritual practices.
- **Symbolism:** This Avarana signifies the control of vital energy and the harmonization of physical and spiritual practices, leading to deeper states of meditation and awareness.

6. The Ten Inner Triangles (Antardasara)

- **Description:** The sixth Avarana consists of ten inner triangles, corresponding to the ten forms of the Goddess Kali (Dasha Mahavidyas) and the ten cosmic energies (Dasha Shaktis).
- **Deities:** These triangles are associated with the Dasara Matruka Devis, deities who embody the primordial sounds (Matrukas) from which the universe is created.
- **Symbolism:** This layer represents the deeper aspects of speech and thought, focusing on the transformation of consciousness through the power of divine sound and vibration.

7. The Eight Triangles (Ashta-Kona)

- **Description:** The seventh Avarana is composed of eight triangles, symbolizing the eight primary energies (Ashta Matrikas) that govern the universe and the inner being.
- **Deities:** The eight triangles are presided over by the Ashta Matrikas, mother goddesses who protect and nurture the cosmic order.
- **Symbolism:** This Avarana represents the integration of cosmic energies into the practitioner's consciousness, leading to the realization of the interconnectedness of all existence.

8. The Inner Triangle (Trikona)

- **Description:** The eighth Avarana is a single, downward-pointing triangle, symbolizing the Yoni, or the source of all creation. It represents the primordial womb of the universe from which all forms arise.

- **Deities:** This triangle is associated with the Goddess Tripura Sundari herself, in her most intimate and personal form as the creator, preserver, and destroyer.
- **Symbolism:** The Trikona represents the union of the individual soul with the cosmic soul, the merging of the personal with the universal. It is the stage where duality dissolves, and the practitioner experiences the oneness of all existence.

9. The Central Point (Bindu)

- **Description:** The ninth and final Avarana is the Bindu, the central point of the Sri Yantra, representing the ultimate reality, the source of all creation, and the abode of the Goddess in her formless aspect.
- **Deities:** The Bindu is Lalita Tripurasundari herself in her supreme, transcendent form, beyond all attributes and forms. It is the ultimate destination of the spiritual journey.
- **Symbolism:** The Bindu represents the state of non-dual awareness, where the individual self realizes its unity with the Divine. It is the goal of the spiritual journey, symbolizing liberation (Moksha) and the return to the source of all existence.

The nine Avaranas of the Sri Yantra encapsulate the entire process of creation, sustenance, and dissolution, as well as the spiritual journey from the outermost layer of physical existence to the innermost core of divine consciousness. Each Avarana corresponds to a different stage of spiritual development, guiding the practitioner from the material world to the realization of the ultimate truth. The Sri Yantra, therefore, serves as both a map of the cosmos and a blueprint for spiritual practice, leading to the highest state of unity with the Divine. Through contemplation and meditation on the Sri Yantra, practitioners of Sri Vidya can transcend the limitations of the ego and experience the profound, all-encompassing presence of the Divine Mother.

Lalita Sahasranama portrays the concept of Leela

In Hindu spirituality, the concept of Leela holds a significant and profound role. Leela, translated as divine play refers to the creative and playful activities of the divine, particularly as manifested by gods and goddesses in Hindu mythology. This concept is rooted in the belief that the ultimate reality, Brahman, engages in the cosmic drama of creation, preservation, and destruction for the sake of its own delight. One of the primary meanings of Lalita is "beautiful" or "graceful." It conveys a sense of charm, elegance, and aesthetic beauty. This aspect of the meaning aligns with the concept of "Leela" or divine play in Hindu philosophy, emphasizing the joyful and playful nature of the divine.

Play is an inherent aspect of human nature that transcends age boundaries. While it is commonly associated with the carefree days of childhood, its importance in adult life is frequently underestimated.

The concept of Leela is intimately associated with Lalita Tripurasundari, where it takes on a specific connotation related to her divine play or cosmic dance. Lalita's Leela is seen as the dynamic and creative manifestation of the ultimate reality, Brahman. Her playful activities are believed to be the source of the universe's creation, maintenance, and dissolution.

The concept of Leela in association with Lalita Tripurasundari adds a specific dimension to the broader understanding of divine play in Hindu spirituality. It emphasizes the dynamic and creative aspects of the goddess's existence, showcasing her role as the source and sustainer of the cosmic dance of life. Devotees view Lalita's Leela as an invitation to participate joyfully in the divine play, seeking spiritual growth and realization through devotion and surrender to the Divine Mother.

Interpreting the concept of Leela in the context of modern physics and the simulation hypothesis can offer intriguing perspectives on the nature of reality. While these concepts may seem distinct, there are parallels that can be explored, providing a bridge between spiritual traditions and scientific theories.

In quantum physics, the nature of reality is inherently uncertain. The concept of Leela, with its emphasis on the dynamic and playful nature of existence, aligns with the inherent uncertainty and fluidity observed at the quantum level. The idea that the universe may be more like a cosmic dance of probabilities resonates with the playful and creative aspects of Leela. Both the spiritual concept of Leela and certain interpretations of modern physics, such as non-duality, emphasize the unity of all things. In Leela, the play of the divine is seen as an expression of the ultimate reality, and in physics, there are theories suggesting that everything is interconnected. The simulation hypothesis, too, posits a unified source from which the simulated reality emerges.

The simulation hypothesis, proposing that our reality is akin to a computer-generated simulation, echoes the idea of Leela in the sense that it suggests a purposeful and creative force behind the manifestation of the universe. In Leela, the divine play is purposeful and imbued with meaning, much like the idea that a simulated reality may have a purpose or underlying design. Leela emphasizes the importance of consciousness and awareness in experiencing and understanding the divine play. In the context of the simulation hypothesis, some theories suggest that consciousness is fundamental to reality and may be a key aspect of the underlying simulation. This aligns with the spiritual notion that consciousness is central to the divine play.

In the modern context, the concept of Leela can offer a lens through which individuals might appreciate the dynamic, uncertain, and interconnected nature of reality as described by certain theories in physics, including the simulation hypothesis. While they approach the nature of existence from different angles, both perspectives invite contemplation on the purpose, meaning, and creative expression embedded in the fabric of the universe.

The Lalita Sahasranama highlights various aspects of Leela through names such as "Sri Vidya", the sacred knowledge or wisdom that reveals the playful nature of the Divine Mother. Lalita's Leela is expressed through the knowledge that she imparts to her devotees. This wisdom, or Sri Vidya, is not just about rituals or practices but about understanding the underlying joy and playfulness in all of creation. It emphasizes that the universe is a manifestation of her divine play, where everything happens as an expression of her will.

"Leela kluptha brahmanda mandala" describes Her as the one who created the universe as a mere sport, directly referencing the concept of Leela, emphasizing that the entire cosmos is created effortlessly by the Divine Mother as part of her play. It suggests that the creation of the universe is not a serious or laborious process for Lalita but a joyful, spontaneous act that reflects her boundless energy and creativity. "Srishti-Karti" highlights Lalita as the creator, and implicitly refers to her role in the ongoing play of creation, where she constantly manifests the universe in a dynamic and playful manner. Her creation is not static but an ongoing, ever-changing play. "Nirlepa" reflects the idea that while Lalita is deeply involved in her cosmic play, she remains unattached and unaffected by it. Her actions in the universe, though full of play and joy, do not bind her. This detachment is a key aspect of Leela, where the divine engages in creation without being entangled by it. "Sahasra Srirsha Vadana" symbolizes the infinite forms and expressions of the Divine Mother. Her Leela is manifest in countless ways, with each aspect of creation reflecting a different face of her divine play. The multiplicity of forms and experiences in the universe is a testament to the endless nature of her Leela.

The concept of Leela in the Lalita Sahasranama teaches devotees to view life and the universe with a sense of wonder, joy, and detachment. It encourages the understanding that all events, whether perceived as good or bad, are part of the divine play of the Mother. This perspective helps devotees cultivate a deeper sense of acceptance and equanimity, recognizing that the ultimate purpose of creation is the expression of divine joy. By contemplating the names and their meanings in the Lalita Sahasranama, one can gain a profound insight into the playful, compassionate, and dynamic nature of the Divine Mother, realizing that the entire cosmos is an expression of her divine Leela.

Lalita Sahasranama is similar in structure to the Brahma Sutra

The 1000 names are arranged in four divisions which are very similar to the Brahma Sutra: Samanvaya (integration of diverse texts into a complete picture), Avirodha (removing all objections and internal contradictions), Sadhana (methods of worship) and Phala (results).

Samanvaya refers to the integration or harmonization of diverse scriptural teachings into a coherent and unified philosophical system. In Hinduism, which encompasses a vast array of scriptures such as the Vedas, Upanishads, Puranas, Itihasas and various Agamas and Tantras, Samanvaya is essential to synthesizing these elements into a consistent worldview of these texts presents different perspectives on the nature of reality, the divine, and the path to spiritual liberation.

The task of Samanvaya involves reconciling these different perspectives and presenting them in a way that they complement rather than contradict each other. This is done by establishing a hierarchy of texts (Prasthana Traya, for example, which includes the Upanishads, the Bhagavad Gita, and the Brahma Sutras) and interpreting them in a way that aligns with the overarching principles of the tradition. The philosopher Adi Shankaracharya is known for his work in integrating the teachings of various scriptures into a coherent non-dual (Advaita) Vedanta philosophy. He harmonized the teachings of the Upanishads, the Bhagavad Gita, and the Brahma Sutras to present a unified understanding of Brahman as the ultimate reality.

Avirodha (Non-Contradiction or Resolution of Objections):

Avirodha means non-contradiction or the resolution of apparent contradictions within or between scriptures, philosophical arguments, or doctrinal statements. This concept is crucial for maintaining the internal consistency of a philosophical system. It is employed to ensure that different teachings within a particular school (like Vedanta, Nyaya, or Samkhya) do not contradict each other. If contradictions appear, they are addressed through logical reasoning and interpretation to remove any inconsistencies.

In classical Indian philosophy, debates between different schools involve the use of Purvapaksha (the statement of an opponent's view) and Siddhanta (the establishment of one's own view). Avirodha plays a key role in the process of Samvadha (dialogue or debate) by resolving objections raised by opponents and demonstrating the internal coherence of one's own position. For example, the Brahma Sutras systematically address and resolve various objections to the teachings of the Upanishads. Each Sutra in the text seeks to clarify and resolve potential contradictions within Vedantic thought.

Sadhana (Methods of Spiritual Practice):

Sadhana refers to the disciplined spiritual practices or methods that are prescribed for attaining spiritual goals, such as self-realization, liberation, or union with the Divine. The term encompasses a wide range of practices, each suited to different temperaments, circumstances, and stages of spiritual development. Hinduism recognizes multiple paths for spiritual practice, such as Jnana Yoga (the path of knowledge), Bhakti Yoga (the path of devotion), Karma Yoga (the path of selfless action), and Raja Yoga (the path of meditation and discipline). Each of these paths constitutes a different form of Sadhana. Sadhana is the practical application of the teachings derived from the scriptures and philosophy. It is through Sadhana that a practitionertransforms theoretical knowledge into experiential wisdom and spiritual realization. The Bhagavad Gita outlines different forms of Sadhana, including Bhakti, Dhyana, Karma each leading to the ultimate goal of union with the Divine.

4. Phala (Results or Fruits of Practice):

Phala refers to the results, fruits, or outcomes of Sadhana or philosophical inquiry. It is understood not only in terms of immediate outcomes but also in terms of ultimate spiritual achievements. The Phala of Sadhana can manifest in various forms, such as increased inner peace, clarity of mind, and detachment from material desires. The ultimate Phala, however, is Moksha which is the release from the cycle of birth and death (Samsara) and the realization of one's true nature as identical with Brahman. The concept of Phala is also closely linked with the Law of Karma, which states that every action has a corresponding result. Good actions lead to positive outcomes, while negative actions lead to suffering. However, in the context of spiritual practice, the focus is on achieving a state of Nishkama Karma (action without attachment to results), which is central to the teachings of the Bhagavad Gita. In the Upanishads, the Phala of realizing the self (is described as the attainment of Brahman and the experience of Sat-Chit-Ananda. This realization is considered the highest Phala, surpassing all material gains or temporary pleasures.

In the broader context of Hindu philosophy, these four concepts are deeply interconnected. Samanvaya and Avirodha ensure that the teachings and doctrines of Hinduism are internally consistent and harmonized, providing a solid foundation for Sadhana. Sadhana, in turn, is the practical means by which these teachings are actualized in the life of the practitioner, leading to the desired Phala or spiritual outcome.

Nama in LSN	How they relate to the structure
1 to 3	Neutral in character
4 to 131	Samanvaya (confirming that everything is the form of Chitshakti)
132 to 256	Avirodha (removing all objections and internal contradictions)
257 to 274	Self-enquiry and realisation
275 to 999	Self-realisation and evidence in shastras
1000	Results obtained

Chapter 2

Poorva Bhaga

Our scriptures describe how the world was in a state of turmoil due to the rise of demonic forces, leading to a decline in dharma and spiritual knowledge. Sage Agastya, though a repository of immense knowledge, was concerned about the increasing ignorance and suffering among the beings on earth. Seeking a way to restore dharma and spiritual balance, Sage Agastya embarked on intense penance to invoke divine guidance.

Vishnu, in his Hayagriva form, appeared before Agastya in response to his prayers. The choice of Hayagriva as the divine teacher in this context is significant, as he is the embodiment of supreme wisdom and the restorer of lost knowledge, especially the Vedas. In the Srimad Bhagavatam, Hayagriva is described as the one who dispels the darkness of ignorance and restores spiritual knowledge, making him the ideal figure to impart such profound wisdom to Agastya.

The interaction between Hayagriva and Agastya is recorded in the Brahmanda Purana where Sage Hayagriva, recognizing Agastya's earnestness and capacity for deep spiritual knowledge, decides to impart the Lalita Sahasranama to him. Hayagriva is narrating the story of Durvasa, who while wandering the earth in a state of ecstasy due to a vow, encountered a Vidyadhari (a celestial nymph) and asked for her heavenly garland. The nymph respectfully gave it to him, and Durvasa placed it on his brow. Continuing his journey, Durvasa came across Indra, who was riding his elephant Airavata and was surrounded by the gods. In his frenzied state, Durvasa threw the garland at Indra, who placed it on Airavata's head. However, the elephant, irritated by the garland's fragrance, tossed it to the ground.

Durvasa was enraged by this disrespectful act and cursed Indra, saying that he would be stripped of his dominion over the three worlds, just as the garland was cast down. Indra pleaded for forgiveness, but Durvasa refused to retract his curse. As a result, Indra and the other devas lost their strength and splendor.

Indra, now remorseful, seeks guidance from his guru, Brihaspati, on how to restore the lost glory of his kingdom. Brihaspati provides an extensive explanation about various transgressions and their consequences, using illustrative stories to make his points. One such story he mentions is about Devi's victory over the demon Bhandasura. Sage Hayagriva begins to narrate this story briefly, but Agastya, intrigued by the mention of Bhandasura, interrupts and asks for more details, inquiring about who Bhandasura is, why Devi is invoked, and the full account of the story, requesting that nothing be omitted. Hayagriva agrees and proceeds to recount the detailed tale.

Sage Hayagriva chose Sage Agastya for this transmission because of Agastya's unparalleled devotion, wisdom, and his role as a preserver of dharma. Agastya, having the spiritual depth to comprehend and preserve such esoteric knowledge, was considered the perfect medium to spread this sacred hymn for the welfare of the world.

Sage Hayagriva

Sage Hayagriva, an avatar of Vishnu, is one of the revered figures in Hindu mythology, especially within the Vaishnava tradition. He is the embodiment of pure knowledge who dispels the darkness of ignorance. His unique form, with a horse's head and a human body, symbolizes the combination of intellect (represented by the human form) and power (represented by the horse's head).

The first Skanda of the Devi Bhagavatam reveals a story about Hayagriva. After completing significant tasks like protecting sacrifices, Vishnu became weary and decided to rest, using his strung bow as a pillow. During this time, the Devas, led by Brahma, needed to wake Vishnu. They enlisted the help of a creature called Vamri (a type of termite) to do so. In exchange, the Vamris demanded a portion of the sacrificial offerings meant for the Devas. The Devas agreed, and the termite cut the string of Vishnu's bow.

The force of the released bow was so powerful that it severed Vishnu's head, sending it flying far away. Despite an intense search, the Devas were unable to locate the head. They turned to Devi for help, who instructed them to attach a horse's head to Vishnu's body. This act gave rise to the name Hayagriva. Hayagriva, who was directly taught by Devi about all the mantras related to Sri Vidya, became an authority on all aspects of this knowledge. In both Sri Vidya and Vaishnava traditions, he is revered as the foundation of all knowledge.

One of the central legends associated with Hayagriva is the story of the theft of the Vedas by the demons Madhu and Kaithabha. The demons, representing ignorance and chaos, stole the sacred texts from Brahma, plunging the universe into darkness. Vishnu in his Hayagriva form, descended to retrieve the sacred texts. This narrative is detailed in the Vishnu Purana and is not merely a mythological tale but carries deep spiritual symbolism. The Vedas represent divine wisdom, and their theft symbolizes the loss of knowledge in the material world. Hayagriva, by restoring the Vedas, signifies the restoration of dharma and the triumph of knowledge over ignorance.

Hayagriva is particularly worshipped by students, scholars, and seekers of knowledge. His iconography, with the Vedas in his hands and a serene expression, inspires devotion among his followers. In southern India, particularly in the Vaishnava tradition, he is revered as the patron deity.

Sage Agastya

Sage Agastya is traditionally considered one of the seven great sages (Saptarishis) of the present Manvantara, the epoch of Vaivasvata Manu.

His origins are shrouded in mythological narratives, with several Puranas providing different accounts of his birth. According to the Mahabharata and the Skanda Purana, Agastya was born from a divine pot (kumbha), which earned him the name "Kumbhaja." He was the son of the celestial beings Mitra and Varuna and is often considered an incarnation of the divine fire. The Saptarishi shloka describes him thus:

Agastya, born from the pot, and the great sage Vasistha, Kashyapa, Atri, Pulastya, and Gautama, these seven sages should always be revered as the Saptarishis

Agastya's contributions to the Vedic tradition are vast. He is credited with composing several hymns in the Rigveda, including those in the first mandala. His hymns are marked by deep spiritual insight and are often invoked for rituals related to health and prosperity. The Rigveda praises him as a seer who has mastered both the spiritual and material worlds.

One of the most significant contributions of Sage Agastya was his journey to South India. According to legend, the Vindhya mountains grew so tall that they obstructed the sun's path. Agastya was requested by the Devas to go southward and halt the mountain's growth. Upon reaching the Vindhyas, he asked the mountain to bow before him until he returned. The Vindhyas complied and have remained low ever since, allowing Agastya to cross them into the southern lands. Agastya's journey to the south is symbolic of the spread of Vedic knowledge to the southern part of the Indian subcontinent. He is credited with introducing the Tamil language and culture, and his influence is deeply embedded in Tamil traditions. Agastya is also believed to have composed the Tamil grammar text Agattiyam.

Agastya is also recognized as a pioneer in the fields of medicine and alchemy. The Agastya Samhita, attributed to him, is an ancient text that contains detailed instructions on various medicinal preparations and treatments, including the use of metals and herbs. Agastya's contributions to Ayurveda are considered foundational, and he is revered as one of the ancient seers who laid the groundwork for the system of Indian medicine.

Several legends and miraculous tales are associated with Sage Agastya. In the Ramayana, he is depicted as a sage who advised Lord Rama during his exile. He presented Rama with the divine weapons necessary to defeat Ravana. Agastya is also known for his miraculous deeds, such as drinking the entire ocean to expose the hiding demons during the Devasura war. Agastya's wife, Lopamudra, is regarded as one of the twelve most significant devotees of Devi. She is considered a sage who discovered the Hadi version of the Panchadashakshari mantra. Devi's affection for Lopamudra is highlighted in the Lalita Sahasranama.

His spiritual legacy transcends time. He is considered an authority on the practice of Yoga and meditation. The Yoga Vasistha, a spiritual treatise, mentions Agastya as a teacher of Raja Yoga. His teachings emphasize the importance of balance between worldly duties and spiritual aspirations. Agastya is often depicted as a figure who harmonizes the earthly and the divine.

The transmission of the Lalita Sahasranama from Hayagriva to Agastya is symbolic of the guru-shishya tradition in Hinduism, where divine knowledge is passed from one generation to another in an unbroken lineage. This tradition underscores the importance of a guru in the transmission of spiritual wisdom, ensuring that the knowledge is preserved in its purest form.

In imparting the Lalita Sahasranama, Hayagriva not only provided Agastya with a powerful spiritual tool but also entrusted him with the responsibility of propagating the hymn for the benefit of humanity. The hymn, when chanted with devotion and understanding, is believed to invoke the presence of the goddess, leading to spiritual awakening and the fulfillment of desires.

The choice of Sage Agastya also reflects the inclusivity of the Lalita Sahasranama as it is accessible to all devotees regardless of their background. Sage Agastya, being a revered figure in both northern and southern India, serves as a bridge, spreading this divine knowledge across different regions and communities.

Shakti's form as Lalita Tripurasundari

In the Tantric texts, there is a story that a grand yagna was organized by Daksha, Sati's father, to which all deities were invited except Shiva. Ignoring Shiva's advice, Sati attended the yagna and was humiliated by her father. Unable to bear the insults to her husband, Sati immolated herself. Enraged, Shiva destroyed the yagna and severed Daksha's head, later restored with a goat's head.

Sati's death plunged Shiva into deep sorrow. He began to wander in the universe. To reduce Shiva's distress, Lord Vishnu using His discus cut Sati's body into 51 pieces, which fell in 51 centers. These centers are the great spiritual places known as the Panchadasa Shakti peethas.

Shiva eventually undertook severe penance in the Himalayas. Shiva represents the unmodified essence of nature. He meditated on himself, setting an example for devotees.

Meanwhile, the demon Taraka terrorized the world, and only Shiva's son could defeat him. To enable this, Shiva needed to remarry. The gods persuaded Parvati to serve Shiva during his meditation. However, Shiva remained indifferent until Manmatha, the lord of desire, attempted to kindle attraction between them.

Shiva's third eye incinerated Manmatha, symbolizing the destruction of desire. Shiva then vanished, leaving Parvati perplexed. She undertook intense tapas to win his affection. Eventually, Shiva accepted her, leading to their marriage.

During Shiva's absence, his retinue created Bhandasura from Manmatha's ashes. Bhandasura performed severe penance to appease Shiva and secured a boon that made him nearly invincible. His boon was such that he could only be defeated by a divine being who was created specifically for that purpose. This boon made him exceptionally powerful and arrogant, as he believed himself to be invincible. Bhandasura's demonic influence spawned Vishukra and Vishanga. Empowered by his boons, Bhandasura started creating havoc and terror across the three worlds:

Heaven, Earth, and the Netherworld. He conquered the celestial realms, defeated the gods, and drove them out of their abodes. His tyranny extended to the mortal realm, where he created widespread suffering.

The gods realized that they had forgotten the power of Shakti and fervently worshipped her. From the sacrificial fire emerged Chidagni Kunda Sambhoota, the divine being who was created specifically for the purpose of defeating the Bhandasura. Shakti took the formidable form of Goddess Durga embodying the combined power of all the gods to confront Bhandasura and restore cosmic order. The battle between Durga and Bhandasura was fierce and intense. Durga, riding her lion and armed with various weapons provided by the gods, fought valiantly against Bhandasura and his army of demons. Bhandasura, using his immense strength and boons, put up a formidable fight.

During the battle, Bhandasura had a unique ability to multiply himself, making it difficult for any opponent to defeat him. However, Durga's strength and divine strategy eventually overwhelmed Bhandasura. She managed to defeat his armies and reach him. With Bhandasura defeated, peace was restored to the three worlds.

After Bhandasura's defeat, Shiva and Parvati's marriage was celebrated by the gods. However, in their joy, they overlooked the crucial role played by Her. To remind them of her significant contribution, She commanded the Vag Devis, the guardian deities of speech, to compose a hymn containing her thousand sacred names.

Commentators observe that the reason why She calls upon the Vag Devis to compose the hymn are that Vasinee and other Vag Devis are masters of word power which is because of Her blessings. They are fully conversant with the secrets of Sri Chakra and since they are always immersed in Her names, they are an embodiment of Her mantras.

She commanded them to compose a hymn which should have Her name as its insignia. It should consist of one thousand names and its recital should give her complete satisfaction. Despite their efforts, their compositions were repeatedly rejected. Desperate, the Vag Devis sought the help of Ganapati, the master poet. With a heartfelt surrender to Her, they crafted a hymn. She then called a divine assembly of gods and requested them to recite this hymn. The Vag Devis presented the Lalita Sahasranama to this celestial gathering. As the recital of the Lalita Sahasranama progressed, the gods were deeply moved and entered a state of profound realization. They beseeched Her to reveal the deeper meanings of this sacred hymn, which were meant to be shared with humanity.

The Poorva Bhaga states that She finds no other Sahasranama as pleasing as this one, making it the most effective way to gain Her favor. The Sahasranama can be approached in two ways: padanam (reading) and keertanam (singing). She is pleased by both spoken recitation and meditative reflection. When the Sri Chakra is worshipped using this Sahasranama along with offerings of lotus flowers, basil leaves, or crataeva leaves, She bestows Her grace immediately. It is recommended to recite this Sahasranama daily after worshipping the Sri Chakra and chanting the Panchadashakshari mantra. Even if one is unable to perform the chanting or do pooja, the full benefits of these practices can still be attained through the recitation of this Sahasranama.

Chapter 3

Dhyana, Nyasa and Panchopachara Puja

The Lalita Sahasranama can be used for both external worship (for example, through the Sri Chakra Puja) or for internal contemplation. The goddess energy can be accessed either through her Saguna or Nirguna forms for meditation. Lalita Sahasranama can be chanted in two different ways - one in Stotra form and the other in mantra form. Both ways are equally effective. In Stotra form, all 1000 namas are separated into stotras of a few namas each and recited. In mantra form, each nama is chanted individually, preceded by Om and followed by Namah. The mantra form is commonly used to recite Lalita Sahasranama during Archana.

The Stotra form works well for those not initiated into Sri Vidya Sadhana by a guru. The poorva bhaga states that if a person is initiated into Sri Vidya, then the following are necessary:

- Worship of the Sri Chakra as detailed in the Tantra texts such as Parashurama Kalpasutra, Tantraraja, Vamakeshvara, etc.
- Japa of Panchadashi and Shodashi mantra either 1008, 308 or 108 times
- Recitation of Lalita Sahasranama with rsyadi nyasa, dhyana shloka, panchapuja, and show the relevant mudras

If one is not initiated into Sri Vidya, then the dhyana shlokas can be chanted followed by the thousand names. The recitation of the poorva and uttara bhagas is also prescribed in the text to emphasise the merits of the hymn but merely chanting the thousand names is also equally acceptable. The practice of reciting any mantra yields results only when done with an understanding of its meaning or essence. It's crucial to know the meaning of the names being chanted, as this helps prevent mistakes in pauses and pronunciation. Moreover, reflecting on the meaning during recitation helps to firmly focus the mind on the nature, divine attributes, and the underlying principle of the deity being worshipped.

It is also very useful to understand the Sri Yantra and its various avaranas before learning to chant the hymn. The Lalita Sahasranama can be divided into nine sections, known as chakras and related to the nine avaranas. The first 111 names describe the Divine Mother in her gross, subtle, and supreme forms. The remaining 889 names are used to offer worship to Her. These nine chakras correspond to the nine enclosures within our bodies. The first 111 names, from 'Srimata' to 'Bisatantu Taneeyasi,' are referred to as the moola grantha (the foundational text). The remaining 889 names serve as elaborations or commentaries on these foundational names.

It is also necessary to understand the concept of Kundalini and chakras as they are intricately linked to the content of the hymn. The process of Kundalini awakening is described as the ascent of Shakti which lies dormant at the base of the spine in the Muladhara Chakra and eventually reaches the Sahasrara Chakra at the crown of the head, where it merges with Shiva.

The ideal times for reciting the Sahasranama include birthdays, anniversaries or any other significant days. Additionally, full moon days, all Fridays, and the Maha Navami day (the 9th day of Navratri festival) are recommended. It is especially beneficial to recite the Sahasranama on Fridays and full moon days. For full moon days, it is best to recite when the moon is completely full, which might occur at an unusual hour. Therefore, any time during the full moon day, preferably late at night, is optimal for recitation to reap the full benefits.

In today's busy world, time can be a constraint, but proper recitation of this Sahasranama should take about thirty minutes. It is important to avoid hurried recitation, as well as reciting without focus or proper visualization of Lalita.

Nyasa, Dhyana and Panchopachara Puja

It is customary to do the Nyasa and Dhyana before chanting any Sahasranama. Nyasa can be translated into "placing" or "depositing" the mantra and involves touching various parts of the body while chanting specific portions of a mantra. This practice is considered an act of assigning or locating divinity within one's own body. Varadachary explains that "Nyasa means placing, applying, or depositing. Mantra is placed on parts of the body. When nyasa is performed, the power of the letter of the mantra, presided over by a particular deity, passes into those body parts". The touch presumably improves sensitivity of touch through improved nerve conduction.

Dhyana or meditation invokes the physical four-dimensional (length, breadth, width and her femininity) presence of Sri Lalitambika in our mind. We need to ensure that we keep this form at the top of our mind throughout the duration of the Japa or Puja

Every mantra has its own nyasa, and there are several types of nyasas, with Karanyasa and Anganyasa being the most prominent. The process of Anganyasa and Karanyasa is undertaken to invoke the deity into us. The human being has 72000 naadis (subtle channels of energy). All these naadi endings are at the tip of our fingers. As it is not possible to touch all the 72000 naadis, we touch the finger tips and invoke the deity into our body.

The concept of nyasa aims to recognize the various components of the macrocosm and visualize them within the body, simultaneously acknowledging the function and utility of body parts in the microcosm. Nyasa mantras end with "Namah," meaning salutation, which signifies a super system's acknowledgment of the service rendered by subordinate systems.

Upon completing nyasa, the worshipper is believed to be endowed with a divine body, suitable for worshipping the divine. Agama shastras highlight two primary benefits of performing nyasa: bhutasuddhi (purification of the five cosmic elements composing the body) and mantrasiddhi (achieving the objectives of the mantras). Varadachary notes in Pancharatragama: "When nyasa is performed, the power of the mantra's letters, presided over by a particular deity, passes into the body parts where it is performed. The practitioner's body is purified."

The goal of nyasa is to sanctify one's body, making it a vessel for invoking the Divine within oneself. It also facilitates the swift fruition of the mantra.

Each mantra is divided into six parts, which are then placed on six specific parts of the body. For kara-nyasa, the six parts of the mantra are placed sequentially on

- thumb – moving index finger from base to the tip
- index finger – moving thumb from base to the tip
- middle finger – moving thumb from base to the tip
- ring finger – moving thumb from base to the tip
- little finger – moving thumb from base to the tip
- palm – one palm is used to swipe across the other palm and dorsal and then the palm is reversed

In anganyasa, the six parts of the mantra are placed on body by touching with fingers of the right hand:

- the heart
- the forehead
- crown of the head
- from ears to elbows
- the eyes
- around the head in a circular manner.

Nyasa

Asya Sri Lalita Sahasranama Stotra Mahamantrasya

Vashinyadhi Vag Devatha Rishaya

Anustup Chandaha

Sri Lalita Parameswari Devata

Aim Sri Mat Vag Bhava Kooteti Beejam

Klim Madhya Kooteti Shaktihi

Sau Shakti Kooteti Keelakam

Moola prakruthihi Ithi Dhyana

Sri Lalitamahatripurasundari Prasada siddhi dwara Chintita phala Avaptyarte Jape Viniyogaḥ

Each mantra is attributed to a specific rishi credited with capturing the mantra from the cosmos in the form of sound beyond the normal human audible range.

The sage or seer who has discovered the mantra and its utility after gaining siddhi (fruition) and has generously disclosed it for the benefit of mankind, is the Rishi of the mantra", says Manblunder on his blog about Mantra Japa Vidhi. Here in the Lalita Sahasranama the Rishis to whom the mantra is attributed are Vashini and Vag Devathas.

Mantras are set to specific meters known as chhandas and address particular deities. "The Vedic meter or prosody that applies to the mantra is taken into consideration. The word chhandas typically conceals the metrical composition of the mantra itself or its uddhara shloka (The verse that reveals the composition and make-up of the mantra). The pronunciation or the rhyme associated with the mantra would resonate with the chhandas that is mentioned in the viniyoga. The secrets and revelation of the mantra are encoded within the chhandas, says Manblunder on his blog about Mantra Japa Vidhi. Here in the Lalita Sahasranama, the chhandas is Anushtup.

This mantra is dedicated to Sri Lalita Parameswari Devatha, specifying the Ishta Devata being worshipped. It signifies that we hold the deity in our heart and wish to forge a permanent bond with deep love, complete trust, surrender and affection.

Bija is the seed of the mantra and all its intended benefits and secrets, are encapsulated within. The bija here refers to the Panchadashakshari mantra which is seen as a representation of Sri Lalita with the Vaghbhava Koota depicting her face, Madhya Koota, her body upto her hips and Shakti Koota upto the legs. These three Kootas form the Bija, Shakti and Keelakam for Sri Lalita Sahasranama and the Moola Prakruti or the basic nature forms the Dhyana.

Viniyoga refers to the deployment or the purpose of performing the mantra japa of the deity. Generally, the words associated with a Viniyoga are 'Abhista Siddhyarthe', 'Chaturvarga Siddhyarthe', 'Devata Prityarthe'. Here in the Lalita Sahasranama, the term used is Prasada Siddhyarte.

You can do the following nyasas with the right hand using the Tattva Mudra/Nyasa Mudra by joining the thumb and the ring finger at the tips.

Vashinyadhi Vag Devatha Rishaya

touch the top of your head with the right hand

Anustup Chandaha

touch the upper lip

Sri Lalita Parameswari Devata

touch the heart

Aim Sri Mat Vag Bhava Kooteti Beejam

touch the right shoulder

Klim Madhya Kooteti Shaktih

touch the left shoulder

Sau Shakti Kooteti Keelakam

touch the navel

Fold your hands into the Namaskara mudra for the viniyoga.

Karanyasa

aim – angusthabhyam namah (use both the index fingers and run them on both the thumbs)

klim – tarjanibhyam namah (use both the thumbs and run them on both the index fingers)

sauḥ – madhyamabhyam namah (both the thumbs on the middle fingers)

aim – anamikabhyam namah (both the thumbs on the ring fingers)

klim – kanisthikabhyam namah (both the thumbs on the little fingers)

sauh – karatalakaraprasthabhyam namah (open both the palms; run the opened palms of the right hand on the front and back sides of the left palm and repeat the same for the other palm).

These nyasas are done on both the hands simultaneously.

Anganyasa

aim – hridayaya namah (open index, middle and ring fingers of the right hand, leaving the thumb and little fingers out and place them on the heart chakra)

klim – sirase svaha (open middle and ring fingers of the right hand and touch the top of the forehead)

sauh – sikhayai vasat (open the right thumb and touch the back of the head) aim – kavachaya hum (cross both the hands and run the fully opened palms from shoulders to finger tips)

klim – netratrayaya vausat (open the index, middle and ring fingers of the right hand; touch both the eyes using index and ring fingers and touch the point between the two eyebrows with the middle finger.

sauh – astraya phat (open up the left palm and strike it three times with index and middle fingers of the right hand.

bhurbhuvassuvaromiti digbandhah

Draw a protective circle around by using right hand thumb and middle fingers make rattle clockwise around the head. (There should be eight rattles made signifying the eight directions).

"The word 'bhur' represents Earth or the material realm, gross body etc., 'bhuvah' represents the atmosphere or the spiritual realm, causal body etc., 'svah' represents the unseen and imperceptible heavenly realms, consciousness, astral body etc. All the triads are to be accounted for, with the mahavrittis – 'bhur', 'bhuvah' and 'svah'. The influences of the triads are to be limited with this command, to help us focus upon the task of mantra japa sadhana", says Manblunder.

Dhyana

Dhyana is a very important step after nyasa. The Universal Absolute, which is formless, is given a form which can be firmly entrenched in one's heart. The dhyana verses serve this purpose by vividly describing the "gross" form or "Swaroopa" of the Goddess. This is like Maanasa Pooja wherein the worshipper performs his worship mentally without any external rituals or paraphernalia.

There are four descriptive shlokas for visualization of Lalita. The first one is said to have been composed by the eight Vag Devis. The second one is believed to have been composed by Dattatreya, considered to be an incarnation of the Divine Trinity – Brahma, Vishnu and Shiva. No information is available about the origin of the third Sloka. The fourth dhyana shloka has been composed by Adi Shankaracharya.

Dhyana Shloka 1

Sindhuraruna vigraham trinayanam manikya mouli spurath
Thara nayaka sekaram smitha mukhi mapina vakshoruham
Panibhayam alipoorna ratna chashakam rakthothpalam bibhrathim
Soumyam ratna ghatastha raktha charanam dhyayeth paramambikam

Meditate on Her, Who has a crimson body, Who has three graceful eyes, Who wears a jeweled crown, Adorned by the moon, Who always has a captivating smile, Who has high and firm breasts, Who has a wine-filled cup made of precious stones, Who holds red flowers in her hands, Who is the ocean of peace, And who keeps her red holy feet on a jeweled platform.

This verse describes Lalita, as having a crimson red form – as red as sindoor and the color of the rising sun. She is three eyed, indicating the Ajna chakra, which is the eye of jnana. The three eyes – sun, moon and Agni (fire) also refer to self-illumined form. Her crown is studded with rubies. She wears the chief of stars, the moon on her crown. She has a smiling face. She is an embodiment of beauty and joy. She has a fully developed bosom. The reference here is to the nama "Sri Mata". Being the Universal Mother, she nourishes one and all with the Supreme nectar. In one hand, She holds a ruby studded cup, filled with honey (spiritual nectar). The honey attracts the spiritual seekers. In the other hand, she holds a lotus. I bow to this beautiful form who has her red feet on a pot studded with red rubies. She is Para Ambikam – The Absolute Supreme – Ambika, who is greater than everything else in this universe.

Dhyana Shloka 2

Arunam Karuna thrangitakshim dhrutha pasangusa pushpabana chapam
Animadhibhi ravrutham mayukai raha mityeva vibhavaye Bhavanim

I imagine my goddess Bhavani, Who has a colour of the rising sun. Who has eyes which are waves of mercy, Who has a bow made of sweet cane, Arrows made of soft flowers, a goad in her hands, Who is surrounded by her devotees who have great powers, Who is the personification of "aham"

This verse describes that Her complexion is like the colour of the sky as it appears in the early morning just before the sunrise when the rays are just coming up. The darkness of the night gives way to light as the brightness envelopes the sky. This form reflects her love and affection for us; it shows us that like the rising Sun, She will dispel all our darkness. Based on the individual needs she gives out compassion in waves, a little at a time. Her gentle and calm eyes reflect the deep love and compassion that exists within Her heart. She holds in Her hands all Her tools – noose, goad, the bow made of sugarcane and arrows that consist of flowers. The 8 supernatural powers (ashta siddhis) of Anima, Laghima etc. surround Her like rays. Just as the Sun retains rays for the benefit of this creation, the Divine Mother retains these supernatural powers for the benefit of her devotees.

Dhyana Shloka 3

Dyayeth padmasanastham vikasitha vadanam padma pathrayathakshim
Hemabham peethavasthram karakalitha lasadhema padmam varangim
Sarvalankara yuktham sathatham abhayadam bhaktha namram
bhavanim
Sri Vidyam shanthamurthim sakala surantham sarva sampat pradhatrim

I meditate upon Her who sits on a lotus, Who has a smiling face, Who has long eyes like the lotus leaf, Who glitters like gold, Who wears red clothes, Who has a golden lotus in her hand, Who grants all desires, Who is dressed to perfection, Who gives protection, Who has a soft heart for her devotees, Who is Sri Vidya, Who is forever peaceful, Who is worshipped by gods and gives all wealth.

This verse describes the Goddess who is seated on a lotus, with shining and bright face which is the cause for our upliftment. Her eyes are elongated like the lotus leaf which also symbolizes that She watches over every being. She has a golden form covered with yellow silk garments and holds a golden lotus in her hand. Her beautiful form is adorned with all the ornaments. She always protects her devotees and blesses them by hearing them intently. She displays the Abhaya mudra of protection towards all beings. An embodiment of Sri Vidya mantra, her peaceful form is worshipped by even the gods. She bestows every form of prosperity, both spiritual and material including vidya, jnana and yoga on her devotees.

Dhyana Shloka 4

Sakumkuma vilepanam adhika chumbi kasthurikam
Samanda hasithekshanam sachara chapa pashangusam
Asesha jana mohinim maruna malya bhoosham bara
Japa kusuma basuram japa vidhou smarath Ambikam

I meditate on her, Who applies saffron on her body, Who applies musk that attracts the bees, Who has a beautiful smile, Who has with her bows, arrows, rope and goad, Who attracts all the souls, Who wears a red garland, Who wears ornaments and is of the colour of the red hibiscus.

In this verse, Lalita is shown as anointed with vermillion and saffron. She wears a bindi made of sandalwood paste and the bhramara bees, drawn by the fragrance of this sandal paste, encircle Her. With a benevolent smile, she looks at her devotees. She holds a bow and arrow in her hands. Adorned with red garland and jewels, everybody is attracted to Her. This form of Lalita that shines like the lustrous hibiscus flower, should be meditated upon during Japa and stotra recital.

Maanasa Pooja

Om Sri Lalita Maha Tripura Sundaryai Nama: Maanasa Panchopa Chara Poojan Karishye

Panchopachara Puja

After the Goddess has been visualized clearly in one's heart with the dhyana, the panchapooja or the Pancha upacharas are conducted mentally. Lamityadi Panchapooja refers to a set of five ritual offerings within Sri Vidya tradition. The term Lamityadi is derived from the syllables that begin each of the five offerings, while Panchapooja means five-fold worship.

Lamityadi Panchapooja concept:

1. **Lam – Gandham** (Sandalwood paste): This represents the earth element (Prithvi Tattva) and is used for purification and grounding.
2. **Ham – Pushpam** (Flowers): This represents the water element (Apa Tattva) and is used as an offering symbolizing beauty and devotion.
3. **Yam – Dhoopa** (Incense): This represents the fire element (Agni Tattva) and signifies the burning away of impurities, bringing clarity and focus.
4. **Ram – Deepam** (Lamp): This represents the air element (Vayu Tattva) and symbolizes the illumination of wisdom and the dispelling of ignorance.
5. **Vam – Naivedya** (Food offering): This represents the ether element (Akasha Tattva) and is an offering of sustenance to the deity, symbolizing the nourishing of the soul.

The universe is composed of the 5 elements – earth, water, fire, air and space. We are also made up of these same 5 elements. All our gnanendriyas (sense organs) and karmendriyas (action organs) are tied to these elements The panchpooja is offered to balance the elements in our bodies and also worship Nature.

Lamitayadi panchapooja in practice:

- lam – pruthivyatmane gandham samarpayami
- ham – akashatmane pushapai pujayami
- yam – vayavatmane dupam aghrapayami

- ram – agnyatmane dipam darshayami
- vam – amrutatmane amrutam mahanaivedyam nivedayami
- sam – sarvatmane sarvopachara pujam samarpayam

Lam pritivi tattvaatmikaye gandham parikalpayami

'Lam' is the seed letter. To Her, who exists as a form of the earth element (prithvi tattva) we offer sandal paste (gandham).

Ham akasha tattvaatmikaye pushpam parikalpayaami

'Ham' is the seed letter. To Her sky element (akasha tattva), we offer flowers (pushpam).

Yam vaayu tattvaatmikayai dhupam parikalpayami

'Yam' is the seed letter. To the air element (vaayu tattva) present everywhere we offer incense stick (dhoopa).

Ram agni tattvaatmikaye deepam sandarshayaami

'Ram' is the seed letter. To Her fire element (Agni tattva), we offer light (deepam)

Vam amrutatatvaatmikaye amruta naivedyam parikalpayami

Vam is the seed letter. To Her, who is nectar (amruta tattva), we offer nectar as naivedya.

Sam sarva tattvaatmikaye sarvopacharaan samarpayaami

'Sam' is the seed letter. To the Divine Mother, who encompasses every essence (Sarva tattva), we offer every form of service (sarva upachara).

After the Divine Mother, seated in the heart has been given a welcome with the panchapooja as above, one can proceed to start with the Madhyama Bhaga or the main part of the Sahasranama.

Recite Moola-Mantra (OM – AIM – HREEM – SREEM)

Then begin the mantra recitation of 182 and a half couplets starting from Sri Mata to Lalitambika.

After the chanting of the stotra, we offer Samarpanam – a deep reverence is once again pledged to the deity to seek their divine grace and help realize all the benefits of the mantra japa sadhana performed at our dwelling.

> guhyati guhya goptri tvam grihanmasmat-kritam japam
> siddhir bhavatu me devi tvatprasadanmayi stira

You sustain the secret of all secrets. Please accept this japa performed by me and bestow Your perpetual Grace on me.

Chapter 4

Madhyama Bhaga

Moola Grantha (1-51)

The first 111 namas of the Divine Mother are considered as the moola grantha (foundation) of the entire substance of Lalita Sahasranama. The remaining 889 names are only commentaries and detailed elaboration of these above contents. These 111 names can be compared to strong foundation that is laid before the construction of a house.

The first avarana is Bhupura and the Chakra is Trailokyamohana (enchanting the three worlds) where the unmanifest becomes manifest.

1. Sri Mata

The auspicious, divine Mother

The Lalita Sahasranama begins with a reverent bow to the creator of the universe, addressing Her as Sri Mata, the Mother of all. This name highlights the first of the three functions of the Brahman—Creation, Sustenance, and Dissolution – indicating that She is the creator of the universe because She is no different from the Brahman.

The Taittiriya Upanishad defines Brahman as "the one from whom the phenomenal world and all the beings have emanated, the one by whom they are sustained and in whom they ultimately merge and disappear. Lalita is this Brahman.

The prefix Sri holds significance here as it denotes the highest form of motherhood. Sri can be traced back to the term "ashreya" or offering shelter. While all mothers care for their offspring with love, they cannot alleviate their destined sufferings and miseries. Lalita transcends the abilities of a mother; She has the power to remove the sorrows and miseries of all beings in the universe, as She is the mother of the entire cosmos, including the galaxy. The universe was created by Her, operates under Her guidance, and merges back into Her during dissolution.

Sri signifies auspiciousness and utmost respect. It is linked to the five auspicious elements of Devi worship known as Sri Panchagam: Sri Matrye Namah Puram (Her dwelling), Sri Chakra (Her Palace), Sri Vidya (ultimate Devi worship), Sri Suktam (hymns in Her praise), and Sri Guru (the spiritual preceptor).

The cycle of samsara, which encompasses birth, sustenance, and death, repeats endlessly. Samsara is likened to an ocean, always putting up a challenge to navigate against its currents. These currents are driven by the sense organs, which influence the mind to generate desires and attachments. Only She can help us overcome the obstacles of samsara and achieve the ultimate goal of realizing Brahman. We can achieve this through Her worship.

Sri Mata signifies that the Vedas originated from the Brahman, and Lalita is the Brahman. The Swetasvatara Upanishad (VI.18) states that Brahman first created Brahma and then presented the Vedas, affirming Her supreme role. It is also said that this nama stands for the Panchadasi mantra.

She wipes away the three deepest fears faced by every being – janma dukha, jara dukha and marana dukha. Every being grieves as a result of the fact that he is born to go through the trials and tribulations of life. This is known as Janma dukkha. Jara dukha is the sorrow that comes with illness and old age. Marana dukha is the fear of death that haunts every living being.

The Uttara Bhaga indicates that those who recite merely this first name as a japa will always remain prosperous and eventually attain liberation as well. The second and third names go on to confirm Her status as not just any mother but one who is a great empress with immense power and potential.

2. Sri Maharagni

The Great Empress

Sri Maharagni signifies the great empress who sustains and protects the universe. This name highlights Her role in governing the cosmos, complementing the first name, Sri Mata, which refers to Her as the creator. As a mother, She creates the universe, and as an empress, She sustains it.

The majestic empress is depicted seated on a throne with Sadashiva as the seat. The throne's legs are supported by Brahma, Vishnu, Rudra, and Ishana. She rules over the three worlds—Earth, Heaven, and the Netherworld—and embodies the three Shaktis: Iccha (will), Gnana (knowledge), and Kriya (action).

She is the consort of the supreme ruler. A king's primary role is to protect his subjects, deliver justice, and uphold righteousness. The Supreme

Mother, as the inner witness, performs these duties from within. She ensures the sustenance and protection of the entire creation.

The prefix Sri in Maharagni signifies Her status as the queen of queens, the empress. Many names in the Sahasranama contain powerful bijaksharas (seed syllables), which are highly secretive and powerful. These syllables, when chanted with proper understanding and pronunciation, bestow significant spiritual power.

The Shodashi mantra, considered the supreme mantra in Devi worship, consists of sixteen syllables (kalas), representing the phases of the moon. The Pancadashi mantra, with fifteen syllables, becomes the Shodashimantra when one more syllable is added. Chanting this mantra for the prescribed 900,000 times is believed to free one from the cycle of rebirth. The sixteenth syllable of Shodashi is hidden in the name Shrim, the bija of sustenance associated with Lakshmi.

The first name, Sri Mata, highlights Her creative power, while the second name, Sri Maharagni, emphasizes Her sustaining power. As a mother, She creates, and as the supreme queen, She sustains the universe.

Kala represents the dynamism inherent in Nature, or prakriti, and in union with Shiva, exhibits creative dynamism. Shiva is twofold: with attributes (endowed with kalas) and without attributes (supreme amongst creation and distinct from prakriti). The sixteen kalas correspond to the sixteen vowels, symbolizing completeness and fullness. As Sri Mata, the Divine Mother embodies these kalas, representing the culmination of their expansion.

Sri Maharagni denotes the great empress who sustains the universe, balancing Her creative power as Sri Mata. This dual role emphasises Her supreme ability to create, govern, and protect the cosmos, illustrated by the powerful legends and mantras associated with Her worship.

3. Srimad Simhasaneshwari

Empress who sits on a throne of lions

Srimad Simhasaneshwari signifies the Goddess who rules the world from a grand throne. This name follows the previous one, Sri Maharagni, highlighting Her as the empress seated on a majestic "Simhasana" (throne), hence the name Srimad Simhasaneshwari.

'Srimat' means exquisitely beautiful, signifying She is the empress seated on an exquisitely decorated throne

'Simha' means lion, derived from 'himsa' (violence). Sitting on the simha (lion/throne) implies She dispels violent and negative thoughts/emotions

She is the force that absorbs creation into Herself.

'Srimat' also refers to the five aspects, indicating She controls and supports these aspects from Her throne. These can be the five Brahmas, five elements, five directions, five actions, pancha rudras, or pancha pranavas.

The Pancha Pranavas are Aim, Hreem, Sreem, Klim, Souh. Aim, Hreem, Sreem represent energies of creation, sustenance, and absorption. They also correspond to the energies of intent (Iccha), knowledge (Jnana), and action (Kriya).

Functions of Creation, Sustenance, and Dissolution

The first three names of the Sahasranama encompass the functions of Creation, Sustenance, and Dissolution. Though there is no direct mention of "Samhaaram" (destruction), dissolution involves destroying sins and enabling Her devotees to merge with Her, known as laya or absorption, which is part of sustenance.

Shakti orchestrates all creation (Prabhava) and dissolution (Pralaya). Brahma, Vishnu, and Rudra execute their roles under Her direction. For true devotees, dissolution means the Goddess destroys their sins and grants liberation. To liberate a devotee, She sends them into the world (creation), clears their karmic debts through experiences in Maya (illusory world), and finally absorbs them into Her (dissolution).

In Shaiva Siddhanta texts like Thirumantram, dissolution is described as the merging of various tattvas and chakras into Supreme consciousness. The elements (muladhara: earth, swadisthana: water, manipura: fire) dissolve into anahata (air), which in turn dissolves into space (vishuddhi, ajna). This process culminates in merging with Supreme Consciousness (Sahasrara). Similarly, Brahma (Earth), Vishnu (Water), and Rudra (Fire) dissolve into Isha (Air) and finally into Sadashiva (Space).

Understanding the Panchabhutas is crucial for comprehending the universe's evolution, sustenance, and dissolution. The Panchamahabhutas are:

- Akasha (Space/Ether)
- Vayu (Air)
- Agni (Fire)
- Apas (Water)
- Prithvi (Earth)

According to Hindu cosmology, these five elements are the building blocks of the universe and all matter within it. The creation process, as described in the Taittiriya Upanishad (2.1), follows a sequence that starts with the subtlest element, Akasha, and culminates with the grossest, Prithvi.

- Akasha (Space): The first element to manifest, Akasha is considered the subtlest and the origin of sound (Shabda), which is the tanmatra (subtle element) associated with it. In the Taittiriya Upanishad (2.1.1), it is stated, "From Atman arose Akasha." Akasha provides the substratum for the other elements to manifest and is essential for the existence of space and time.
- Vayu (Air): Vayu emerges from Akasha and is associated with the tanmatra of touch (Sparsha). It represents motion and life force (Prana). The Prashna Upanishad (3.5) highlights the role of Vayu as the breath of life, sustaining all beings.
- Agni (Fire): From Vayu emerges Agni, associated with the tanmatra of sight (Rupa). Agni symbolizes transformation and energy,

essential for digestion, perception, and the sun's radiance. In the Chandogya Upanishad (6.2.3), Agni is described as the source of heat and light, crucial for sustaining life.

- Apas (Water): Apas emerges from Agni and is associated with the tanmatra of taste (Rasa). Water is the essence of life, representing fluidity and cohesion. The Rig Veda extols water as a purifier and sustainer of all life forms.

- Prithvi (Earth): The final element, Prithvi, emerges from Apas and is associated with the tanmatra of smell (Gandha). Prithvi represents solidity and stability, forming the physical foundation of the universe. The Bhagavad Gita (7.4) mentions earth as one of the eightfold material elements (Ashtadha Prakriti) that constitute the material world.

The Panchamahabhutas are not isolated entities; they are interdependent and manifest in varying proportions in all forms of existence. The human body is composed of these five elements, with each element corresponding to specific senses. The ear is related to Akasha (sound), the skin to Vayu (touch), the eyes to Agni (sight), the tongue to Apas (taste), and the nose to Prithvi (smell). The Brihadaranyaka Upanishad describes how the cosmic being (Hiranyagarbha) manifested the elements in the same order, which then combined to form the universe. Each element is seen as a step in the densification of consciousness into matter. The Vedic rituals, particularly the Agnihotra, symbolically represent the interplay of these elements. The fire (Agni) ritual itself is a microcosm of creation, where the offerings (Ahuti) symbolize the merging of the elements to sustain the cosmos.

The first name addresses Lalita as the creator. The second name discusses sustenance while the third name conveys dissolution. Together, these names subtly convey the primary qualities of the Brahman: creation, sustenance, and dissolution. These three acts are further elaborated in later names of the Sahasranama (264, 266, and 268).

4. Chidagni kunda sambhootha

She who emerged from the sacrificial fire of knowledge

Since we now know Her as the all-powerful Mother, we would like to understand at this point where she comes from and what her lineage is. She is the one who has risen from the altar of pure consciousness. Yet again it is reiterated that She is the Brahman as the Upanishads state "Prajnanam Brahma".

In this nama, Chit signifies consciousness, and Agni Kunda represents the fire that dispels darkness or ignorance. This name means Lalita arose from the sacrificial fire of knowledge to dissipate ignorance. When attributes stemming from past lives' vasanas (impressions) and karmas (actions) are offered into this sacrificial fire, it dispels all darkness, transforming the soul into Satchitananda—pure consciousness or light—embodied by Lalita.

This name alludes to a story in the Brahmanda Purana involving the demon Bhandasura. The devas, tormented by Bhandasura, invoke Lalita to defeat him. They initiate a sacrificial fire called Chidagnikunda. Lalita emerges when the devas offered all their organs into the fire. This narrative is elaborated further in nama 64, detailing Bhandasura's destruction.

The term Sambhootha in this context means "emergence" rather than "birth," emphasizing Her eternal existence. Although eternal, She remains unseen, similar to butter hidden in milk, which requires significant effort to extract. Lalita emerged from the Chidagni only after the devas performed the sacrifice with complete faith, dedication, and surrender.

This name highlights Her subtle form of illumination (chaitanya, jyoti), through which She dispels ignorance. This pure consciousness form elucidates Her role in illuminating and guiding the soul towards enlightenment.

5. Devakarya samudyata

She who manifested to help the gods

This name signifies that Lalita manifested to fulfill the objectives of the Devas. On a deeper level, this name highlights her Prakasa form, where Prakasa represents Shiva and Vimarsa represents Shakti. The rising of the Kundalini Shakti is subtly referenced here. The asuras symbolize ignorance, while the Devas represent knowledge. The implication here is that She bestows seekers with knowledge of Brahman by destroying ignorance.

The names mentioned previously describe Her subtle form. The upcoming names elucidate Her gross form. The Lalita Sahasranama is akin to the Vedas in that it describes the Supreme essence (Parabrahma). Hence, the description of Her gross form begins from the head/hair and proceeds downward to the feet, contrary to the common practice of worshipping the deity starting from the feet upwards.

6. Udyadbhanu sahasrabha

She who shines as brilliantly as a thousand rising suns

This name conveys her radiant and overwhelming splendor. Here, "sahasra" (or thousand) symbolizes infinity, indicating that her luminosity is unimaginable and limitless. The imagery of a thousand suns rising simultaneously suggests a profound and dazzling effulgence. Lalita's red complexion, described in the dhyana sloka "Sakumkuma vilepanaam," symbolizes auspiciousness, compassion, and love.

So far, we have discussed the Prakasa and Vimarsa forms. The upcoming names will delve into three additional forms:

- Stula: the physical form
- Sukshma: the mantra form (Sri Vidya)
- Para: the Vasanas

7. Chaturbahu samanvita

She who is endowed with four arms

This marks the beginning of the description of her physical form. Lalita is endowed with four arms which symbolize her four divine attendants: Ashwarooda, Sampatkari, Mantrini, and Varahi. Emerging from the illumination, the visibility of her four arms reassures the Devas, offering them abhaya (assurance of fearlessness). Her four arms signify her mission to restore the four Purusharthas and the four Vedas. Additionally, they symbolize the four components of the human mind:

- Manas (mind)
- Chitta (consciousness)
- Buddhi (intellect)
- Ahamkara (ego)

8. Ragaswaroopa pashadhya

She who holds a noose in Her rear left arm

In one of her arms, she holds the noose to display her love. The noose she uses to draw people towards herself shows her love, affection, and care for her children. Although she emerges to kill the demons, she first wants to give them a chance to reform through her love. Her love is not meant to create bondages but to free from them.

This name illustrates Lalita's compassionate nature. She uses the noose of desire to attract and lovingly guide her devotees towards spiritual liberation, ensuring they are not ensnared by their desires.

9. Krodhankaranoshjwala

She who holds a goad in Her rear right arm

In her right rear arm, She holds an elephant goad used to control a rogue elephant (representing the mind in human beings). This name refers to the subtle "Gnana" or knowledge. She uses the hook to destroy the hatred and anger in her devotees, which often arise from ignorance, and bestows knowledge. The Kali bija mantra "krom" is hidden in this name, signifying that Kali is also a destroyer of evils.

She controls the desires and hatred in her devotees by fulfilling their wishes and ultimately raising them to her level. This name, along with the previous name references the vasanas (impressions from past lives). In Ragaswaroopapashadhya, the vasana forms that the noose captures are raga (wish) and anuraga (desire). In this name, anger is the captured by the hook. When the mind is not satisfied or when wishes remain unfulfilled, the immediate reaction is often anger. Therefore, a powerful weapon like the elephant hook is needed to control the powerful mind to help it rise above maya.

10. Manorupekshu kodanda

She who holds a goad in Her rear right arm

Lalita holds a bow made of sugarcane on her left forearm. While a typical bow is made of dry bamboo, her bow is made of sugarcane, which is filled with sweetness and moisture. When sugarcane is crushed, the juice that is obtained is sweet and tasty. This sweet weapon is used by Lalita to purify her devotees.

Any thought that arises in the mind involves both the process of thinking and the difference in perception. These are influenced by the sense organs, which finetune thoughts and result in actions. Similarly, the ever-compassionate Goddess uses this gentle weapon to help her devotees control their minds and achieve self-realization.

11. Panchatanmatra sayaka

She who holds arrows in Her rear forearm

This name refers to the five tanmatras (subtle elements) which constitute her arrows (made of flowers). The five flowers which are depicted represent emotions like excitement, confusion, ecstasy, stimulation, and destruction.

The presiding deity of these arrows is Dandini or Varahi. Arrows are typically used to hit and vanquish enemies, and similarly, Lalita aims to destroy Maya in her devotees, which is the greatest impediment to achieving self-realization. Pancha tanmatras refer to the five sense organs:

sound, touch, taste, sight, and smell. These correspond to the five elements that constitute the physical world:

- Earth – Smell
- Water – Taste
- Fire – Sight
- Wind – Touch
- Space – Sound

The bow, represented by Mantrini (the power of intellect), and the arrows, represented by Varahi (physical power), together emphasize that intellect and power should act in unison. The significance of this name is that She controls the mind through the medium of the tanmatras, guiding her devotees towards self-realization by harmonizing their senses and emotions.

12. Nijaruna prabha pura majjad brahmanda mandala

She who engulfs the universe with Her brilliance

13. Champakashoka punnaga saugandhika lasat kacha

Her hair is adorned with the fragrant Champaka, Ashoka, Punnaga and red lotus flowers

From this nama, a description of Her gross form begins. Since Lalita's hair emerged first out of the sacrificial fire, the description of Her gross form commences with the hair.

The Panchadashi mantra is divided into three kutas, out of which the Vagbhavakuta is meditated on from the top of her head to her neck. Beginning the description of Her gross body with the hair also symbolizes the importance of the Sahasrara chakra.

14. Kuruvinda manishreni kanat kotira mandita

Her crown glitters with rows of kuruvinda gems

The kuruvinda is a rare type of ruby, red in colour. Wearing rubies is believed to result in fulfilment of desires and attachment to good things like desire, love and wealth. This implies that by meditating on the Goddess wearing a red crown, the purusharthas are fulfilled, devotion increases and the devotee is blessed with spirituality and prosperity.

15. Ashtami chandra vibraja dalikasthala shobhita

Her forehead shines like the moon on the eighth day of the lunar fortnight

While hair symbolized the Sahasrara chakra, the forehead represents Ajna chakra (the two petalled lotus), which is located in the centre of the forehead. The moon on this day, appears as a beautiful semicircle and is the same shape in both the waxing and waning period. This nama describes how Her forehead looked when She emerged from the sacrificial fire. The crown, hair and flowers came out one after the other and then the forehead appeared as a beautiful inverted semicircle. Ashtami is also known as tvarita which means quick. Hence 'Ashtami Chandra' symbolizes that She quickly grants blessings.

16. Mukha chandra kalankabha mriganabhi visheshaka

The dot adorning face appears like a tiny spot on a full moon

The Moon is described as "Mriganka" because the shape of its stain resembles a deer. However, on Her beautiful forehead, this dot enhances her beauty rather than diminishing it. While her forehead is compared to the half moon, her face is likened to a glowing full moon. The dot symbolizes the Ajna chakra. Just as it takes effort to locate the small black mark on the beautiful full moon, a sadhaka needs to focus on the Ajna chakra to achieve quick concentration and contemplation.

17. Vadana smara mangalya griha torana chillika

She who has beautiful eyelids which look like the ornaments to her face which is like the Love God's home

It is believed that Manmatha, the lord of desires, designed his palace based on Her face. This nama states that if Her face is the beautiful palace of Manmatha, then Her striking eyebrows are the festoons (torana) that lead to it. At times of festivities, traditionally archways made of mango leaves are tied at the entrance of the house to denote auspiciousness. These leaves blow away the poisonous germs and prevent their entry into the house.

18. Vaktra lakshmi parivaha chalan minabhalocana

She who has beautiful eyes which look like fish in the pond of her face

Her face is an ocean of beauty and her eyes are the fish that are swimming in it. They are beautiful and lustrous and are the cause of all auspiciousness. Just like a mother fish keeps track of all her children with just her single glance, She takes care of and protects her children with one view from Her lustrous eyes.

19. Nava champaka pushpabha nasa danda virajita

She who has nose like freshly opened flowers of Champaka

Her nose is like the freshly bloomed champaka flower and adds to Her beauty. Danda refers to a stick which acts as a support for moving upwards. 'Nasadanda' means that the nose is to be used as a tool to move to higher planes. This has reference to the importance of Pranayama as a yogic practice.

20. Tara kanti tiraskari nasa bharana bhasura

She who has a nose ring which shines more than the star

Her nose ring made of rubies and pearls studded outshines the stars. Tara refers to the planets Mars and Venus. This means that these two planets adorn Her nose. So, worshipping Her mitigates the ill effects of these planets.

21. Kadamba manjari klupta karnapura manohara

She who wears kadamba flowers around her ears

22. Tatanka yugali bhuta tapanodupa mandala

She who wears the sun and the moon as her ear studs

Large earrings are called Tatanka. She wears the Sun and Moon as Her earrings thereby controlling and sustaining all the activities of the universe. The importance of the tradition of ear piercing is being highlighted. When the nerve endings at the ear lobe are pierced and cut, the prana shakti within the individual increases and results in increased longevity. The intellect improves as there is a connection between the nerves of the brain and nose.

23. Padmaraga shiladharsha paribhavi kapolabhuh

She who has cheeks which shine more than the mirror made of Padmaraga

Her shining and soft cheeks reflect a red colour that can be compared to the shine of a very rare gemstone, Padmaraaga. It may be recalled from the earlier namas, that everything about Her is red indicating compassion.

24. Nava vidruma bimbashri nyakkariradanacchada

She whose lips are like beautiful new corals

Her striking red lips outshine the redness of corals as well as redness of the bimba fruit. One whose red lips challenge the luster of red corals and the ripe Bimba fruit.

25. Shuddha vidyankurakara dhvija pankti dvyojvala

She who has teeth which look like germinated true knowledge

Her teeth shine like the sprouts of of the knowledge of Sri Vidya which is considered the purest, most secret and powerful worship of Lalita. Sri Vidya involves many prayers, rituals which are based on nonduality and follow the tradition of Tantra. Swami Rama said that in Sanatana, the most ancient tradition is Tantra and the highest knowledge in Tantra is that of Sri Vidya in the Samayachara method.

This Nama contains a reference to the Shodasi mantra and its efficacy. All the lines of the Lalita Sahasranama start with only 32 of the 51 Sanskrit alphabets. Hence, the reference to the 32 teeth, each of which represents an alphabet. Many scholars treat this as an indication that the Lalita

Sahasranama can be chanted without initiation by a Guru while others hold the radically opposite view that initiation into Sri Vidya has to be given by a Guru verbally to the disciple.

This nama also implies that one who embraces Sri Vidya is twice born just like a Brahmin who is considered to be born again after undergoing the purification ritual of Upanayanam. Teeth in humans also can be seen as twice born – once the milk teeth fall out, the permanent set of teeth emerge.

From a purely poetic angle, this nama can also bring to mind an image of two rows of brahmins, clad in white enjoying a sumptuous meal. The Soul and Brahman are considered different owing to our ignorance and when the veil of avidya is lifted after Sri Vidya sadhana, this duality disappears as we come into the light of Divine Consciousness.

26. Karpura viti kamodha samakarshi digantara

The fragrance that arises from her mouth as a result of chewing on betel leaves and camphor attracts Her devotees.

Karpuravitika refers to the rare combination of ingredients that goes into the making of supari or special "paaku" for her betel leaves. The ingredients which include saffron, camphor, clove, cardamom and sugar candy are powdered and chewed with the betel leaves. The immense fragrance emitted when She chews this, pervades the whole universe. The intention is to attract the ignorant and bestow Her grace.

27. Nija sallapa madurya vinirbharshita kacchapi

Her voice is melodious; far sweeter than the sounds of Saraswati's Veena

The Kacchapi is not an ordinary veena; it is an instrument that is the favourite of Ma Saraswati, the Goddess of Knowledge. This veena grants the power of speech (vak) and music (naada) on to every being. The music of such a powerful Veena fades in comparison to the divine voice of the Supreme Mother!

There is a story in the Puranas about Saraswati was once playing the Veena with Lalitambika as her audience. The Mother sometimes intervened to verbally praise the soulful music. Upon hearing the mellifluous voice of the Mother, Saraswati felt that the music rendered by her veena was far inferior in nature. She hid the instrument and asked the Mother to speak in her melodious voice.

The Kacchapi is also known as raghunatha veena and is used mostly in Carnatic Indian classical music. There are several variations of the veena, which in its South Indian form is a member of the lute family. One who plays the veena is referred to as a vainika. The veena instruments developed much like a tree, branching out into instruments as diverse as the harp-like Akasa (a veena that was tied up in the tops of trees for the strings to vibrate from the currents of wind) and the Audumbari veena (played as an accompaniment by the wives of Vedic priests as they chanted during ceremonial Yajnas). Veenas ranged from one string to one hundred and were composed of many different materials like eagle bone, bamboo, wood, and coconut shells. Shiva is depicted playing or holding a veena in his form called "Veenadhara," which means "bearer of the vina." The sage Narada is known as a veena maestro, and refers to 19 different kinds of Veena in Sangita Makarandha. Ravana, the antagonist of the epic Ramayana, is described as a versatile veena player.

The Ramayana, the Puranas and Bharata Muni's Natya Shastra all contain references to the veena, as well as the Sutra and the Aranyaka. The Vedic sage Yajnavalkya speaks of the greatness of the veena in the following verse: "One who is skilled in Veena play, one who is an expert in the varieties of srutis (quarter tones) and one who is proficient in tala (rhythm) attain salvation without effort. Each physical portion of the veena is said to be the seat in which subtle aspects of various gods and goddesses reside in Hinduism. The instrument's neck is Shiva; the strings constitute his consort, Parvati. The bridge is Lakshmi, while the secondary gourd is Brahma, and the dragon head is Vishnu. Upon the "table" (or the resonating body) is Saraswati. "Thus, the veena is the abode of divinity and the source of all happiness." R. Rangaramanuja Ayyangar

28. Manda smita prabha pura majjat kamesha manasa

Kamesha is so overwhelmed by Her smile that it leads him to merge into Her

Kamesha refers to the Paramatma, the one who is the cause of all intentions, who grants consciousness and who gives us the power to see, experience comprehend all aspects of the Universe. Paramatma, who till this point was motionless now merges with Shakti and gives rise to all of creation. This nama implies that She is the root cause for creation.

29. Anakalita sadrishya chibukashri virajita

The beauty of Her chin is beyond comparison and description.

She has the most beautiful chin. It leaves even the Vag Devatas, who have composed this stotra, without words to describe its beauty.

30. Kamesha baddha mangalya sutra shobhita kandhara

Kamesha has tied a Mangalasutra around Her neck, and this causes Her to shine in all glory

Lalita's neck is adorned by the Mangalya Sutra tied by Kameshwara. She is a Nitya Sumangali, never taking off the Mangalasutra. This mangal sutra tied by Kameshwara, is said to bless the whole world as it contains the essence of all mantras and it is His way of showering auspiciousness on Shakti. With their coming together, auspiciousness becomes doubled and further strengthened.

Marriage in the Sanatana tradition is seen as a transfer of energy between two beings or jivas. The groom ties the mangala sutra around the bride's neck in a ceremony called the Mangalya Dharanam (wearing the auspicious) during a Hindu wedding while the mantra Mangalyam tantunanena mama jeevana hetuna: kanthe badhnami subhage twam jeevasarada satam is chanted. It means: This is a sacred thread. This is essential for my long life. I tie this around your neck, O maiden having many auspicious attributes may you live happily for a hundred years. This necklace serves as a visual marker of status as a married Hindu woman.

The first 30 names of this Sahasranama comprise the 'Vagbhava kuta' of the Shodashi mantra. The first 5 bijaksharas of this mantra were outlined in the form of describing her face (Vagbhava kuta). We now step into the Madhyama kuta, the middle portion of the mantra.

31. Kanakangada keyuraka maniyabhujanvita

Her arms are bedecked with the golden armlets Angada and Keyura.

Her beautiful body is adorned with angada for the wrists and keyura for the upper arms. The subtle meaning here is that although these ornaments are made of gold, they differ in their form. So, though living beings differ in their forms, their atman is no different from the Divine Consciousness.

Arms represent the determination and the strength to uplift dharma. The Devatas, who are establishers of righteousness are said to be Her armlets. It is the grace of the Devatas that inspires the human being to uplift and protect dharma. The true essence behind worshipping any deity is to seek the creation of good thoughts and intentions. Developing a positive attitude that strengthens dharma and which seeks the upliftment of all, leads to welfare of society.

32. Ratna graiveya chintaka lola mukta phalanvita

She wears an exquisite chain made of gems and pearls.

This nama describes Lalita as wearing a pearl necklace with a golden pendant studded with gemstones. Pearl symbolizes the mind and is used to control the mind. It renders the mind pure. The scriptures related to gems (ratna shastra) and astrology (jyotishya shastra) declare that those suffering from infliction of moon should wear pearls.

By wearing pearls, the Divine Mother indicates that She grants a pure mind and progress in yoga to the devotee. The person who fixes his mind on the throat of Devi, which is Her Vishuddha Chakra, when seeing the idol, is blessed with a pure mind and is relieved of tensions.

The hidden meaning of this nama is that it outlines three different types of devotees and how their practice brings them the fruits of their sadhana. The first type are devotees who chant the japa with a distracted mind. They are Graiveya Chintakas, who have limited discipline to access Her in entirety and exclusively focussing on her form above the neck. Their lack of attention means that the anugraha they receive is also limited. The second type of devotees are the Lolas, whose minds are not entirely fixed on her and they keep oscillating between their devotion to Her and their attachment to the material world. They are likened to a pendant hanging from a necklace, in constant state of motion. They reap some benefits from their devotion but there is much room for their spiritual growth. The third type of devotees are those who are Mukta, detached and dispassionate. They have been able to acquire vairagya over the material world and are fully dedicated to Her in thought, word and deed. They receive Her full anugraha.

33. Kameshvara prema ratna mani prati panastani

She has given her breasts in exchange for the love of Kameshwara.

Kameshwara is a precious gem and to procure this gem, the Divine Mother has traded away her breasts. She offers her bosom to Kameswara in reciprocation of His love. In a subtle sense, She showers Her blessings generously on her devotees, in return for the small amounts of devotion they offer to Her.

Breasts in this context are not to be approached from a sexual angle. They imply that which is needed for growth and sustenance. In this nama, they represent Her task of sustenance of Her own creation. The process of creation began with her reciprocating the love of Kameshwara and She now plays the role of the sustainer or preserver by ensuring that creation is nurtured and nourished through Her ample bosom.

In the Mahabharata, there is a wonderful story about Maharishi Jadabharata. He practiced Madhukari, begging for food going from house to house. Out of respect, he never looked at women directly, only at their feet, and thus did not know what a woman looked like. One day, when a woman came to offer him alms, he accidentally looked at her face and then her body. Surprised to see that her body was different from his, Jadabharata, who had a pure and innocent mind, asked her why this was so.

The woman, shocked, ran to her mother-in-law to report the incident. The elderly woman, understanding the situation better, realized that the mendicant might have a genuine question. She approached him, and Jadabharata repeated his query. After thinking for a moment, she explained, "A woman's body is designed by God to provide food for the baby she will have in the future."

This answer had a profound impact on Jadabharata. He thought, "If the Supreme Mother ensures food for a being yet to be born, wouldn't she also provide for those already created?" Leaving his begging bowl at the doorstep, he walked away silently, went into the forest, and began to meditate, trusting that the Divine Mother would provide for him.

After a few days, the king of the land saw the meditating mendicant and, moved by his devotion, placed some fruits beside him. Seeing the king's respect for the mendicant, the villagers also began to bring food daily. In this way, the Supreme Mother ensured that Jadabharata was taken care of all his life.

34. Nabhya lavala romalilata phala kuchadvayai

Her two breasts are like fruits dangling on a creeper which is a line of hair climbing up from the trench of her navel.

Her navel and waist are so slender and thin that they appear like a thin hairlike creeper. To this thin creeper, the breasts appear like fruits. The navel is one of the focal points (kendra sthaana) for yoga; the significance of this focal point is highlighted through this nama. The esoteric meaning of this nama is its reference to the upward rise of kundalini during meditation from the Swadishtana chakra which is just below the navel to the Anahata chakra which is located in the chest region.

35. Lakshya roma lata dharata samunne yamadhyama

She who is suspected to have a waist because of the creeper like hairs raising from there

Her waist is so slender that its existence can only be inferred from the previous nama. The hidden meaning of this nama is that the atma is so subtle that it cannot be seen but can only be experienced through sadhana.

Her waist is slim and subtle which denotes that She is the form of time (kala swaroopam). She is eternal and always found in the most supreme state. By depicting her thin hairlike waist, it can be understood that for She manifests in the madhyama state for the benefit of Her devotees.

36. Stana bhara dalan madhya patta bandha valitraya

The three folds of Her abdomen form a waistband and support Her waist from collapsing under the weight of Her breasts.

The three-fold waistband represents the three Vedas (trayee is also another name for the Vedas). She therefore retains the Vedas themselves as Her waistbands. The Samudrika Shastra states that upper class men and women have three folds on their forehead, neck and abdomen which are signs of extremely good fortune.

37. Arunaruna kausumbha vastra bhasvat kati tati

Her saree that is of a deep red colour adds to Her majestic and graceful form.

The word Aruna has been reiterated twice here to highlight the depth of the colour of the sari. The red colour 'Aruna' is like that of the Charioteer of the Sun God, who rises before the Sun. The juice of the Kausumbha herb is used as a dye to create the red colour which is an indication of Her compassion and love.

38. Ratna kinkini karamya rashanadamabhushita

Her waist belt that is abounding in hanging diamonds and precious stones adds to Her divine brightness. A melodious sound 'Kinkini' reverberates from that waist belt.

The word kinkini represents the various melodious sounds in nature such as chirping of birds, water gushing through the valleys and many more. The esoteric meaning of this nama is the reference it contains to the location of the Muladhara chakra where the odyana bandha is located. This is an important mystical knot for every spiritual practitioner.

The names 31 till 38 described Her Madhya kuta of the Shodashi mantra and we now step into Her Shakti kuta.

39. Kamesha jnata saubhagya mardavoru dvayanvita

Only her husband Kamesha knows the softness and beauty of Her thighs.

This highlights Her chastity and at the same time it once again highlights that Shiva and Shakti are, in reality, one single entity.

40. Manikya mukuta kara janu dvaya virajita

Her knee caps are decorated with rubies

41. Indra gopa parikshipta smaratunabhajanghika

Her calf muscles resemble Manmatha's quiver and is surrounded by thousands of tiny insects called Indragopas.

The Devi's calf muscles are firm and reddish in hue, resembling the quiver carried by Manmatha, the God of Desire. The brightness of her legs attracts Indragopas which are red tiny insects that are seen during rains. They have a short lifespan and come in groups of thousands.

In the Saundarya Lahiri, Ali Shankaracharya describes that Manmatha, who was decimated by Shiva, seeks revenge upon him and when Shiva finds himself attracted to Her beauty, Manmatha makes her calf muscles his quiver and Her toes his arrows.

42. Gudhagulpha

Her ankles firm and beautiful, always kept hidden from the eyes of others. The esoteric meaning of this nama is that She secretly protects her devotees who take Her name.

43. Kurma prashtha jayishnu prapadanvita

Her feet resemble the back of a turtle

The arch of her feet is beautiful and curved like a tortoise shell. Vishnu's incarnation in Kurma avatar teaches us that the tortoise is seen as supporting and holding up the entire universe. This nama, which compares Her feet to a tortoise shell signifies that She is the one upholding and supporting the universe. Worshipping Her feet is the same as worshipping the entire universe.

In the Saundarya Lahiri, Ali Shankaracharya takes exception to this simile as he states that the shell of a tortoise is hard while Her feet are soft and gentle. In the 88th verse, he asks: Only Shiva knows the softness of Your feet, that is why He held Your feet with great care during Your marriage ceremony. How can the Vac Devis compare such soft feet to a tortoise shell?

The esoteric meaning of this nama is that Devi blesses her devotees with Her feet as Her four hands are occupied with the four weapons. Since she does not have the abhaya and varada mudra, the two acts of blessings and granting boons are done by Her feet.

44. Nakha didhiti samchanna namajjana tamoguna

She removes the darkness of ignorance by those to pray to her by the lustre of Her toe nails.

The bright illumination emanating from Her toe nails destroys the tamas of all those who offer obeisance to Her. Tamas is inertia and ignorance. We prostrate before a deity so that the energy from the murthi merges with our Sahasrara chakra and spreads to the entire body.

45. Pada dvaya prabha jala parakrta saroruha

The brilliance originating from Her feet outshine even the most beautiful lotuses.

The lotus is generally used to describe the face or eyes of beautiful women. The beauty of a lotus arises from its softness, elongated shape and symmetry. This nama points to the fact that while a lotus blooms and shrivels in one day, Her feet remain permanently lustrous. Spiritual aspirants who have imprinted Her feet in their mind achieve accomplishment quickly. Her position as a Guru is highlighted in this nama.

46. Sinjana mani manjira mandita Sri padambuja

The anklets on Her feet, ornamented with various precious stones, make a sweet and melodious sound.

The sounds emanating from Her anklets are the Vedas.

47. Marali manda gamana

Her gait is as graceful as a Swan

In the Mooka Panchashati, the swans in Devi's palace try to copy Her gait. The hidden meaning in this nama is that Manda is one of the names of Shani (Saturn). It is implied that She removes the troubles and afflictions caused by Saturn when worshipped. Hamsa, which is a synonym for marali, is a reference to our prana (breath and life force). There are four levels of saintliness – kutichaka, bahudaka, hamsa and paramahamsa. She is the protector to all these yogis.

48. Maha lavanya shevadhih

She is the repository of all beauty

The description of Her form concludes with the final declaration that Her beauty is limitless and beyond description. She is an ocean of most Supreme Bliss and bestows such bliss on those who worship Her.

49. Sarvaruna

Her body, garments, jewels, flowers and lustre are all red.

Everything associated with Her is red. Her redness is not just because She emerged from the sacrificial fire. It is Her natural attribute symbolizing Her compassion.

50. Anavadyangi

She is faultless and flawlessly beautiful. Her limbs are in perfect shape.

51. Sarvabharana bhushita

She is adorned with all ornaments.

The ornaments worn by Her are described in the Kalpa Sutra and Kalika Purina. The jewels try to enhance Her beauty but fail. However, the beauty of the jewels is enhanced by their presence on Her beautiful body.

In the names so far, Her gross form was described from head to toe. The process of visualizing the Shodashi mantra in Her gross form was also detailed. The next few names detail Her place of residence.

Chapter 5

Moola Grantha (52-111)

52. Shivakameshwarantastha

She who sits on the thigh of Shivakameshwara

Shivakameshwara (Shiva+ Kama+ Eshwara) Shiva is the Auspiciousness One. Kama means one who is beautiful and Eshwara rules over the actions of others and makes them act as per His wishes. Her position of sitting in Shivakameshwara's lap signifies that she is astride knowledge, consciousness and auspiciousness, carrying an authority over all three.

53. Shiva

She is Shiva's consort and hence inseparable from Shiva

This is one of the most powerful names in this Sahasranama. As the wife of Shiva, She takes on His name. Through this name, it is conveyed that there is no difference between Shiva and Shakti.

"Yata Shiva-tata Devata; yata Devata-tata Shiva" encapsulates a profound truth within Advaita Vedanta, and Shakti traditions. It can be understood as wherever there is Shiva, there is Divinity; wherever there is Divinity, there is Shiva. This phrase highlights the non-dual nature of the Divine, emphasizing that Shiva, who represents the formless, infinite consciousness, is inseparable from Devata, the manifest deity. In essence, Shiva and the various deities worshiped in Hinduism are not different entities but different expressions of the same ultimate reality. In the context of Shaktism, this is often expressed as the unity of Shiva and

Shakti. Shiva is the unchanging, formless aspect of reality, while Shakti is the dynamic, creative force. Together, they represent the totality of existence.

In non-dualistic philosophy, this phrase can be understood as an affirmation that the Brahman is beyond all distinctions. Shiva, in this sense, is synonymous with Brahman, the absolute, and all deities (Devatas) are seen as manifestations of that one reality. For practitioners, this phrase serves as a reminder that all forms of divine worship ultimately lead to the same truth. Whether one worships Shiva, Vishnu, Devi, or any other deity, they are connecting with the same underlying divine consciousness. It encourages a non-sectarian approach to spirituality, acknowledging the divinity in all forms and rejecting the notion of superiority among different deities or paths. Devi Mahatmyam in the Markandeya Purana glorifies the Goddess as the supreme power but also acknowledges her inseparable connection with Shiva, indicating their unified essence.

Sri Ganapati Sachidananda Swamiji says: The ignorant presume that Shiva is the Lord who wears tiger skin around his waist and roams about in a cremation ground while the Supreme Mother is a personification of endless beauty with all her ornaments and silks. Progress in sadhana will result in a spiritual awakening of the person. He is then able to visualize them as Ardhanareshwara roopa (a form in which one half is Shiva and other half is Devi). Gradually the realization that there is only one entity that truly exists will dawn upon him. This name Shiva clarifies that She is the force who helps in controlling the senses, controlling the mind and in achieving single pointed concentration (ekagrata). The word 'Vashi' means 'one who helps us in controlling our senses (indriyas)'. Interchanging these 'va' and 'shi', the word 'Shiva' is formed. Therefore, Shiva is said to be the force that aids us in sense control. As His wife, She is the energy who ensures that it is rendered possible. She is the kinetic energy as opposed to the static energy of Shiva. Shiva means one who is eternally in bliss (Ananda), who possesses excellent qualities and who is an embodiment of auspiciousness. Shiva is one who grants this auspiciousness on to the devotee (Shivam karoti). As She bestows all these upon to Her devotees, She is Shiva. Just repeating the word 'Shiva' blesses one with auspiciousness (mangalam).

She is Iccha, the willful form of Shiva. There are three types of Shaktis: Iccha (desire), Jnana (knowledge) and Kriya (action). Shiva does not have any desires. But His iccha form is reflected in Lalita. Here desire means the desire for self-realization.

54. Swadhina vallabha

She who is a loving consort

This nama is a confirmation of the previous one and indicates that Her consort Shiva belongs exclusively to Her. The esoteric meaning of this nama is that while Brahman is omnipresent, our karmas are embedded in the jiva. Neither the Brahman nor soul can create life in their individual capacity. Brahman needs the soul to function with a gross form, and the soul needs Brahman to get birth.

Some scholars have said that this nama can be understood to mean that She controls Her husband. This does not imply that She is superior to her husband, instead it reflects a healthy association and marriage of equals. Shiva is the cause of this universe and She is the energy that propels him.

The word 'Swa' stands for self. Swadhina is made up of two words swa+ adhina, which means subjugation of the self. This nama also implies that She is fond of people who practise self-control and actively seek self-realization.

55. Sumeru madhya shringhasta

She who dwells in the central peak of Mount Meru

Sumeru is the legendary golden mountain which supports the earth at its base. There are three peaks located in a triangular formation within which lies the fourth and highest peak at its exact centre. It is here that She dwells. The hidden meaning in this nama is the reference to the Sri Chakra or

Sri Yantra which is also variously known as the Bhuprasthara in its two-dimensional form and Maha Meru in its three-dimensional form. The Sri Chakra is the most auspicious sacred geometry which is considered to be a blueprint of the entire universe. On a microcosmic level, the human body is seen as the Sri Chakra within which the backbone is considered to be the Sumeru. She resides at the Sahasrara chakra which lies at the top of the head.

56. Sriman nagara nayika

She who is the ruler of the beautiful city called 'Srinagara' or 'Srimannagara'.

She is the head of the city which is described in the Rudrayamala as Sudhasamudra. The word nagara here refers to the Sri Chakra and therefore She is also described as Sri Chakra Nayika.

After the annihilation of Bhandasura, the Trimurtis (Brahma, Vishnu, and Shiva) summoned the cosmic architect Vishwakarma and the demon architect Maya. They were instructed to construct 16 palaces in 16 sacred places (kshetras) for the residence of Lalita and Shiva Kameswara. These kshetras include the Meru and other gigantic mountains (9 in total) and Jalasamudra and other oceans (7 in total), making up the 16 kshetras. The palatial buildings of the Divine Mother located in these kshetras are called Sripura.

Wherever a Sripura is located, its dimensions are as follows:

Mount Meru

Mount Meru has four peaks:

1. One on the eastern side
2. One on the northwestern side
3. One on the southwestern side

Each of these peaks is 100 yojanas tall and 100 yojanas wide, representing the worlds of the Trimurtis.

4. The fourth peak, located at the center, is 400 yojanas tall and 400 yojanas wide.

Sripura on the Middle Peak

- Sripura is situated on the central peak of Mount Meru.
- It is surrounded by seven square-shaped metallic compound walls, each separated from the next by a distance of 7 yojanas.

Within this sacred island, there are multiple forts, each made from a unique material:

Kalayasa (Iron) Wall:

- Perimeter: 16,000 yojanas
- This is the outermost wall. The space between the Kalayasa and Kansya walls forms the first chamber, where several trees and gardens are located.
- Gatekeepers: Mahakali and Mahakala, who are seated on the Kalachakra throne.

Kansya (Bronze) Wall:

- The area between the Kansya and Tamra walls forms the second chamber, which is home to a forest of Kalpavruksha (wish-fulfilling trees), also known as Kalpavatica.
- Protector: Vasanta (Spring Season)
- Consorts: Madhusri and Madhavasri

Tamra (Copper) Wall:

- This wall surrounds the third chamber, a forest of Santana trees (progeny-granting trees).
- Protector: Grishma (Summer Season)
- Consorts: Shukrasri and Shuchisri

Seesa (Lead) Wall:

- The fourth chamber contains a forest of Hari Chandana Vruksha (yellow fragrant sandalwood trees).
- Protector: Varsharutu (Rainy Season)
- Consorts: Nabhasri and Nabhasyasri

Aarkuta (Brass) Wall:

- The fifth chamber houses a garden of Mandara trees (Calotropis gigantea).
- Protector: Sharadrutu (Autumn Season)
- Consorts: Ishasri and Urjasri

Panchaloha (Five-Metal) Wall:

- The sixth chamber contains a forest of Parijata trees.
- Protector: Hemantarutu (Early Winter Season)
- Consorts: Sahasri and Sahasyasri

Raupya (Silver) Wall:

- The seventh chamber features a Kadamba forest.
- Protector: Sisira (Winter Season)
- Consorts: Tavasri and Tavasyasri
- This is where Mantrini Devi resides in a temple. She has another quarter close to Lalita's residence in Mahapadmatavi (the forest of lotuses). When on duty, she stays in that quarter.
- In this seventh chamber, near Mantrini's residence, Matanga Kanyas are constantly singing and dancing

57. Chintamani grihantastha

She who dwells in a house constructed with Chintamani

Within the city of Srinagara, She resides in the house made of Chintamani gems. Chintamani is the gem that dispels worries and also grants all wishes. The syllables in Devi's mantras are capable of bestowing all desires and hence these mantras are also known as Chintamani. She resides within the bijaksharas of these mantras.

Chintamani, also known as Mahapadmatavi, is surrounded by hundreds of thousands of lotus-like palaces.

1. **To the East:** There is a large vessel called the Arghya Patra, used for washing hands.

2. **At the Southeast Corner:** The Chidagnikunda is located.

3. **At the Southwest:** The Sri Chakra Ratha is situated.

4. **At the Northwest:** The Geya Chakra Ratha of Mantrini can be found.

5. **At the Northeast:** The Kiri Chakra Ratha of the Goddess Dandini is positioned.

6. **Between the East and Southeast:** The abode of Goddess Mantrini (Mantrini Gruha) is located.

7. **Between the East and Northeast:** The abode of Goddess Dandini (Dandini Gruha) is situated.

Description of the Palace of Cintamani:

1. The palace is centrally located in Sripattana, the City of Sri (Wealth).

2. The walls of the palace are constructed from Cintamani gems.

3. The roof is also made of Cintamani stones.

4. The palace has three towers, named Iccha Sikhara (Tower of Desire), Kriya Sikhara (Tower of Action), and Jnana Sikhara (Tower of Knowledge).

5. The palace has four doors, known as Amnaya Devas, corresponding to the four directions: East (Purva), South (Dakshina), West (Pascima), and North (Uttara). The term "Amnaya" refers to the Vedas.

6. The Bindu Peetha (central seat of power) is located at the heart of the palace.

7. This seat of power has steps on all four sides.

8. The entire structure is designed in the form of Sricakra.

9. All male and female deities of Sricakra reside here.

10. The Bindu Peetha is also known by several other names, including Sri Peetha, Maha Peetha, Vidya Peetha, and Ananda Peetha, representing prosperity, greatness, knowledge, and bliss.

11. On the pedestal exists the cot of the five Brahmas.

12.   The cot has four legs, which represent Brahma, Vishnu, Mahesana, and Iswara. These deities attained their female forms through worship of the Divine Mother.

13.   The plank resting on these legs represents SadaShiva.

14.   To the east of this cot, there are 36 steps, representing the 36 aspects of spiritualism.

Manidweepam is the celestial island where Lalita, resides. This magnificent island was created by Her mere thought. It is more splendid than Kailasa, more glorious than Vaikunta, and more wondrous than all the worlds, earning it the title "Sarva Lokam." Manidweepam is surrounded on all sides by the nectar of immortality, whose gentle waves create a cool and soothing breeze.

Within this sacred island, there are multiple forts, each made from a unique material which are listed above in name 56. The outermost fort is made of iron, with entrances guarded by vigilant sentinels armed with weapons. Devotees of the Divine Mother reside within this fort. Moving further inward, one encounters a fort made of brass, adorned with a unique gopuram (tower). This fort is surrounded by a variety of fruit-bearing trees and is home to numerous birds, butterflies, and bees. Beyond this brass fort lies a sacred forest, or Kalpavanam, overseen by Vasantam (the deity of spring). In this forest, Gandharvas (celestial musicians) reside, singing praises of Sridevi.

Deeper within the island, one finds a fort made of copper and, beyond that, another of glass. Between these two forts is a forest known as Santana Vatika, presided over by Grishma (the deity of summer). This forest is the dwelling place of Siddha Ganas (perfected beings). Moving further inward, one comes upon another fort made of copper. Between forts lies another forest, overseen by Varsha (the deity of monsoon).

At the heart of Manidweepam stands the Chintamani Gruham, the abode of Sridevi. The air is fragrant with the scents of flowers and dhoopam (incense). This divine residence houses four mantapams (halls): the

Shringara Mantapam, Jnana Mantapam, Mukti Mantapam, and Ekanta Mantapam.

In the Shringara Mantapam, the Gods sing hymns in praise of Tripura Sundari. Here, the Goddess of the Universe sits on Her majestic throne, presiding over all. From the Jnana Mantapam, Sridevi imparts spiritual wisdom to Her devotees. In the Mukti Mantapam, She consults with Her ministers on matters of liberation and grace.

58. Pancha brahmasana shitha

She who sits on a throne made up of five Brahmas

Within her house made up of Chintamani, She sits on a throne that is supported by the Five Brahmas (Pancha Brahmas). In Hindu tradition, the concept of Pancha Brahma holds significant importance, as it describes five manifestations of the Supreme Truth, Brahman. These aspects of Shiva are found in the Krishna Yajur Veda, particularly in the Pancha Brahma Upanishad. The primary Pancha Brahmas are Sadyojata, Vamadeva, Aghora, Tatpurusha, and Ishana, and they further manifest as Brahma, Vishnu, Rudra, Maheshwara, and Sada Shiva respectively.

When the Supreme Being decides to manifest this world, he brings into being the five Brahmans who help materialise this desire by carrying out the five functions of creation (srishti), sustenance (stithi), dissolution (laya), creating a veil (thirodhana) and finally offering grace (anugraha).

Associated with the western direction, Sadyojata represents Iccha Shakti or willpower. This aspect is linked to the mind and is connected to the fire element, symbolizing the fire of the mind and body. Sadyojata's function is that of the creative force and is associated with the Manipura chakra.

Aligned with the northern direction, Vamadeva embodies the shakti or strength and beauty, as well as the goddess Maya. It is associated with

Vijnanamaya Kosha, the sheath of universal consciousness limited to the individual mind. Mantras to Vamadeva are believed to have healing benefits. This aspect represents the preserving energy of Shiva and is connected to the air element and the Anahata Chakra.

Associated with the southern direction, Aghora represents jnana Shakti or the power of knowledge, and the Buddhi rupa, meaning the form of intellect. This aspect is linked to the Pranamaya Kosha and embodies the rejuvenating and dissolving qualities of Shiva. It is connected to the water element and the Svadishthana chakra.

The eastern face of Shiva, Tatpurusha, represents the paramatman or supreme soul behind the physical being. This aspect is associated with Ananda Shakti, the power of bliss, and the Annamaya kosha. Tatpurusha is connected to the earth element and the muladhara chakra, and it is considered beneficial for increasing focus.

Ishana is the upper or skyward face of Shiva, associated with the Citta Shakti or power of individual consciousness realizing the universal consciousness. This aspect represents Akasha or ether and is linked to the Vishuddha chakra. Ishana embodies the total energy of Shiva, encompassing all his attributes and is associated with the Anandamaya kosha.

Sadashiva is the central plank on which She is seated and the other four are the legs of Her throne. The reason for the Brahmans acting as legs of her throne is their desire to be in close proximity and of faithful service to Her at all times.

59. Maha padmatavi samstha

She who resides in the forest of the great lotuses.

This forest is said to be located in the centre of the Chintamanigriha. Mahapadmatavi also refers to the Sahasrara chakra which is depicted as a thousand petal lotus, located on the top of our head where She resides.

60. Kadamba vana vasini

She who lives in the Kadamba Forest

The Kadamba tree is uncommon in most regions and it flowers for a very brief period in a year. This tree is unique, in that it does not take in water through its roots, but only imbibes rainwater that falls on its leaves. In the monsoon the tree dries up. Kadamba tree reflects the connection between the Devatas and earth. Rains are the outcome of our prayers. When the society follows the path of Dharma, then the rain gods bless the land with abundant rainfall. It is said that one glimpse of the Kadamba tree gives us a vision of the abode of the Devatas. Performing a pradakshina (circumambulation) to this tree is considered very sacred.

Kadamba vana subtly refers to the spiritual pursuits undertaken by the individual. Chanting, meditation and prayer are tools that help us develop a connection with the deities. Our spiritual efforts are likened to a Kadamba vana within which She resides.

61. Sudha sagara madhyasta

She who resides in the middle of the ocean of nectar.

The Rudrayamala states that Chintamanigraha is located in this ocean of nectar. The esoteric meaning of this nama points to the bindusthana in the Chandramandala, located just under the Sahasrara chakra which is also known as the Sudhasindhu. A spiritual sadhaka is able to move his energy towards the highest chakra with his endeavours.

The ten names from Shivakameshwarankastha (barring Shiva) specify Her place of residence in the top-down approach. Now let us understand this in a down to up approach. In a large ocean of nectar, there is an island within which is a beautiful forest of lotuses. Within this forest is a garden of Kadamba trees which is home to a large city. This city consists of a vast mansion known as the Chintamani Griha. In this mansion, She is seated on a throne supported by Pancha Brahmas. With all the weapons in Her hand, She is smiling while the sages surrounding Her recite the Vedas.

62. Kamakshi

She who has beautiful eyes

Her eyes are full of grace and compassion and with one look she is able to fulfil the desires of Her devotees. The hidden meaning of this nama is that She has Saraswati (Ka) as one of Her eyes and Lakshmi (Ma) as the other. It also refers to Kanchipuram which is one of the 51 Shakti Peethas where Devi's waist is said to have fallen. Brahma is said to have performed a Yagnya in Kanchipuram seeking the powers of creation. Since Devi fulfilled Brahma's desire, She is also known as Kamakshi.

63. Kamadayini

She fulfils every desire of Her devotees.

64. Devarshi ganasanghata stuyamanatma vaibhava

She who is worshipped by both Gods and Sages

The word vaibhava comes from the root vibhu which means omnipresent. She is all pervading and therefore can fulfil the desires of the devotees in an instant if they earn Her grace. Sanghata here refers to hell from which the Gods and Sages seek her blessings to get a release. The reference to atma signifies the undivided form of the Devi thereby indicating that Her manifestation is omnipresent, omnipotent and filled with a boundless energy. She imparts knowledge of the self to even the Gods and Sages.

65. Bhandasura vadhodyukta shakti sena samanvita

One who leads an army of energy to destroy Bhandasura

Manmatha is reduced to ashes by the fire of Shiva's third eye as His meditation is disturbed. Shiva's retinue collects these ashes and build a figure out of it. This figure comes alive as Bhandasura and does such intense penance that Shiva has no choice but to grant him many boons. He wreaks havoc in the world and the Devatas call out to Devi to help them in dispelling the threat of Bhandasura. Devi emerges from the fire and releases an army of energy to fight the evil brought about by this demon.

The hidden meaning here is that Bhanda is an ignorant egoist who seeks to rob us of our prana which is symbolic of arresting our spiritual growth and not allowing us access to the supreme knowledge. Her role in the life of a devotee is to help him acquire knowledge of the self and She does so by sending out Her army to protect the devotee.

66. Sampatkari samaarudha sindhura vraja sevita

She is worshipped by the elephant brigade commanded by Sampatkari

An array of elephants arranged by Lakshmi, the Goddess of prosperity, known as Sampatkari Devi is ready to serve Her.

There are two hidden meanings of this nama. The first is that Sampatkari Vidya is a powerful three-syllable bijakshara mantra which can be found in the Swatantra Tantra. It also points to the knowledge of triputi (triad, set of 3 which are commonly found in Hinduism – ranging from Brahma, Vishnu Maheshwara to Rajas, Tamas, Sattva to Bhu, Bhuva, Swaha, etc.,), which constitute the true wealth (sampat) that a devotee can earn with his practice. The ultimate triad is that of the knowledge which enables one to identify the knower, the known and the object of knowledge and their correlation is also known as sampatkari or most essential wealth.

67. Ashvaroodha dhisthitaatsva kotikoti biraavruta

She is surrounded by millions of horses commandeered by Ashvaroodha

Ashva or horse refers to the five senses in other Hindu scriptures. The five senses which our only source of information from the outside world, are equated to horses on which is mounted the mind. Hence, the mind is Ashvaroodha. It is only though the senses that the mind carries out all its activities. She therefore is the master of the senses and is seated upon them. Millions of horses signify the millions of living beings existing in the universe.

The Sri Suktam which can be found in the Rig Veda has a similar reference to Lakshmi:

Ashva-Purvaam Ratha Madhyaam Hastinada Prabodhinim Shriyam Devim Upahvaye Shrirma Devi Jushataam

She, who is sitting in the Chariot which is driven by horses in front and whose appearance is heralded by the trumpet of elephants.

68. Chakraraja ratharudha sarvayudha parishkrita

She who is mounted on the Sri Chakra chariot surrounded by all kinds of weapons

The Sri Chakra Raja Ratha has the following dimensions and features according to a blog titled: Synopsis of Lalitopakhyana – A Concise Story of the Goddess Lalita Tripura Sundari

- A. **Width:** 4 Yojanas (1 Yojana is approximately 9 miles)
- B. **Height:** 10 Yojanas
- C. **Parvas (Landings):** 9 in number
- D. **Chakras (Wheels):** Represent the four Vedas
- E. **Horses:** Symbolize the fourfold aims of life (Purusharthas)
- F. **Flag:** Represents absolute bliss
- G. **Seat at the Topmost Landing:** The Bindu Peetha
- H. **Form:** Designed in the form of Meru Prastara
- I. **Material:** Constructed from Tejas (divine radiance)

The Sri Chakra is considered to be the king of all yantras as all other yantras can be extracted from it. This sacred diagram is also the seat from where she watches over Her creation. The nine avaranas of the Sri Chakra are seen to be the nine tiers of the chariot with the Sarvanandamaya Chakra shining as a flag on top of the chariot. The weapons that surround her are symbolic of the different types of energies that the deities bring to the field.

69. Geyachakra ratharudha Mantrini parisevita

She who is worshipped by Mantrini seated in Her chariot Geyachakra

Shyamala who takes on the name of Mantrini is a Shakti created by Devi out of her sugarcane bow as an embodiment of mind energy. She is the presiding deity of all Vedas and for the set of mantras pertaining to all Gods. It is She who bestows knowledge. She has a Veena in one hand and a parrot in another. She is capable of bestowing on her devotees, sweet voice, knowledge of music and power to attract the mind. Geya means 'to be praised/ sung about' and is related to song and music. As music originates from the Vishuddha chakra, it can be understood that Geyachakra is an allusion to the throat Chakra. This chakra gives the power of speech and the power of knowledge.

In Devi's army, Mantrini occupies a position next to Her. In statecraft, the king has consultations on many matters without other's knowledge. This process is known mantralochana. Just as mantras are said to be secret, matters in statecraft are referred to by the same name. In a war, the ability to reflect, think and plan effectively is very critical. The word 'mantri' means 'minister' i.e. the person who has the good intellect and ability of strategic planning. He is the guide for the war. Here it states that Mantrini seats herself within our intellect and guides the war against our inner enemies.

If the mantras are contemplated with controlled mind and clear intellect, they convert the mind into Devi's form. This is mantrasiddhi (fruition of the power of mantra).

70. Kirichakra ratharudha Dandanatha puraskrita

She who is worshipped by Dandanatha seated in Her chariot Kirichakra

Goddess Varahi, known as Dandanatha for wielding a staff, has a boar-like face and rides a chariot drawn by boars. She is one of the seven Divine Mothers (sapta matrukas) who assisted the Supreme Mother in battling the demons Shumbha and Nishumbha.

The significance of her boar-like face is rooted in the meaning of the name Varaha, which is derived from 'Vara' (most superior/auspicious) and 'Aha' (day), collectively meaning 'an auspicious festive day'. Among the ten incarnations of Mahavishnu (Dashavataras), His incarnation as a boar (Varaha) holds special importance. It marks His first complete terrestrial form, following His aquatic (Matsya, the fish) and amphibious (Kurma, the turtle) forms.

In this boar form, Vishnu dived into the ocean to slay the demon Hiranyaksha, retrieved the submerged land, and restored it. This remarkable act led to the day being celebrated as an auspicious day, hence the name Varaha.

The symbolism of lifting the earth from the water refers to elevating the people living on earth. While animals lack the capability to change their nature and elevate themselves, humans possess this potential. Goddess Varahi aids in driving away the negative forces that hinder a devotee's progress, thus helping them rise and improve.

71. Jvalamalinika kshipta vahni prakara madhyaga

She who dwells in the centre of the fort of fire built by Jwalamalini

In the Sri Chakra, fifteen Nitya Devis are seated, with five positioned on each of the three sides of the triangle encircling the Bindu. These goddesses symbolize time and include Kameshwari, Bhagamalini, Nityaklinna, Bherunda, Vahnivasini, Mahavajreshwari, Shivaduti, Tvarita, Kulasundari, Nithya, Neelapataka, Vijaya, Sarvamangala, Jwalamalini, and Chitra. At the center, Devi occupies the Bindusthana as the 16th Mahanitya.

During the bright half of the lunar month (Shuklapaksha), worship begins with Kameshwari and concludes with Chitra. In contrast, during the dark half (Krishnapaksha), worship starts with Chitra and ends with Kameshwari, proceeding in reverse order. Jwalamalini is specifically worshipped on the fourteenth day of the bright half and on the second day of the dark half.

Although she is the source of the three cosmic functions of creation, sustenance, and destruction, she remains unaffected by these acts. Surrounded by Jwalamalas (sparks of fire), she stays unaltered.

72. Bhanda sainya vadhodyukta Shakti vikrama harshita

She who is pleased with the bravery of the Shaktis engaged in destroying Bhandasura's army

A battle erupts between Her forces and the demons while She remains seated in stillness. Her forces, well-aware of their assigned duties are prepared to annihilate all evil. Their skill, enthusiasm, and bravery bring joy to Her. The demonic forces of Bhanda symbolize the obstacles and challenges that we encounter on our spiritual journey, as well as those in our everyday lives. These include the ego and the ignorance that clouds our intellect. Overcoming these obstacles requires Her divine energy. Only when we acquire this energy and fill our hearts with it will Her grace be bestowed upon us.

73. Nitya parakramatopa nirikshana samutsukha

She who is overjoyed with the Nitya Devis

The fifteen Nitya Devis as described in nama 71 preside over the fifteen days of the lunar fortnight, each responsible for vanquishing one of the fifteen leaders of the demon army. This battle symbolizes an internal conflict within the sadhaka – a struggle between ignorance, ego, and other negative traits on one side and divine forces on the other.

This nama points to the importance of discipline and practice (Abhyasa) in knowing Her. The disciplined actions of sadhakas, who adhere to their daily duties bring Her great joy. These duties include studying the Vedas, practicing yoga, and engaging in continuous learning. Abhyasa signifies consistent, dedicated practice or repetition. Derived from the Sanskrit root bhyas, meaning "to practice," and involves the continual effort to cultivate and sustain spiritual practices, leading to the steady transformation of the mind and soul.

Abhyasa emphasizes the importance of regular, persistent practice in the spiritual path. Whether it is the repetition of a mantra, daily meditation, or the disciplined study of scriptures, it involves making these practices an integral part of one's life. In the Yoga Sutras of Patanjali, Abhyasa is defined as the effort to achieve a steady and tranquil state of mind. Patanjali states, "Tatra sthitau yatnah abhyasa" – the effort to remain steady in practice is Abhyasa." He further explains that practice becomes firmly grounded when done for a long time, without interruption, and with sincere devotion. It plays a crucial role in stabilizing the mind and overcoming the distractions and fluctuations that are inherent in human consciousness. Through repeated practice, the mind becomes more focused, leading to a state of inner tranquility (chittavritti-nirodha), which is the ultimate goal of yoga. The Bhagavad Gita emphasizes the power of Abhyasa in controlling the restless mind. Krishna advises Arjuna that the mind, although difficult to control, can be subdued through Abhyasa and Vairagya.

In any spiritual pursuit, mastery is achieved not through sporadic effort but through sustained and dedicated practice. Whether it is the mastery of yoga asanas, the deepening of meditation, or the understanding of spiritual teachings, Abhyasa ensures gradual progress and eventual mastery. It is seen as a means to overcome obstacles on the spiritual path. These obstacles, which can include doubt, laziness, and distractions, are gradually weakened and eventually eradicated through persistent practice. The Yoga Sutras describe various obstacles (antarayas) that impede spiritual progress and prescribe Abhyasa as a remedy to overcome them, enabling the practitioner to remain focused on the path.

While Abhyasa involves active practice, it is paired with Vairagya in Hindu philosophy. Together, they create a balanced approach to spiritual growth. Abhyasa involves effort and engagement, while Vairagya involves letting go of attachment to the fruits of that effort. In the Yoga Sutras Patanjali states, that the restraint of mental modifications is achieved through both Abhyasa and Vairagya.

74. Bhanda putra vadhodyukta bala vikrama nandita

She who is pleased with the bravery of Bala who destroys Bhanda's sons.

When Bhanda sees his soldiers being defeated, he sends his thirty sons to continue the battle. They are slain by Bala Tripurasundari, who perpetually appears as a nine-year-old child. She wears an armor that emerged from Sridevi's own armor and fights Bhanda's sons while riding a small chariot called Karniratha. Sridevi is delighted by Bala's prowess.

The hidden allusion is this nama is to Devi's mantra in its Panchadasakshari form, which comprises of three groups of 5, 6, and 4 syllables, respectively known as Vagbhava, Kamaraja, and Shakti kutas. The Bala mantra consists of three syllables Aim Klim Sauh, each corresponding to one of the groups in Panchadasakshari. The initiation into Sri Vidya is through this Bala mantra.There are three types of sins: arrogance, illusion, and ignorance. These sins bind the soul to the cycle of repeated births. When these sins are perceived through the ten organs of the body, they are represented as Bhanda's thirty sons. The Bala mantra has the power to destroy all these sins.

75. Mantrinyamba virajita vishanga vadha toshita

She who is pleased by the killing of Vishanga by Mantrini

Vishanga and Vishukra, the two brothers of the demon Bhanda, are created by him. After the death of all his sons, Bhandasura sends his brothers to continue the battle. Vishukra approaches the Her forces at night and uses a mystical yantra (vighna Yantra, an esoteric geometric design) to penetrate the firewall created by Jwalamalini. This yantra induces delusion, ignorance, and laziness among the Mother's troops.

Mantrini and Dandini, unaffected by this obstacle, approach Her, seeking blessings to go forward into the battle. She creates Ganesha by merely smiling at Kameshwara. Ganesha destroys the yantra created by Vishukra, awakening the divine troops from their ignorance and slumber. They then charge into battle and defeat Vishanga.

Vishanga represents the demon that prevents us from participating in good associations and keeps us from performing mantra japa. Mantrini destroys Vishanga and in order to receive Her grace, mantra japa is a must.

76. Vishukra prana harana Varahi virya nandita

She who is pleased by the prowess of Varahi in killing Vishukra

Vishukra serves as the commander-in-chief of Bhandasura, and he is slain by Varahi, the commander-in-chief of Devi's army, bringing Her great joy. In the form of Bala, She removes the three sins. In her form as Mantrini, she helps stabilize the fluctuating mind. When she takes the form of Dandanathini, she inspires devotion to Shiva and imparts the strength to carry out all duties with steadfast determination.

77. Kameshvara mukhaloka kalpita Sri Ganeshwara

She who created Ganesha with one glance at Kameshwara

Seeing that his army is being decimated, Bhandasura commands Vishukra to deploy the Vighnayantra, an instrument of illusion crafted by demons. This yantra is placed within Devi's forces, resulting in eight detrimental effects: laziness, disinterest in combat, inferiority complex, fatigue, drowsiness, unconsciousness, cowardly lack of motivation, and loss of self-respect. Mantrini reports these issues to Devi, who merely glances at Kameshwara seated beside her. Their affectionate and smiling exchange causes Ganapati to emerge, with an elephant face. In his ten hands, he holds a pomegranate, mace, sugarcane bow, spear, wheel, conch, noose, lily flower, paddy crops, and one of his tusks. His trunk, which serves as an eleventh hand, carries a sacred gem-studded pot.

The esoteric meaning of this nama is that the presence of obstacles like laziness hinders intellectual functioning, and only the energy of yoga can eliminate these obstacles, sharpening the mind. Ganesha, the deity who bestows this energy, is revered for clearing mental obstacles, and the term "kalpita" is a reference to the beauty of his incarnation.

78. Mahaganesha nirbhinna vighna yantra praharshita

She who is jubilant when Ganesha destroyed the Vighna yantra.

79. Bhandasurendra nirmukta shastra pratyastra varshini

One who directs counter missiles to destroy the armaments of Bhandasura

Weapons used in the war fall into two categories:

- **Armaments**: These are handheld weapons like swords, maces, spears, etc., used for combat against nearby enemies.
- **Missiles**: These are long-range weapons aimed at distant enemies.

Bhandasura attacks Devi with armaments when she is near him. However, She counters his attacks using missiles from a distance.

The hidden meaning here is that for those who think She is near or are attracted to her, she will seem far away. Conversely, for those who long for her and feel her at a distance, she will appear very close. She plays this dual game with Bhanda.

The main part of the war is now described, and it is a direct battle between ignorance (ajnana) and knowledge (jnana).

Astra refers to the power or energy generated by the repetition of mantras (mantra shakti), which is the real weapon. She uses mantras as her weapons. Through her recitation of mantras, the weapons sent by Bhanda were destroyed.

In the Mahabharata, Ashwatthama sent a blade of grass filled with the Brahmastra mantra. The grass itself was a physical weapon, but it gained immense power from the mantra, becoming capable of causing unimaginable destruction. Similarly, in Puranic stories, sages often curse using water, indicating that they have infused the water with the power of mantras. Mantras can be packed into various objects such as grass, turmeric, kumkum, and rice grains mixed with turmeric as they naturally conduct mantra energy.

80. Karanguli nakhotpanna narayana dashkritih

The Dashavataras emerged from Her fingernails.

Bhandasura launches his missile, Sarvasurasthram, creating the demons Somakan, Ravanan, and Hiranyakshan to fight against Devi In an instant, She manifests the ten forms of Narayana from her ten finger nails. Each form battles and defeats a demon.

The Dashavatara refers to the ten principal incarnations Vishnu, who is revered as the preserver and protector of the universe. Each avatar represents a divine intervention in the cosmic cycle, occurring in response to the rise of adharma and the need to restore dharma.

The Ten Avatars are:

- **Matsya – Vishnu took this form to** save the Vedas and the sage Manu from a great deluge, symbolizing the preservation of knowledge and the continuity of life during times of destruction.

- **Kurma – Vishnu took** the shape of a tortoise to support Mount Mandara during the churning of the ocean which produced the nectar of immortality. Kurma represents stability and support in times of cosmic upheaval.

- **Varaha** – Vishnu, in the form of a boar, rescued the Earth (personified as the goddess Bhudevi) from the demon Hiranyaksha, who had submerged it in the cosmic ocean. Varaha symbolizes the restoration of the earth and the defeat of evil forces.

- **Narasimha** – a hybrid of man and lion, destroyed the demon Hiranyakashipu to protect his devotee Prahlada. Narasimha represents divine intervention that transcends the limitations of the physical world to uphold dharma.

- **Vamana – Vishnu** appeared as a dwarf brahmin to subdue the demon king Bali by taking three giant steps to reclaim the heavens, earth, and netherworld. Vamana signifies the humbling of the arrogant and the restoration of cosmic balance.

- **Parashurama** – Vishnu incarnated as a warrior sage with an axe to rid the world of corrupt Kshatriya rulers, symbolizing the restoration of social order and the protection of righteousness.

- **Rama** who embodies the ideals of dharma, duty, and kingly virtue.

- **Krishna** – Vishnu appears as the central figure of the Bhagavad Gita and the hero of the Mahabharata. He represents divine love, wisdom, and the principle of bhakti (devotion). Krishna's teachings emphasize the importance of duty, righteousness, and devotion.
- **Buddha** – Vishnu's ninth avatar is identified as the Buddha, who taught compassion and non-violence, leading humanity away from ritualistic practices and towards spiritual enlightenment. This interpretation points to Vishnu's role in guiding humanity according to the needs of the age.
- **Kalki** is prophesied to appear at the end of the current age to destroy adharma and restore dharma, ushering in a new era of truth and righteousness.

The Dashavatara illustrates the evolution of life and consciousness, from the aquatic form of Matsya to the human form of Krishna and the anticipated future of Kalki. Each avatar symbolizes a stage in this evolution and a divine response to the specific challenges of the age. The Dashavatara also reflects the cyclical nature of time in Hindu cosmology, where each age (Yuga) demands a different form of divine intervention to maintain the balance of the universe. This concept is a testament to the adaptability and the continuing relevance of the divine in responding to the changing moral and spiritual needs of humanity.

In this name, the term Narayana signifies both the individual soul and the Supreme Being. Every soul experiences five states:

- Awake (Jagrath)
- Dream (Swapna)
- Deep sleep (Sushupti)
- Swoon (Turiya)
- Transcendental (Turiyateetam)

Narayana performs five cosmic actions:

- Creation (Srishti)
- Sustenance (Sthithi)

- Destruction (Samhara)
- Concealment of the impact of material pleasure and displeasure (Thirodhana)
- Blessings (Anugraha)

Devi effortlessly executes all these actions through her ten finger nails.

81. Maha pashupatastragni nirdagdhasura sainika

She who burned to death the army of the demons with the missile called Mahapashupatha

The missile Pashupatha is capable of burning the entire world. The presiding deity is Shiva in the form of Pashupathi, a combination of the three Gunas – rajas, tamas and satva. This missile (Mahapashupata) is more powerful than Pashupatha. The presiding deity of this missile is Sadashiva, who is beyond the three gunas.

The inner meaning of this nama is that the Pashupata mantra is a very powerful one which can burn down of the entire army of hindrances on our path towards spiritual evolution.

82. Kameshvarastra nirdagdha sabhandasura shunyaka

She who burnt Bhandasura and his city Shunyaka

Bhandasura constructed the cities of Sonitha and Shunyaka as his capitals. The Mahakameshwara is even more powerful than the Mahapashupatha missile. It completely obliterates Bhandasura and his two cities. Shunyaka means nothingness – the city was annihilated and reduced to nothing. Shunyaka represents the illusion of presence when there is none. The Kameshvarastra reduces Bhanda and his two cities to ashes without leaving a trace.

This nama illustrates the journey of the Jiva towards liberation, signifying that in the end, nothing remains but the void. The destruction using the weapon Kameshvarastra symbolises the complete eradication of ignorance and ego through supreme knowledge of self-realisation.

83. Brahamopendra mahendradi deva samstuta vaibhava

Gods such as Brahma, Upendra, Mahendra together with a host of Devatas sing hymns in Her praise.

The story of Bhanda's destruction symbolically represents the eradication of ignorance within an individual. Bhanda embodies the individual ego and ignorance. The Mother initially removes all layers of ignorance surrounding us, then draws us closer to herself. With the elimination of ignorance, the Devatas recognize the power of Shakti which they had previously forgotten.

All the names until this point, explain the purpose and completion of her emergence to help fulfil the wishes of the devas.

84. Hara netragni sandagdha kamasanjivanaushadhih

She who revived Manmatha after he is reduced to ashes by Shiva

After Devi kills Bhandasura, she revives Manmatha at the request of all the Devas, beginning with Brahma. Just as a child punished by the father seeks support from the mother, Manmatha, who was burned by Shiva, regains his life through the grace of mother.

Before his destruction, Manmatha was an embodiment of ignorance, primarily composed of ego. His name signifies "churning the mind" (with "man" meaning mind and "matha" meaning to churn), which caused significant disturbances. Shiva had to destroy him because of these tendencies. Despite worshipping Shiva, his chosen deity, Manmatha attempts an experiment on him, which leads to Shiva's wrath and his subsequent incineration.

As a Guru, Devi restores Manmatha, bringing about a profound transformation in him. She cleanses him of his old latent mental impressions (vasanas) and grants him a new, non-physical body in the form of thought waves (taranga). With her grace, he receives Supreme Knowledge, understanding advaita and attains liberation.

The term "Hara" refers to the removal of self-embodiment and guiding one to overcome ignorance, which pervades all places like fire, thus called "Haranethragni." This ignorance is completely burned away by the feeling of the soul in the form of Kameshwara. By completely destroying the root cause of ignorance, Devi as the embodiment of Vidya, helps the ignorant reach the reality of God and attain liberation. In her role as Guru, Devi refines us and guides us on the spiritual journey. She acts as the navigator of the soul, reforming and elevating us to a state of bliss and peace.

The Divine Mother has 3 states of existence – gross (stula), subtle (sukshma) and supreme (para). The first part of the Moola Grantha detailed Her gross form. Her subtle form is described as chidagni while the next few names, Her supreme most form where she exists as bijaksharas is described in detail.

The most important mantra in Sri Vidya is the Shodashi mantra. This 16-syllable mantra is taught by a guru once the deserving disciple has completed the requisite number of repetitions of the Panchadashi mantra. One seed letter is added to the Panchadashi mantra to make it the Shodashi mantra. As discussed earlier, the Panchadashi mantra is divided into three kutas. These are explained in the following lines.

85. Shrimad vagbhava kutaika swaroopa mukha pankaja

She who has a face created by the bijaksharas of the Vagbhava kuta

The first five bijas of the Panchadashi mantra are known as the Vagbhava Kuta. These bijas are placed at specific locations: the forehead, cheeks, nose, lips, and neck. Lines are then drawn around these letters in the shape of a Yantra, creating Her face. When these lines and seed letter positions are combined, Her complete form emerges and corresponds to the Gnana shakti. In the names describing Her gross form, the 13th to the 30th name correspond to this Vagbhava kuta.

86. Kanthadhah kati paryanta madhyakuta swaroopini

She who has an upper body created by the bijaksharas of the Madhyama kuta

The bijaksharas of the Madhyama kuta represent Her body from neck to hip. The six most important bijaksharas of Sri Vidya take up residence in the mid portion of Her body. It is akin to a lamp, which, when lit at the center of the house, lights up the entire house. All wishes and desires are expressed through this part of the body and hence it corresponds to the Iccha shakti. The 31st name till 38th name correspond to the Madhyama kuta.

87. Shakti kutaika tapanna katyadhobhaga dharini

She who has a lower body created by the bijaksharas of the Shakti kuta

Shakti kuta comprises of four syllables which represent Her body from hops to feet and the energy of creation, Kriya Shakti emerges from here. The 39th name to the 47th name correspond to the Shakti kuta.

88. Mula mantratmika

She who is the root mantra of the Sri Vidya tradition

A mantra is a sacred utterance that protects the person who recites it continuously. It cleanses the individual of past sins and bestows peace and purity of mind. Through constant japa, the sense of self-identity is dissolved and ultimately the Sadhana is blessed with a vision of the true self.

89. Mula kuta traya kalebara

Her body, in its subtle form, is identical to the root mantra

This name reiterates the previous one. After teaching us about external worship and visualization of the Devi at the macrocosmic level, the Lalita Sahasranama now delves into inner worship and inner visualization. This inner worship corresponds to the antardasharam (inner 10 concentric circles) of the Sri Chakra.

Until now, Devi's gross, subtle and supreme forms have been described. Now, the energy called Kundalini comes up for discussion as the next few stanzas describe the process of invoking the dormant Kundalini energy and how to visualize the inner Sri Chakra.

90. Kulamritaika rasika

She who relishes the nectar that flows from the Sahasrara

The Sushumna nadi runs from the base of the spine to the skull at the Muladhara chakra, passing through the center of the body along the backbone. At the base of the spine, Kundalini energy lies dormant, coiled in three and a half rounds. This Kundalini energy can be awakened by heightened spiritual practice or spontaneous uprising or by Shaktipata from a guru. When this energy reaches the Sahasrara chakra, it gathers like butter, seeping and flowing throughout the body as nectar. This nectar is called kulamrutha. She revels in this nectar.

91. Kula sanketa palini

She who guards the esoteric knowledge of the Kaulas

She protects and supports those who undertake spiritual pursuits by providing them with all the facilities and the time needed. Scholars and commentators warn that 'Kula' in this context should not be interpreted to mean any caste or community. It should also not be inferred as Koula marga; adhering to the customs and traditions that have come down from generations or those practices given to us by our Guru is 'kula'. Such kula should be followed.

92. Kulangana

She who is from a chaste family

While the surface meaning of kulangana can be a reference to a chaste woman who abides by her dharma, it also implies that a kulastri is not normally visible to others. Similarly, Devi hides behind the veil of avidya and reveals herself only to those who seek out knowledge. Also, some scholars point out that since Sri Vidya upasana is a secret practice and should not be revealed to all, the nama Kulangana is used.

93. Kulantastha

She who resides within the kula

Kula represents both the Muladhara and Sahasrara Chakras (as noted in nama 90). Since She is the energy that flows between these two chakras, encompassing the beginning and the end, She is called Kulantastha signifying that She is the all-pervading energy.

Additionally, the word Kula has various meanings, such as country, house, body, etc. In this context, the nama can be interpreted to mean that She resides in every country, every house, every body, and, more specifically, in every heart. She is omnipresent.

94. Kaulini

She is the presiding deity of Kaula marga.

Kula is Shakti and Akula is Shiva. The union between Shiva and Shakti, (Prakriti and Purusha) is the path of Yoga which is the Kaula marga. In the external worship of the Sri Chakra, there are three aspects – the Upasaka, the Devi and devotion. This method of worship is the Kaula marga. Since She is worshipped in this method, She is also known as Kaulini.

95. Kula yogini

She is the mother of Yogini matas.

Yogini matas are the various manifestations of Devi and are featured in the Sri Chakra as Prakata Yogini, Gupta Yogini, Guptatara Yogini, Nigarbha Yogini, etc., In this form She paves the way for contemplating the various deities of the Sri Chakra.

With this name, the description of the antar yaaga is complete.

96. Akula

She who is beyond family, tribe, etc.,

Kula in the literal sense can be taken to mean family, tribe or social group. She is beyond all these just as She is beyond birth and death. Akula also refers to the Sahasrara Chakra, where She resides. Akulachara can also refer to samayachara which is seen as one step beyond Kulachara.

97. Samayantastha

She who is the analogous forms of Shiva and Shakti

Samayachara is explained as offering worship inwardly and jointly to Shiva and Shakti. This has been explained in five books written by Vashista, Suka, Sanaka, Sanandana and Sanatkumara. She dwells in this path. Samaya also means time. Realizing the value of time, following discipline and fulfilling one's duties are very dear to Her. She protects all those who follow this.

98. Samayachara tatpara

She who is interested in the Samayachara method

One of the prominent methods of worshipping Her in Sri Vidya is Samayachara. This nama is a reiteration of the earlier name.

The names 99 to 108 deal with Kundalini yoga. The result of the inner worship (antar yaaga) is taught.

99. Muladharaika nilaya

She who resides in the Muladhara chakra

The spine in the human body is called the Merudanda and the main nadi, Sushumna runs through it. She resides in the form of Kundalini at the base of the spine at the Muladhara. She merges with this location and therefore this is Her permanent residence until the death of the being. Upon death of the gross body, this energy merges into the energy of the universe. When a new body is taken, it once again enters and remains seated at the Muladhara. This cycle continues endlessly until the soul attains moksha.

100. Brahmagranthi vibhedini

She pierces the knot (granthi) called Brahmagranthi

The Kundalini starts at the Muladhara, then travels through the Swadisthana, Manipura, Anahata, Vishudda, Ajna chakras to finally pierce the Sahasrara chakra. Granthis are the small knots that lie between the chakras. The first knot that one encounters is the Brahma granthi that lies between the Muladhara and Swadisthana chakras.

The Brahmagranthi is a knot characterized by doubts. Deep breathing through Pranayama is the way to untie this knot. This yogic practice enables the Kundalini energy which lies dormant in the Muladhara to begin moving upwards. With Her boundless compassion, She cuts the knot when the Kundalini reaches this point.

Undoing this knot frees the sadhaka from unnecessary doubts, health problems, and various obstacles that hinder spiritual progress. Additionally, it can be understood to mean that She erases the destiny or fate (Brahma lipi) referred to as Brahmagranthi.

With this, the first 100 namas (shatakam) is complete. These first 100 names form the first of the nine enclosures that take us to Her abode. These enclosures exist both at microcosm and macrocosm planes.

The second enclosure (avarana) that we are entering into is Sarvaasha paripoora chakra (fulfiller of all desires). Creation begins at the Triputi (top-most triangle) in the Srichakra. The first thing that happens after creation is origin of desires and intents (sankalpa). She is fulfilling all the desires (Sarva asha). Lalita Sahasranama is now moving ahead with a description of the antar puja.

101. Manipuranta rudita

The Kundalini energy makes itself visible at Manipura Chakra, after cutting the Brahmagranthi

This description intertwines the spiritual concept of chakras with the practices of worship and the significance of deities and rituals in Hinduism.

The Manipura Chakra is located near the belly button and is referred to as Sthithi Chakra, the place of Vishnu and Surya Kandam. Kundalini energy, as it ascends, pierces the Brahmagranthi in the lower chakras, Muladhara and Swadhisthana, before rising to Manipura. In Manipura, the kundalini energy, personified as a feminine force, receives 47 offerings starting from Padhyam and culminating in the offering of jewels.

In a later name (Chatushastiupacharadhya) She is offered 64 types of upacharas. She is adorned with various gems in this chakra, which is also a reason for the nama Manipuranta rudita.

102. Vishnugranthi vibhedini

She pierces the knot (granthi) called Vishnugranthi

The Vishnu Granthi is located between the Anahata and Vishuddha Chakra and is associated with Vishnu, the preserver and sustainer of the universe. This granthi is connected Her role in maintaining order and balance. It corresponds to the dream state (swapna avastha) and the emotional and mental aspects of an individual. t represents the attachment to power, control, and the material world. It can manifest as ego, ambition, and the desire for control over one's environment and circumstances.

When the Vishnu Granthi is pierced or transcended, it signifies the aspirant's ability to move beyond the emotional and mental constraints, overcoming the ego's need for control and power. This transition allows the Kundalini energy to rise further, reaching higher states of consciousness and spiritual awakening.

103. Ajna chakrantaralastha

She in the form of Kundalini energy who resides at Ajna Chakra

The hidden meaning of this nama is that at this stage, one must seek permission from Devi (in the form of a guru) to advance further. Only those who receive this permission can proceed to the Sahasrara. In other words, the spiritual practice becomes more challenging from this point onward.

104. Rudragranthi vibhedini

She pierces the knot of Rudragranthi

The granthis hold significant meaning particularly in the context of the states of existence: waking, dreaming and deep sleep. In the waking state, the person is aware of his surroundings and identity, but it is the inner being who is truly awake. This inner being transitions into a dream state, where it eventually becomes exhausted and moves into deep sleep, losing awareness of existence and surroundings. This illustrates that the inner being drifts between these states.

At the Brahmagranthi, the knot associated with the wakeful state (body consciousness and creation) is eliminated. At the Manipura level, the dream state is cleared, allowing the aspirant to transcend the state of sustenance, which relates to Vishnu's role of sustenance and protection. Thus, the Vishnugranthi is cut.When the aspirant crosses the Anahata Chakra, they begin to hear beautiful, auspicious sounds created without friction, hence the name Anahata. Here, She cuts the Rudragranthi, associated with deep sleep, allowing the aspirant to progress.

The three granthis represent A U M (Omkara). According to the Mandukya Upanishad, when the heart's knot is completely cut, all doubts and reservations vanish, the sense of "I and mine" in actions is destroyed, and the individual ego dissolves into the universal ego, leading to the loss of separate identity. Cutting the three granthis corresponds to transcending of three stages, after which the being receives divine permission to proceed further on the spiritual path.

105. Sahasrarambujarudha

She who is seated at the Sahasrara Chakra

The sadhaka has now traversed through the various chakras after having pierced the three granthis and has reached the Sahasrara where She can be visualised seated on a thousand-petalled lotus. This is the place of Sadashiva. Out of the 16 phases of the moon, 15 are always either in waxing or waning stage. Only one phase which is called Sada is permanent and the Sahasrara is this phase.

106. Sudhasarabhi varshini

At the Sahasrara, She drenches the upasaka with nectar

The sole purpose of Sri Vidya upasana is to reach this point when the nectar flows from all the nadis and the upasaka experiences indescribable bliss and oneness with the Universe.

107. Tadillatasamararuchi

She glistens like lightning

Once the upasaka experiences the bliss of Her awareness, it only lasts for a brief while, just as lightning strikes and then is no longer visible. The symbolism here is that the sadhana has to be a continuous process if She is to be experienced.

108. Shatchakropari samsthita

She who is seated above the six chakras at the Sahasrara.

109. Maha Shaktih

She is the supreme energy that is immeasurable and infinite.

The word Mahat means expanding in all directions. Her greatness is spread in all parts of creation.

110. Kundalini

She who is the form of Kundalini

Her true essence resides, coiled three and a half times like a serpent at the Muladhara chakra. The three rounds represent A, U and M and the half round stands for half a scale. She breathes like a snake sleeping in the Muladhara and this is the breath of life itself as prana. Just as an ascent is always followed by a descent, after reaching the peak of the Sahasrara, the energy descends back to the Muladhara, its true home. This descent teaches the importance of remembering one's origins, regardless of how high one ascends. Similarly, one should not forget their original state even after reaching the Sahasrara through their efforts.

111. Bisatantu taniyasi

She who is as fine as the fibre of a lotus stalk

The lotus flower is associated with purity, enlightenment, and spiritual awakening. It grows in muddy water yet emerges clean and beautiful, symbolizing the ability to rise above impurities and attain a higher state of consciousness.Many deities in Hinduism, including Lakshmi and Saraswati, are depicted seated on a lotus flower. The lotus stalk, as the support of the flower, represents the connection between the divine and the earthly realms.

The lotus stalk's ability to rise from the depths of muddy waters to the surface and bloom beautifully parallels the spiritual journey of rising from ignorance to knowledge and enlightenment. The lotus stalk is strong and resilient, able to support the weight and structure of the lotus flower. This resilience is symbolic of spiritual and moral strength, the ability to withstand challenges, and remain steadfast. Just as the stalk lies beneath the water's surface and is essential for the flower's growth, it represents latent potential and the unseen support system that nurtures growth and beauty.

Chapter 6

Names 112 to 200

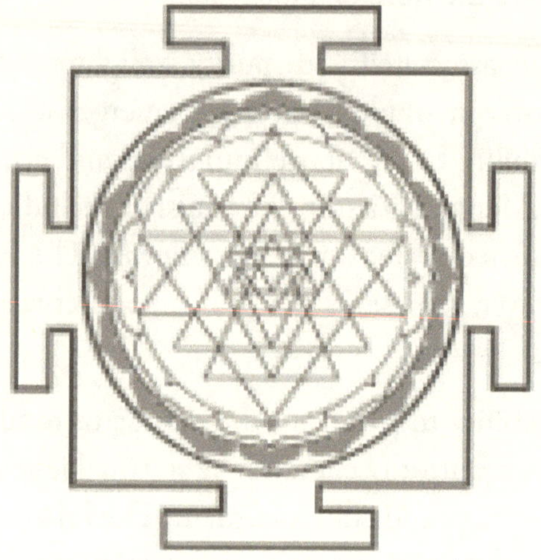

The names from 112 to 200 form the second enclosure which is the Shodasha dala padma and the Chakra is Sarvasa paripuraka (fulfilment of every desire)

112. Bhavani

She who is the wife of Bhava is Bhavani

Shiva is also known as Bhava when He takes the form of water. In some texts, it is said that She gives life to the living form of water and hence is called Bhavani.

113. Bhavanagamya

She who can be realised through devotion in meditation

The Pavanopanishad explains the method of adoration through meditation. The term Antarmukha samaradhya suggests inner worship, emphasizing meditation and contemplation rather than external rituals. The term Yadbhavam tadbhavati (as you think, so you become) highlights the transformative power of thoughts and meditation. The idea is that whatever one constantly contemplates upon, one becomes.

She can be reached through three types of meditation:

- Formless Meditation which involves contemplating on the formless aspect of the Divine, is typically accessible to those who have a regular practice of adoring Her. It requires a deep and consistent spiritual discipline, as meditating on the formless divine requires the mind to transcend physical forms and focus on the abstract, ultimate reality.
- Meditating on Her energy form involves focusing on Her as the embodiment of pure consciousness and supreme intelligence. This meditation helps the practitioner connect with the infinite and eternal aspect of Devi beyond her physical forms.
- Meditation on Her form which involves meditating on Her attributes. It allows practitioners to visualize and worship the divine in a specific form, such as an idol or an image of the deity. This form of meditation makes it easier for many to concentrate and develop a personal relationship with the divine.

These different methods of meditation cater to practitioners at various levels of spiritual progress. For those who have a consistent worship practice, moving towards formless meditation represents an advanced stage where the divine is perceived beyond physical forms.

114. Bhavaranya kutharika

She who clears us from the bondage of samsara

Just as forest is dense with trees that grow back after being axed, the cycle of life also makes us take birth again and again as a result of our karmic bondages. Just like the forest will only be fully destroyed when all trees are felled, so also samsara ends with all karmas being axed down completely. Only She can help us break this eternal bondage.

115. Bhadra-priya

One who is fond of everything auspicious

116. Bhadra-murti

One who personifies auspiciousness

117. Bhakta saubhagya dayini

She who grants all round advancement to Her devotees

The 6 attributes of prosperity, beauty, fame, power, knowledge and dispassion are together are known as saubhagya. She showers such auspiciousness on Her devotees.

118. Bhakti priya

She who is fond of devotion

119. Bhakti gamya

One who is reached through true devotion

There are nine paths to devotion:

1. Shravanam – hearing about Her
2. Keertanam – singing about Her
3. Smaranam – thinking about Her
4. Pada sevanam – offering service at Her feet
5. Archanam – offering Her worship
6. Vandanam – offering Her obeisance
7. Dasyam – becoming Her servant
8. Sakhyam – friendship
9. Atma nivedanam – self surrender

120. Bhakti vashya

She who can be won through true devotion

121. Bhayapaha

One who dispels all the fears

122. Shambhavi

As the wife of Shambhu (Shiva) She takes on the name Shambhavi

123. Sharadaradhya

She who deserves the adoration of Sharada

Sharada is Saraswati, the Goddess of knowledge who worships Devi. This carries the implication that Devi is the ultimate authority over all knowledge. This nama also points to the festival of Navratri when Devi is worshipped for 9 days, which commences in the month of autumn, also known as Sharad ritu.

124. Sharvani

She is the wife of Sharva (Shiva) and hence is Sharvani.

Shiva, representing his role as the protector and destroyer is also known as Sharva. In the context of deep sleep, Sharva is the divine presence that ensures the being remains safe and protected during this vulnerable state. Shiva, as Sharva, symbolizes the underlying consciousness that persists even when the individual is not aware of it.

125. Sharma-dayini

Bestower of happiness to Her devotees.

The term 'Sharma' means knowledge about the self. Through constant study of the Vedas or through acquiring the knowledge about the self, the being is blessed with auspiciousness.

126. Shankari

As the wife of Shankara (Shiva), She is Shankari

127. Sri-kari

She who grants prosperity

128. Sadhvi

She who is a paragon of virtue

The term Sadhvi describes a woman who embodies predominantly pure traits of sattva guna and exhibits saint-like, gentle behavior free from anger, jealousy, hatred, and similar negative emotions.

There is a close connection between this nama and three other namas – Bhavanagamya (113) Sadashivapativrata (709) and Sati (820). Achieving a saint-like state is possible through the development of proper feelings and attitudes. Correct mental perceptions and feelings lead to peace. Without peace of mind, one cannot find happiness, regardless of material possessions. True peace stems from knowledge, suggesting that supreme knowledge leads a person to a peaceful and selfless state.

129. Sharad chandra nibhanana

She who has a face that glows like the full moon in autumn

130. Shatodhari

She who has a slender waist

This nama is similar in meaning to Laksya roma latadharata samunneya madhyama (35) and Talodaree (847). Udara means cave. As She is the daughter of Himavan (king of mount Himalaya which has thousands of caves), she is known as Shatodhari. The hidden meaning in this nama is that our body is like the Himalayan mountain within which is the cave where She resides.

131. Shantimati

She who has a controlled and peaceful mind

From this point, many names in the Sahasranama begin with the word "Nir," which means "without." These names highlight a series of traits that the Divine Mother does not possess, forming a significant portion of the Sahasranama. This section plays a crucial role in conveying the essence of the self (atma tattva).

132. Niradhara

One who is without any support

There are two primary ways to worship Devi: external (Bahyam) and internal (Antaram). The external method further divides into Vedic and Tantric practices. The internal method is divided into two types: with support (Sadhara) and without support (Niradhara).

The External Worship method can be Vedic which involves rituals and practices based on the Vedas or it can be Tantric which includes rituals and practices based on Tantra texts from the Agamas.

The Internal Worship method can be with support which means it involves using mental images and mantras. Devotees focus their minds on mental representations of Devi meditating on her form and attributes through the guidance of mantras. The Niradhara method is a more advanced form of worship, where pure intellect is used to focus the mind on Devi's image obtained through knowledge. In this method, pure intellect is equated with the Devi. This nama can also be understood as a reference to the fact that the Divine Energy needs no support for its existence is without beginning or end and it is what supports all of creation.

133. Niranjana

She who is free of all stains

Anjana refers to collyrium or kajal which is used to beautify the eyes. Even though it is a cosmetic, it is still considered a stain. Anjana implies ignorance or illusion in this context. She is one who is free of illusion and also One who frees Her devotees of their ignorance.

134. Nirlepa

She who is free from karmic affectations

135. Nirmala

She who is free from all impurities

136. Nitya

She who is eternal

137. Nirakara

She who is not limited to any form

138. Nirakula

She who is never agitated

139. Nirguṇa

She who is beyond the three guns of Sattva, Rajas and Tamas

The three gunas are fundamental qualities that define all of nature and human behavior. These are sattva (purity), rajas (activity), and tamas (inertia). Understanding the gunas helps in comprehending the dynamics of the universe and the human mind. Here's a brief note on each:

1. Sattva (Purity, Harmony):

Characteristics: Sattva is associated with qualities such as purity, wisdom, harmony, and balance. It promotes clarity of thought, peacefulness, and virtuous behavior.

Effects: When sattva predominates in a person, they exhibit calmness, serenity, and a sense of inner peace. Sattvic individuals are often compassionate, selfless, and possess a keen understanding of spiritual truths.

Role: Sattva is the ideal state for spiritual growth and enlightenment. Practices such as meditation, selfless service, and consumption of pure food can enhance sattva in one's life.

2. Rajas (Activity, Passion):

Characteristics: Rajas is characterized by activity, passion, and restlessness. It is the force that drives action, change, and desire.

Effects: When rajas dominates, a person tends to be ambitious, energetic, and driven by desires and goals. However, this can also lead to stress, anxiety, and dissatisfaction due to constant striving and attachment.

Role: While rajas is essential for action and progress, it needs to be balanced by sattva to avoid excessive restlessness and to channel energy towards positive and productive outcomes.

3. Tamas (Inertia, Darkness):

Characteristics: Tamas represents inertia, darkness, and ignorance. It brings about stagnation, laziness, and confusion.

Effects: A predominance of tamas results in lethargy, procrastination, and a lack of motivation. Tamas can lead to destructive behaviors, delusion, and a lack of clarity in life.

Role: Although tamas is necessary for rest and stability, an excess can be detrimental. Overcoming tamas involves cultivating sattva and rajas in balanced measures through activities that promote clarity, discipline, and engagement.

The three gunas are constantly interacting and influencing one another, creating a dynamic balance in both the cosmos and individual beings. The predominant guna in an individual can change over time based on actions, thoughts, diet, and spiritual practices. The goal of spiritual practice in Hinduism is to increase sattva, manage rajas, and reduce tamas to achieve a balanced and harmonious state conducive to spiritual growth and self-realization.

140. Nishkala

She who is part less and whole

Every person possesses sixteen essential factors, known as 16 kalas, which are crucial for life. Among these, the pranakala (life energy) is the most important and is referred to as the 16th kala. When this 16th kala departs, the person dies, resulting in a state of nishkala (devoid of kala) for the ordinary being.

A body without life force (Shakti) cannot move and is considered a dead body (shava). Therefore, the union of Shiva and Shakti is essential for life, forming the 16th kala.

Devi who transcends a human form, exists beyond all these kalas.

141. Shanta

She who is the embodiment of peace.

The concept of "rasa" refers to the emotions felt by all humans. There are nine primary rasas:

1. Sringara (Beauty)
2. Hasya (Happiness):
3. Raudra (Fury)
4. Karunya (Compassion)
5. Bibhatsa (Aversion)
6. Bhaya (Fear)
7. Veera (Courage)
8. Adbhuta (Amazement)
9. Shanta (Peace, Tranquility)

Devi only displays one rasa and that is Shanta.

142. Nishkama

She who is free from desire

143. Nirupaplava

She who cannot be destroyed

144. Nitya-mukta

She who is always free of worldly bonds

145. Nirvikara

She who is not subject to changes

Every living being born in this world undergoes six types of changes. They are:

- **Jayate (Birth)**: The being, which was until then without a physical body, now finds itself enveloped by a physical, visible, and distinct body.
- **Asti (Existence)**: Having been enveloped by this physical body, the being perceives itself as 'existing' within the physical form.
- **Vardhate (Growth)**: The nourishment of the body that leads to its growth.
- **Viparinamate (Transformation)**: Physical changes that occur during the various stages of growth.
- **Apaksheeyate (Decay)**: The process of the body decaying and shrinking with age.
- **Nashyati (Death)**: The final stage, where the body ceases to live.

She is not subject to the above changes and strives to guide her devotees to a state that is beyond these modifications, free from the cycles of birth, existence, growth, transformation, decay, and death.

146. Nishprapancha

She who is beyond this universe

The word prapancha can be understood as 1) to unite 2) to extend and 3) to expand and since She is complete in Herself, she is beyond these three facets of the universe that can be controlled.

147. Nirashraya

She who is not dependent on anything

Ashraya means shelter or refuge. She does not depend on anything but instead serves as a refuge and shelter for every aspect of creation

148. Nityashuddha

She who is eternally pure

149. Nityabuddha

She who is knowledgeable and wise

150. Niravadhya

She who is without deficiency

151. Nirantara

She who is without any divisions

This nama has a beautiful and profound explanation. It touches on the concept of Nirantara, which can be seen as an eternal, continuous presence that exists independently, yet supports and allows the existence of other entities. This idea resonates with many philosophical and spiritual traditions that see the underlying essence of existence as something that is self-sustaining and all-encompassing.

152. Nishkarana

She who is without cause

Devi is the root cause of everything so she has no cause for Herself.

153. Nishkalanka

She who is unblemished and sinless.

154. Nirupadhi

She who is devoid of limitations

She is a form of pure conscious and hence has no limitations brought about by ignorance. The hidden meaning in this name is that upa means near and adhi means to give. A hibiscus brought close to an idol made of crystal imparts its colour to the idol, thereby limiting its form. She is devoid of such limitations.

155. Nireeshwara

She who has no superior or protector

The next few names teach about the six inner enemies (arishadvargas) that exist within all of us. The Arishadvargas are negative qualities or vices that hinder one's spiritual progress. They are:

1. **Kama:** Excessive desire or lust for material pleasures.
2. **Krodha:** Uncontrolled anger or rage
3. **Lobha:** Intense and selfish desire for wealth or power.
4. **Moha:** Attachment or infatuation, often leading to confusion and lack of clarity
5. **Mada:** Ego or arrogance.
6. **Matsarya:** Envy or jealousy towards others

Overcoming the Arishadvargas

1. Kama

Practice Contentment: Develop contentment by being grateful for what you have.

Mindfulness and Moderation: Practice mindfulness to recognize and control desires. Live in moderation.

Devotion and Surrender: Direct desires towards a higher purpose or divine by engaging in devotional practices.

2. Krodha

Cultivate Patience: Practice patience and forgiveness.

Meditation: Engage in meditation and breathing exercises to calm the mind.

Self-Reflection: Reflect on the causes of anger and address underlying issues.

3. Lobha

Generosity: Practice giving and sharing with others

Simplicity: Embrace a simple lifestyle and focus on needs rather than wants.

Self-Discipline: Cultivate self-discipline (Tapas) to control impulses.

4. Moha

Wisdom and Knowledge: Seek knowledge and wisdom through study and reflection.

Detachment: Practice detachment by recognizing the transient nature of material things.

Self-Inquiry: Engage in self-inquiry to understand your true nature.

5. Mada

Humility: Cultivate humility by acknowledging the contributions of others and recognizing your own limitations.

Service: Engage in selfless service to others.

Gratitude: Practice gratitude for the blessings and opportunities in your life.

6. Matsarya

Appreciation: Learn to appreciate the achievements and qualities of others.

Self-Improvement: Focus on your own growth and improvement rather than comparing yourself to others.

Compassion: Develop compassion and empathy towards others.

By practicing these virtues and engaging in spiritual disciplines, one can overcome the Arishadvargas and progress on the path to spiritual liberation and inner peace.

156. Niraga

She who has no attachments

157. Raga mathani

She who churns the desires of her devotees until they are removed

158. Nirmada

She who is without pride

159. Mada-nashini

She who destroys all pride

160. Nischinta

She who is free from all anxieties.

161. Nirahankara

She is devoid of ego

162. Nirmoha

She is untouched by delusion

163. Mohanashini

She destroys the delusion that exists in the mind of her devotees.

164. Nirmama

She who has no self-conceit

165. Mamatahantri

She who destroys selfishness

166. Nishpapa

She who is untouched by sin

167. Papanashini

She who destroys the sins of her devotees.

168. Nishkrodha

She who is devoid of anger

169. Krodhashamani

She who destroys the tendency to become angry

170. Nirlobha

She who is without greed

171. Lobhanashini

She who destroys greed and covetousness

172. Nissamshaya

She who is without any doubts

173. Samshayagni

She who destroys doubt

174. Nirbhava

She who is without origin

175. Bhavanashini

She who destroys worldly bondage

176. Nirvikalpa

She who is changeless.

The term Vikalpa means a change of state. In the Yoga sutras, the term Shabda anupati vikalpa is used to refer to the changes in the mind triggered by sounds, even when the sounds themselves lack inherent meaning. Certain sounds can evoke fear, agitation, confusion, or disturbance, such as the fear caused by sudden thunder. Conversely, some sounds can induce excessive joy. Even meaningless words can create changes in the mental state. For instance, phrases such as rabbit's horn or horse's horn despite their absurdity, stimulate the imagination. Additionally, there are meaningless sounds generated internally that can also affect the mind. These fluctuations disrupt the mind and hinder spiritual growth. The goal is to reach a state where, even if a word is heard, it does not register mentally. This includes tuning out unnecessary ambient sounds like other people's chatter, radio in background, etc., Achieving this state is known as Nirvikalpa. She transcends all these mental fluctuations, embodying the state of being Nirvikalpa.

177. Nirabadha

She who has an undisturbed mind

178. Nirbheda

She who is non-dual.

179. Bhedanashini

She destroys feelings of dualism

Bheda refers to the concept of distinction or difference. It is discussed in the context of philosophy and theology to describe the nature of reality and the relationship between the individual self (Atman) and the ultimate reality (Brahman). There are various interpretations and schools of thought regarding bheda:

1. **Dvaita (Dualism)**: In the Dvaita philosophy, founded by Madhvacharya, bheda is emphasized as the fundamental distinction between the Atman and the Brahman. According to this view, God and the individual souls are eternally distinct entities.

2. **Advaita (Non-Dualism)**: In contrast, Advaita Vedanta, propounded by Adi Shankaracharya, teaches that the perception of bheda is due to ignorance (Avidya). In reality, there is no difference between Atman and Brahman; they are one and the same. The goal is to realize this non-dual nature.

3. **Vishishtadvaita (Qualified Non-Dualism)**: Ramanujacharya's Vishishtadvaita philosophy acknowledges both oneness and difference. It posits that the individual soul and the Supreme Being are distinct yet inseparably connected, much like the relationship between a body and its soul.

4. **Dvaitadvaita (Dualistic Non-Dualism)**: Nimbarka's Dvaitadvaita philosophy holds that the soul and God are simultaneously distinct and non-distinct. This school maintains a balance between the concepts of difference and non-difference.

5. **Achintya Bheda Abheda (Inconceivable Oneness and Difference)**: This philosophy, espoused by Chaitanya Mahaprabhu, asserts that the relationship between God and the individual soul is beyond human comprehension. They are simultaneously one and different.

In many Hindu practices, the distinction between the worshipper and the deity is emphasized, reflecting the concept of bheda. The devotee performs rituals, prays, and seeks blessings from the deity, acknowledging their distinct identities. Understanding the distinction between the self and others can influence ethical and moral behavior. Recognizing the unique identity of each being encourages respect and compassion in interpersonal relationships. Bheda, thus, plays a crucial role in shaping Hindu philosophical thought, religious practices, and spiritual pursuits, offering diverse perspectives on the nature of reality and the relationship between the individual and the divine.

180. Nirnasha

She who is indestructible and eternal.

If one truly assimilates the principles of non-duality, he understands this indestructible nature.

181. Mrityu-mathani

She who removes the fear of death

182. Nishkriya

She is over and above all action

This nama looks at Her in the nirguna form. Since She has no form, She merely witnesses actions. Thereby She is beyond karma-akarma and vikarma.

183. Nishparigraha

She who does not accept anything as gifts

In the Bhagavad Gita, Chapter 5, Verse 15 it is said:

Nadatte kasyachit papam na chaiva sukritam vibhuh

Ajnanenavritam jnanam tena muhyanti jantavah

The omnipresent God does not involve Himself in the sinful or virtuous deeds of anyone. The living entities are deluded because their inner knowledge is covered by ignorance.

God is not responsible either for anyone's virtuous deeds or sinful actions. His work in this regard is threefold: 1) Providing the soul with the power to act. 2) Once we have performed actions with the power supplied to us, our actions are noted 3) We are given the results of our karmas.

This nama emphasizes that Devi being all-pervading and transcendental, does not personally take on the good or bad deeds of any individual. Instead, it is the ignorance that covers one's knowledge which causes beings to be deluded. Each person is responsible for their own actions and their consequences. Devi does not interfere with this process.

184. Nistula

She who is unequalled.

185. Neelachikura

She who has long black hair.

186. Nirapaya

She who is imperishable

187. Niratyaya

She who is beyond transgressions

188. Durlabha

She who is difficult to obtain

189. Durgama

She who is hard to approach

190. Durga

She who goes by the name Durga

The 3 names Durlabha, Durgama and Durga teach us that mental efforts are extremely crucial if one is truly desirous of reaching Her.

191. Duḥkhahantri

She who dispels all grief and suffering

The three types of suffering are known as the "Trividha Tapas." These are:

1. **Adhyatmika** are sufferings that arise from within oneself. They can be physical, such as illnesses and diseases, or mental, such as anxiety, depression, and other psychological issues.

2. **Adhibhautika** sufferings come from external sources. They include physical harm caused by other living beings, such as animals or humans, and natural calamities like earthquakes, floods, or any other disturbances caused by the external world.

3. **Adhidaivika** sufferings that are caused by supernatural forces or cosmic influences. They can include events like natural disasters (storms, droughts), astrological influences, and other events that are beyond human control.

She dispels all the Trividha Tapas.

192. Sukhaprada

She who bestows happiness

193. Dushadoora

She who is not attainable to evil people

194. Durachara shamani

She who puts an end to evil customs

Achara refers to the customs, practices, and code of conduct that people need to follow in order to lead a dharmic life. Sadachara signifies the righteous way of conduct and observances that have been passed down through generations. The opposite of Sadachara is Durachara.

195. Dosha varjita

She who relieves from all faults

196. Sarvagna

She is omniscient

197. Sandrakaruna

She has limitless compassion

198. Samanadhika varjitha

She who has no equal

199. Sarvashaktimayi

She is the form of all energies

200. Sarvamaṇgaḷa

She is the source of all auspiciousness

Chapter 7

Names 201 to 300

The names from 201 to 300 form the third avarana which is Ashta dala padma and the Chakra is Sarva-samshobhana (the agitator of all)

The first enclosure is the Trailokya mohana chakra where the un-manifest becomes manifest. The second enclosure is the Sarvasa paripuraka chakra which symbolises fulfilment of every desire. As desires get fulfilled, the mind is filled with agitation and this brings us to the Sarva samshobhana chakra.

201. Sadgatiprada

She who leads to the path of salvation

202. Sarveshwari

She who is the Supreme Empress of the universe

203. Sarvamayi

She who is omnipresent and omnipotent

In the Shaivite and Shakta traditions, the concept of the 36 Tattvas (elements or principles) is fundamental. These tattvas represent the different stages or levels of reality, ranging from the most abstract, formless essence to the most concrete, material form. The Tattvas can be broadly divided into three groups: Shuddha (pure), Shuddhashuddha (pure-impure), and Ashuddha (impure).

Shuddha Tattvas (Pure Principles)

These are the highest and most subtle levels of reality, associated with pure consciousness and divine aspects.

- **Shiva**: The supreme consciousness or pure awareness.
- **Shakti**: The dynamic energy or power inherent in Shiva.
- **Sadashiva**: The principle of the ever-auspicious, indicating the first awareness of duality (I-ness and this-ness).
- **Ishvara**: The sense of personal divinity, where the divine self becomes aware of the universe.
- **Shuddhavidya**: The principle of pure knowledge, representing the state where the distinction between the knower and the known starts to emerge.

Shuddhashuddha Tattvas (Pure-Impure Principles)

These tattvas represent the bridge between the pure consciousness and the material world, embodying both spiritual and material aspects.

- **Maya**: The principle of illusion that veils the true nature of reality.
- **Kala**: The principle of limitation in action.
- **Vidya**: The principle of limited knowledge.
- **Raga**: The principle of attachment or desire.
- **Kala**: The principle of time.
- **Niyati**: The principle of restriction or order.

Ashuddha Tattvas (Impure Principles)

These represent the material and mental realms of existence, dominated by duality and limitation.

- **Purusha**: The individual soul or self.
- **Prakriti**: The principle of nature or the material cause of the universe.
- **Buddhi**: The intellect or discriminative faculty.
- **Ahamkara**: The ego or the sense of individuality.
- **Manas**: The mind or the faculty of thought and emotion.

The following tattvas represent the five sensory functions (Jnana Indriyas), five motor functions (Karma Indriyas), and the elements (Tanmatras and Mahabhutas):

Sensory Functions (Jnana Indriyas):

- **Shrotra**: Hearing
- **Tvak**: Touch
- **Chakshu**: Sight
- **Rasana**: Taste
- **Ghrana**: Smell

Motor Functions (Karma Indriyas):

- **Vak**: Speech
- **Pani**: Grasping
- **Pada**: Walking
- **Payu**: Excretion
- **Upastha**: Procreation

Subtle Elements (Tanmatras):

- **Shabda**: Sound
- **Sparsha**: Touch
- **Rupa**: Form
- **Rasa**: Taste
- **Gandha**: Smell

Gross Elements (Mahabhutas):

- **Akasha**: Ether
- **Vayu**: Air
- **Agni**: Fire
- **Apas**: Water
- **Prithvi**: Earth

These 36 Tattvas map out the process by which the One, indivisible reality diversifies into the multitude of forms and phenomena that constitute our experience of the universe. She is worshipped through all these tattvas.

204. Sarvamantraswaroopini

She is the essence of all mantras

Mantras are a foundational aspect of Hindu practice, embodying both spiritual and practical significance. Derived from the Sanskrit root "man" (to think) and "tra" (tool or instrument), a mantra is described as a tool for the mind, aiding in concentration, meditation, and spiritual growth. Mantras are considered potent sounds or vibrations that can influence the mind, body, and spirit.

Types and Functions of Mantras

- **Vedic Mantras:** These are the oldest and most revered, originating from the Vedas Vedic mantras are used in rituals and ceremonies and are chanted for various purposes such as invoking deities, seeking blessings, and purifying the environment. The Gayatri Mantra, dedicated to the Sun deity, is one of the most prominent Vedic mantras.
- **Puranic Mantras:** These mantras come from the Puranas, later Hindu texts that contain myths, legends, and hymns. Puranic mantras often praise specific deities like Vishnu, Shiva, or Devi (the Goddess). Examples include the Vishnu Sahasranama and the Lalita Sahasranama

- **Tantric Mantras**: Used within the Tantric tradition, these mantras are more esoteric and are associated with specific rituals and practices. Tantric mantras can involve bija sounds, which are single-syllable sounds like "Om," "Hrim," and "Shreem," believed to have inherent power.

The Power and Effect of Mantras

Mantras hold several benefits:

Spiritual Elevation: Repeated chanting of mantras is thought to elevate the mind, bringing it closer to the divine. The repetition (japa) of a mantra can lead to a state of deep meditation and spiritual awakening.

Mental Focus: Mantras help in concentrating the mind and reducing the distractions caused by the constant chatter of thoughts. This mental focus is crucial for meditation and other spiritual practices.

Purification: Chanting mantras is believed to purify the mind and body, removing negative energies and influences. This purification can lead to a sense of peace and well-being.

Invocation: Mantras are used to invoke deities, seeking their blessings, protection, and guidance. The vibrations of the mantras are believed to attract the presence and favor of the divine beings.

Structure and Components

A mantra typically consists of one or more of the following components:

Bija Syllables: These are potent single-syllable sounds like "Om" that are believed to contain the essence of the divine. They are often used as the core of more complex mantras.

Name of the Deity: Many mantras include the name of a deity, such as "Om Namah Shivaya" (I bow to Shiva) or "Hare Krishna" (praise Krishna).

Invocation: Some mantras begin with an invocation, such as "Om," which is considered the primordial sound and is often used to start a mantra.

Practice and Ritual

- **Japa**: The repetition of a mantra, often using a mala with 108 beads.
- **Dhyana**: Mantras are used as focal points in meditation to deepen concentration and achieve a meditative state.
- **Yajna**: Vedic mantras are chanted during yajnas, fire rituals that involve offerings to deities.
- **Daily Chants**: Many Hindus incorporate mantra chanting into their daily routines, during prayers, or while performing daily chores, integrating spirituality into everyday life.

Mantras are not merely words or sounds but are powerful instruments for spiritual growth, mental clarity, and divine connection. She is the essence of all mantras.

205. Sarva yantratmika

She is the soul of all Yantras

Yantras are intricate geometric diagrams used in the Shakti tradition of Hinduism, serving as powerful tools for meditation, ritual worship, and spiritual growth. The term yantra comes from the Sanskrit root "yam," meaning "to control" or "to restrain," and "tra," meaning "instrument." Thus, a yantra is an instrument of control, associated with harnessing and focusing divine energies.

In the Shakti tradition, yantras are deeply connected to the worship of Devi in her various forms. Each yantra is a symbolic representation of a particular deity and encapsulates their essence, attributes, and cosmic functions. The geometrical precision of yantras is believed to resonate with the vibrational energy of the corresponding deity, making them a potent medium for invoking divine presence and blessings.

Yantras are typically composed of various geometric shapes, each carrying specific symbolic meanings:

- **Dot (Bindu)**: The central point of the yantra, representing the source of creation and the focal point of concentration. It symbolizes the unity of the cosmos and the starting point of manifestation.
- **Triangles**: Representing Shakti (feminine, dynamic energy) and Shiva (masculine, static consciousness). Downward triangles (Shakti) denote feminine energy, fertility, and material prosperity, while upward triangles (Shiva) symbolize masculine energy, spiritual ascent, and cosmic order.
- **Circles**: Symbolizing the cyclical nature of life and the universe. They represent wholeness, infinite potential, and the rhythmic cycles of time.
- **Lotus Petals**: Denoting purity, spiritual enlightenment, and the unfolding of divine consciousness. The number of petals varies, often corresponding to the chakras or energy centers within the body.
- **Squares and Enclosures**: Representing stability, order, and protection. They often form the outer boundary of the yantra, symbolizing the material world and the containment of sacred space.

Prominent Yantras in the Shakti Tradition

- **Sri Yantra**: The most revered yantra in the Shakti tradition, associated with Lalita Tripura Sundari. It consists of nine interlocking triangles surrounding a central bindu, forming 43 smaller triangles. The Sri Yantra represents the entire cosmos and the union of Shiva and Shakti. Meditating on the Sri Yantra is said to bestow prosperity, spiritual power, and liberation.
- **Chandi Yantra**: Dedicated to Goddess Chandi or Durga, this yantra is used in rituals to invoke the goddess's protective and transformative energies. It is especially prominent during Navaratri, the festival dedicated to the worship of Durga.

- **Kali Yantra:** Associated with Goddess Kali, the fierce aspect of Shakti. This yantra is used to invoke Kali's power for destruction of negativity, transformation, and liberation from time and death.
- **Tripura Bhairavi Yantra:** Linked to Goddess Tripura Bhairavi, representing the fierce, transformative power of the divine feminine. This yantra aids in overcoming obstacles, fear, and ignorance.

Yantras are used in various rituals and meditative practices to harness their spiritual power:

- **Puja:** Yantras are placed on altars and used as focal points for deity worship. They are energized through rituals involving offerings, mantras, and prayers.
- **Meditation:** Practitioners meditate on the yantra by focusing on the bindu and visualizing the geometrical patterns. This practice helps to align the mind with the divine energy of the yantra, leading to heightened spiritual awareness and inner peace.
- **Installation:** Yantras are often installed in homes, temples, and sacred spaces to attract positive energy and protection. They are also used in vaastu (the traditional Indian system of architecture) to harmonize environmental energies.

Through the worship and contemplation of yantras, practitioners seek to harmonize their inner world with the cosmic order, thereby attaining spiritual growth and enlightenment. She manifests in the form of all the Yantras.

206. Sarvatantrarupa

She who is the spirit of all tantra

Tantra is a complex and multifaceted spiritual tradition that encompasses a wide range of practices, texts, rituals, and philosophical concepts. Emerging around the 5th century CE, Tantra offered an alternative to the more orthodox Vedic traditions, emphasizing direct personal experience of the divine and the transformation of consciousness.

Core Concepts

- **Unity of the Divine and the Individual**: At the heart of Tantra is the belief in the non-dualistic unity of the divine and the individual. This is often expressed through the relationship between Shiva (consciousness) and Shakti (energy). The goal of Tantric practice is to realize this unity within oneself.
- **Mantra and Yantra**: Mantras and yantras are fundamental tools in Tantra. Mantras are chanted to invoke deities and align the practitioner's consciousness with divine vibrations. Yantras serve as visual focal points for meditation and ritual, symbolizing cosmic principles.
- **Ritual and Sadhana**: Tantra is known for its elaborate rituals and sadhanas, which include the use of mudras (hand gestures), pranayama (breath control), and dharana (concentration). These practices aim to purify the mind, awaken Kundalini, and achieve higher states of consciousness.
- **Kundalini and Chakras**: A distinctive aspect of Tantra is the concept of Kundalini, which can be awakened through specific practices leading to spiritual enlightenment.
- **Transcending Dualities**: Tantra seeks to transcend the dualities of good and evil, sacred and profane, seeing all aspects of existence as manifestations of the divine. This inclusivity extends to embracing physical and sensual experiences as pathways to spiritual growth.

Tantra has profoundly influenced many aspects of Hindu culture, including temple architecture, iconography, and festivals. Its practices have also permeated other spiritual traditions, notably Vajrayana Buddhism in Tibet and Shingon Buddhism in Japan. Despite its esoteric nature, Tantra's emphasis on direct experience, ritual, and the sacredness of all aspects of life continues to attract practitioners and scholars worldwide. She is the spirit of Tantra.

207. Manonmani

One who is the form of transcendent consciousness.

The Yogashastra says that when the mind is in a controlled state, free from attachments, it attains the state of "unmana". In this state the senses are completely subdued and the mind is immersed in dhyana. This nama suggests that She is this form and also meditation on Her brings about this state of being.

208. Maheshwari

She who is the consort of Maheshwara

209. Mahadevi

She who is the greatest of all Devis

210. Mahalakshmi

She who is the form of Lakshmi

211. Mridapriya

She is very dear to Shiva

Shiva is variously known as Bhava, Mrida and Hara when He is involved in the task of creation. In His Mrida form, His character is predominantly sattvik. She is consort to that aspect of Shiva.

212. Maharoopa

She who has a magnificent form

213. Mahapoojya

She who is worthy of worship.

214. Mahapatakanashini

She who destroys the most heinous sins

The term Pataka refers to sins or moral transgressions. The classification and details about Patakas are found in various Hindu scriptures and Dharmashastras, such as the Manusmriti, Yajnavalkya Smriti, and the Puranas.

Classification of Patakas

- ### Mahapataka (Great Sins)

  These are considered the gravest sins and have severe consequences. They are explicitly condemned in the scriptures and are believed to lead to significant negative karma, requiring stringent penance and atonement.

  Examples of Mahapataka include:

  Brahmahatya: Killing a Brahmin or, by extension, committing murder.

  Surapana: Consuming alcohol or other intoxicants.

  Steya: Theft, particularly of valuable or sacred objects.

  Guru Talpagamana: Adultery, especially with the spouse of a teacher or mentor.

  Maha Pataka: Associating with those who commit the above sins.

- ### Upapataka (Minor Sins)

  These are lesser sins compared to Mahapatakas but still considered serious. They also carry negative karmic consequences and typically require appropriate penance for rectification.

  Examples of Upapataka include:

  Neglect of Vedic duties: Failing to perform prescribed religious and social duties.

  False testimony: Giving false evidence or lying.

  Injustice: Acting unjustly or unfairly, particularly in positions of power or authority.

  Neglect of ancestors: Failing to perform rituals and duties toward one's ancestors.

- **Kricchra Pataka (Occasional Sins)**

These sins are committed occasionally and may not be as severe as the Mahapatakas or Upapatakas, but they still affect one's karma and spiritual progress.

Examples include acts like dishonesty, engaging in frivolous or harmful behavior, and neglecting one's daily spiritual practices.

215. Mahamaya

She is the form of the great illusion

Maya is a profound and complex concept representing the illusion or appearance of the phenomenal world. It plays a crucial role in understanding the nature of reality, perception, and liberation. Maya is extensively discussed in the Upanishads, the Bhagavad Gita, and later Vedantic texts, particularly in the Advaita Vedanta tradition.

The term "Maya" originates from the Sanskrit root "ma," meaning "to measure, form, or limit." In its philosophical context, Maya refers to the cosmic illusion that creates a sense of duality and multiplicity in the world, obscuring the true, non-dual nature of reality.

The Upanishads first introduce the concept of Maya. They describe Maya as the mysterious power of Brahman that projects the cosmos and veils the true nature of the self. The Mundaka Upanishad (2.2.9) states, "As the spider creates the web from within itself, so does Brahman manifest the universe through its own power, Maya."

In the Advaita Vedanta school Maya is a central concept. Brahman is the sole, non-dual reality, infinite and eternal. Everything else is an appearance or manifestation of Brahman. Maya is the force that causes Avidya, or ignorance, leading individuals to perceive a dualistic world of separate entities. This ignorance is the root cause of human suffering and bondage. Maya involves the superimposition of names and forms (nama-rupa) on the formless Brahman, creating the illusion of the material world. The world perceived through Maya is Mithya, meaning it is neither absolutely real nor absolutely unreal but exists in a dependent reality. Liberation is attained through the realization of the true nature of the self (Atman) as non-different from Brahman. This realization dispels Maya and leads to the knowledge (Jnana) that the self is one with the ultimate reality.

The Bhagavad Gita, also discusses Maya. Lord Krishna describes Maya as his divine power (daivi maya) that is difficult to overcome (Gita 7.14). However, those who surrender to him and attain knowledge can transcend Maya and realize the eternal truth.

216. Mahasattva

She is the personification of Sattva guna

Sattva Guna is one of the three fundamental qualities or gunas, the other two being Rajas and Tamas. These three gunas are essential in understanding the dynamics of nature (Prakriti) and human behavior. The concept of the gunas is elaborately discussed in texts such as the Bhagavad Gita, the Samkhya Karika, and various Upanishads.

Sattva is translated as purity, harmony, or balance. It is the quality associated with clarity, wisdom, and spiritual luminescence. When Sattva predominates in an individual, it brings about virtues such as knowledge, happiness, contentment, and a sense of inner peace.

Key Characteristics of Sattva:

- **Purity and Clarity**: Sattva is characterized by mental clarity, purity, and the ability to see things as they truly are.
- **Knowledge and Wisdom**: It fosters a love for truth, learning, and a deep understanding of the nature of reality.
- **Harmony and Balance**: Sattva leads to a balanced and harmonious state of mind, promoting health and well-being.
- **Positivity and Lightness**: It brings about positive emotions, joy, and a lightness of being.
- **Virtue and Morality**: Sattvic individuals are often ethical, compassionate, and altruistic.

The Bhagavad Gita offers a detailed description of the three gunas, explaining their effects on human behavior and spiritual development. According to the Gita (Chapter 14), when Sattva is predominant, it illuminates knowledge and dispels ignorance. A person under the influence of Sattva is said to be free from attachment and ego, exhibiting qualities such as patience, self-control, and a tendency towards spiritual practices.

In Samkhya philosophy, Sattva is one of the three gunas that constitute Prakriti, the material nature. The interplay of these gunas creates the diversity of the universe. Sattva is associated with light and consciousness, and it balances the dynamism of Rajas and the inertia of Tamas. Liberation (Moksha) in Samkhya is achieved when the Purusha (consciousness) realizes its distinctness from Prakriti and is no longer influenced by the gunas, particularly through the cultivation of Sattva.

Practices to enhance Sattva involve lifestyle choices that promote purity, peace, and clarity:

- **Diet**: Consuming fresh, natural, and wholesome foods that nourish the body and mind.
- **Meditation and Yoga**: Engaging in regular meditation, yoga, and other spiritual practices to calm the mind and foster inner awareness.
- **Ethical Living**: Adopting a lifestyle that adheres to ethical principles, non-violence, truthfulness, and compassion.
- **Positive Environment**: Surrounding oneself with a positive and serene environment, including nature, clean spaces, and harmonious relationships.

Sattva is considered crucial for spiritual growth and self-realization. By increasing Sattva in one's life, an individual can transcend the lower gunas of Rajas (activity and restlessness) and Tamas (darkness and ignorance). However, in the ultimate spiritual goal of liberation, one transcends all three gunas, including Sattva, to realize the pure, undisturbed state of the self (Atman or Purusha).

217. Mahashakti

She is the greatest energy

218. Maharati

She who has boundless delight

219. Mahabhoga

She who enjoys all luxuries

Bhoga refers to the experience of worldly pleasures and enjoyment. The term bhoga is derived from the Sanskrit root "bhuj," meaning "to enjoy" or "to partake." It encompasses a broad spectrum of sensory and material enjoyments, such as the pleasures of food, wealth, sensory gratification, and other forms of indulgence.

Bhoga is discussed in contrast with yoga, where yoga represents spiritual discipline and union with the divine, and bhoga represents the pursuit of material and sensual pleasures. While bhoga is not inherently negative, Hindu philosophy generally views it as a stage or aspect of life that must be transcended to achieve higher spiritual goals.

The Vedic texts, particularly the early Vedic Samhitas, acknowledge the pursuit of earthly pleasures and material success as legitimate aspects of human life. The Vedas contain hymns and rituals aimed at securing prosperity, health, and enjoyment. The Upanishads, however, emphasize the transient nature of bhoga and advocate for the pursuit of moksha through knowledge and self-realization. They teach that while bhoga may bring temporary satisfaction, it cannot provide lasting peace and fulfilment. Bhagavad Gita addresses the tension between bhoga and yoga extensively. In Chapter 2, verse 45, Lord Krishna advises Arjuna to rise above the dualities of pleasure and pain, success and failure, and focus on selfless action (karma yoga) and devotion (bhakti yoga) to attain true peace.

Bhoga is primarily associated with Kama and Artha. The pursuit of Kama involves seeking pleasure and enjoyment, while Artha involves the acquisition of wealth and resources to support a comfortable life. Both Kama and Artha are considered legitimate goals, provided they are pursued in accordance with Dharma and do not hinder the ultimate goal of Moksha.

While bhoga can provide immediate gratification, our philosophical traditions emphasize the importance of recognizing its impermanent and often illusory nature. Key texts and teachings suggest:

- **Detachment (Vairagya):** Developing a sense of detachment from worldly pleasures, recognizing that attachment to bhoga can lead to suffering and bondage.
- **Self-Control (Yama and Niyama):** Practicing self-control and ethical behavior as prescribed in the Yamas and Niyamas (ethical guidelines in Yoga), to balance the pursuit of bhoga with spiritual growth.
- **Transcendence:** Ultimately, the spiritual path involves transcending the desire for bhoga through practices such as meditation, devotion, and selfless action, leading to the realization of the Atman (true self) and union with the divine.

The entire universe is Her wealth. She enjoys the luxuries provided by it and bestows such luxuries on Her children.

220. Mahaishwarya

She who possesses supreme sovereignty

221. Mahaveerya

She who is supreme in bravery

222. Mahabala

She who possesses the greatest strength

The word Bala means strength but the inner meaning of this nama is that the word also means a crow. Great yogis like Bhusunda worshipped Devi in the form a crow and got great strengths as it is mentioned in the Yogavashistha.

223. Mahabuddhi

She who has great wisdom

224. Mahasiddhi

She is the form of all Siddhis and also grants them

Siddhis refers to supernatural powers or spiritual abilities that can be attained through intense practice of yoga and meditation. Among these siddhis, eight are considered primary:

- **Anima**: The ability to shrink one's body to the size of an atom, becoming invisible or very small.
- **Mahima**: The power to expand one's body to an infinitely large size, enabling one to become immense.
- **Garima**: The capacity to become infinitely heavy, making one's body immovable.
- **Laghima**: The ability to become weightless or to levitate and float in the air.
- **Prapti**: The power to instantly obtain any desired object or to be able to reach any place or acquire anything, regardless of distance.
- **Prakamya**: The ability to achieve whatever one desires, to realize dreams, and to have one's wishes fulfilled.
- **Ishita**: The power to control natural forces, such as influencing the elements (earth, water, fire, air, and ether) and having authority over nature.
- **Vashita**: The ability to control or subjugate all living creatures, humans, and animals, and to exercise dominion over the physical and metaphysical realms.

These siddhis are described in various Hindu scriptures, including the Yoga Sutras of Patanjali, the Bhagavata Purana, and other yogic and tantric texts. While the attainment of siddhis is often seen as a by-product of advanced spiritual practice, traditional teachings caution against becoming attached to these powers. The primary focus should remain on the ultimate goal of spiritual liberation rather than the acquisition of supernatural abilities.

225. Mahayogeshwareshwari

She is the empress of all yogis

226. Mahatantra

She is the greatest tantra

227. Mahamantra

She is OM, the Pranava mantra which is the greatest mantra

228. Mahayantra

She is the Sri Yantra, the greatest of all yantras

229. Mahasana

She is seated on a greatest throne

230. Mahayagakramaradhya

She is to be worshipped by the method of Mahayagya

Maha yaga refers to the internal worship of the Sri Chakra which according to Her is the most supreme yaga.

There are three types of *Pralaya* (cosmic destruction) and the roles of the divine beings in these events.

Avaantara Pralaya: A minor or intermediate dissolution. Vishnu is responsible for rescuing the world from this type of destruction.

Maha Pralaya: The great dissolution at the end of a Kalpa (cosmic cycle). Shiva, in his role as the destroyer, rescues the world during this period.

Kama Pralaya: A special kind of destruction linked to the concept of desire (*Kama*). This destruction is particularly relevant in the context of the destruction caused by Bhandasura, a demon who embodies the distortion of desire. Lalita is the only one who can rescue the world from this situation. The Devatas are instructed to take shelter in her and beseech her for help, as She alone can create another Lalita to counteract the effects of Kama Pralaya.

Maha Shambhu (another form of Shiva) explains the concept of Maha Yaga or the great fire sacrifice. In this Yaga, He assumes the form of Vayu (the wind) and acts as the Hota (priest) who makes offerings. His own Chidagni (the fire of consciousness) serves as the fire in this sacrifice.

This nama reflects the intricate interplay of cosmic principles and divine beings in maintaining and restoring cosmic order during different phases of destruction.

231. Mahabhairavapoojita

One who is worshipped by Mahabhairava

Bhairava is a fierce manifestation of Lord Shiva who embodies the destructive and regenerative aspects of Shiva, emphasizing his role as the protector and destroyer. The name Bhairava is derived from the Sanskrit root "bha," which means "fear. Rava can mean "sound" or "cry." Thus, Bhairava can be interpreted as "one who shouts or roars in fear" or "one who destroys fear."

The origin of Bhairava is described in various Hindu texts, including the Puranas, Tantras, and the Mahabharata. One of the prominent myths involves Bhairava emerging from Shiva's forehead to cut off the fifth head of Brahma, which symbolizes the destruction of ego and ignorance.

Bhairava has numerous forms, each with distinct attributes and significance. As Kala Bhairava, he is the lord of time, consuming everything in the path. He is worshipped for protection and to ward off the fear of death. In the Ashta Bhairava, each form governs a particular direction and aspect of life. These include Asitanga Bhairava, Ruru Bhairava, Chanda Bhairava, Krodha Bhairava, Unmatta Bhairava, Kapala Bhairava, Bhishana Bhairava, and Samhara Bhairava.

Within all of us, there exists a guardian deity that offers protection. This guardian is the intellect (buddhi). The subtle implication here is that this intellect is symbolically referred to as Mahabhairava and the advice conveyed is to use this powerful intellect to perpetually worship Her.

232. Maheshwaramahakalpamahatandavasakshini

She is a witness to Shiva's tandava

Shiva's tandava is a cosmic dance which symbolizes the dynamic interplay of creation, preservation, and destruction within the universe. It is not a single dance but encompasses various forms, each with distinct meanings and purposes. Some of the notable forms include:

- **Ananda Tandava**: This form represents the ecstatic joy and dynamic energy of creation. It symbolizes the cosmic cycles of creation and dissolution and the eternal rhythm of the universe.
- **Rudra Tandava**: This fierce form of the dance symbolizes Shiva's destructive power. It is performed during times of cosmic dissolution, emphasizing Shiva's role as the destroyer who paves the way for new creation.
- **Sandhya Tandava**: This dance is performed during the twilight hours, symbolizing the transition and balance between day and night, creation and destruction.
- **Tripura Tandava**: This form celebrates Shiva's victory over the demon Tripurasura, representing the triumph of good over evil.
- **Samhar Tandava**: This dance of annihilation signifies the destruction of the universe at the end of a cosmic cycle.

233. Mahakameshamahishi

She is the consort of Mahakamesha

Let us look at the progression of these names. After the great deluge (Maha pralaya), Shiva performs the maha tandava, with Shakti as the witness. In this state, Shiva is in supreme bliss. To initiate a new creation, Shakti stimulates Him and the subsequent name explains the state that emerges after this stimulation: the first step in creation, which always begins with a triad (Triputi).

Now, let us relate this process to the individual level. Through performing inner worship an individual enters a state of meditation and merges into the infinite. This merging represents the Maha pralaya. At this stage, the Maha tandava occurs. The person, now motionless like a rock and immersed in bliss, is then stimulated by Shakti. This stimulation awakens the individual from deep meditation and initiates their descent back into the material world. The first point of creation in this context is the triputi. With this awakening, the individual re-enters the material world.

We can see the correlation as below:

Cosmic Level:

Maha Pralaya: The great deluge

Maha Tandava: Shiva's dance of bliss witnessed by Shakti

Stimulation by Shakti: Initiates new creation

Triputi: The first step in creation

Individual Level:

Inner Worship: Leads to deep meditation

Maha Pralaya: Total merger into the infinite

Maha Tandava: Experience of supreme bliss

Stimulation by Shakti: Awakens the individual

Triputi: Re-entry into the material world

234. Mahatripurasundari

She who is the most divine beauty of all triads

235. Chatushastiupacharadhya

She is worshipped with 64 offerings

Chatushasti Upachara refers to the sixty-four traditional offerings performed in the worship of deities. This elaborate ritual is designed to honor and serve the deity with utmost devotion and reverence. The Chatushasti Upachara is described in various Agamas, Puranas, and other religious texts. The sixty-four offerings can be broadly categorized into several groups, encompassing various aspects of welcoming, worship, and farewell.

Here is a general outline of these offerings:

Awakening and welcoming the deity:

1. **Avahana:** Inviting the deity to the puja
2. **Asana:** Offering a seat to the deity
3. **Padya:** Washing the deity's feet
4. **Arghya:** Offering water for washing hands
5. **Achamaniya:** Offering water for sipping

Morning Rituals:

6. **Snana:** Bathing the deity
7. **Vastra:** Offering clothes
8. **Upavita:** Offering sacred thread
9. **Gandha:** Applying sandalwood paste
10. **Pushpa:** Offering flowers

Food and Drink:

11. **Dhupa:** Offering incense
12. **Dipa:** Offering a lamp
13. **Naivedya:** Offering food

14. **Tambula**: Offering betel leaves and nuts
15. **Jala**: Offering water to drink

Adornment and Comfort:

16. **Alankara**: Adorning the deity with ornaments
17. **Chandan**: Applying sandalwood paste
18. **Pushpanjali**: Offering flowers
19. **Chhatra**: Offering an umbrella
20. **Chamara**: Offering a flywhisk

Sacred Rituals and Mantras:

21-40: Various rituals involving mantras, mudras (hand gestures), and other sacred acts to honor the deity

Evening Rituals and Farewell:

41-50: Preparing the deity for rest, including offerings of food, drink, and comfortable arrangements for the night

Final Offerings:

51-60: Concluding the puja with final offerings and prayers

61-64: Farewell rituals, thanking the deity and inviting the deity to return

In contemporary worship, the Chatushasti Upachara is not always performed in full due to time constraints or simplified rituals. However, the essence of these offerings remains integral to the practice of puja, ensuring that the core principles of devotion, respect, and love for the deity are maintained. The routine puja performed at homes comprises of 16 types of services offered to the deity (shodasha upachara puja). The more detailed procedure of puja that can be witnessed during the navavarana puja.

236. Chatushastikalamayi

She is a personification of the 64 arts

The Chatushshashti Kalas encompass a wide range of skills and knowledge areas that were traditionally considered essential for a well-rounded education and refinement. These arts are mentioned in various ancient texts, including the Kama Sutra, and reflect the cultural and intellectual heritage of ancient India.

The 64 Arts

1. **Geet vidya**: Art of singing
2. **Vadya vidya**: Art of playing musical instruments
3. **Nritya vidya**: Art of dancing
4. **Natya vidya**: Art of theatricals
5. **Alekhya vidya**: Art of painting
6. **Visheshakacchedya**: Art of painting the face and body with colored unguents and cosmetics
7. **Tandula kusuma bali vikara**: Art of preparing offerings from rice and flowers
8. **Pushpastarana**: Art of making a covering of flowers for a bed
9. **Dasana vasananga raga**: Art of applying preparations for cleansing the teeth, clothes, and painting the body
10. **Manibhumi**: Art of making and setting a crown with jewels
11. **Shayana rachana**: Art of preparing beds
12. **Udaka vadya**: Art of playing music in water
13. **Udaka ghata**: Art of splashing water with hands or sticks
14. **Chitra shakapu**: Art of playing with magic lanterns, creating phantoms
15. **Malya grathana vikalpa**: Art of making garlands
16. **Keshasekara pida yojana**: Art of making crowns of flowers
17. **Nataka akshepa**: Art of decorating with flowers
18. **Karna patra bhanga**: Art of making ear ornaments
19. **Sugandha yuktibhyanga**: Art of perfuming
20. **Bhushana yojana**: Art of applying and preparing perfumes
21. **Aindra jala**: Art of jugglery
22. **Kaucumara**: Art of sleight of hand
23. **Hasta laghava**: Art of juggling

24. **Citra yatra**: Art of making designs on the floor
25. **Matrika**: Art of designing mats
26. **Chalitra**: Art of designing friezes and borders
27. **Vastu vidya**: Art of architecture
28. **Manimukti kala**: Art of mending or setting jewelry and gems
29. **Sayya karpana**: Art of making beds
30. **Anga ragakatha**: Art of applying cosmetics and make-up
31. **Ayurveda**: Science of health and medicine
32. **Sutragrahana**: Art of sewing
33. **Vastra vikalpa**: Art of designing clothes
34. **Lepya**: Art of using enamels and glazes
35. **Kshirodasambhava**: Art of making soft drinks and syrups
36. **Khadyakavidhana**: Art of cooking
37. **Supa sastra**: Art of preparing soups and broths
38. **Paka yojana**: Art of arranging and serving meals
39. **Tambula bhanga**: Art of preparing betel leaves
40. **Kavya samasyapuranam**: Art of solving riddles
41. **Patralekha**: Art of writing letters
42. **Manasi kavya kriya**: Art of composing poetry
43. **Akshara mushtika kathana**: Art of reciting tongue twisters
44. **Mlecha khaddha**: Art of speaking in foreign languages
45. **Desa bhasya gnana**: Art of speaking in different dialects
46. **Pushpa sastraka**: Art of flower arranging
47. **Dhvani vidya**: Art of creating musical tones
48. **Sampatika**: Art of making musical instruments
49. **Bhuta vidya**: Art of exorcism
50. **Vrata vidya**: Art of performing rituals and vows
51. **Yantra matrika**: Art of making mechanical contrivances
52. **Dhatu vada**: Art of working with metals
53. **Mani bheda**: Art of gemology
54. **Vajra muktadi karma**: Art of working with diamonds and other precious stones
55. **Ankura paka**: Art of gardening
56. **Krida vikalpa**: Art of playing games

57. **Balaka krida**: Art of playing with children
58. **Vainayaki vidya**: Art of etiquette
59. **Hasi lekha**: Art of humorous writing
60. **Chitra yogya**: Art of creating caricatures and cartoons
61. **Vina pada**: Art of playing the lute and other string instruments
62. **Sthapya veda**: Art of sculpture
63. **Shilpa sastra**: Art of crafting statues
64. **Yogasana**: Art of practicing yoga postures

These 64 arts represent a comprehensive education that prepares an individual for all aspects of life. They illustrate the importance of a balanced development, combining practical skills, creative arts, intellectual pursuits, and physical health.

All these 64 arts exist in Her and are a part of Her; She can be called an embodiment of these arts.

237. Maha chatushasti kotiyogini ganasevita

Innumerable troops of yogini-devatas serve Her

It is said that on one occasion, some scholars from Kashi sought to challenge Bhaskararaya, the esteemed commentator of the Lalita Sahasranama. They asked him to enumerate the names of the 64 crore yoginis who surround the Divine Mother, as referenced in this name. Without hesitation, Bhaskararaya began reciting the names of the yoginis one by one. As he continued, one of the devotees present, Kumkuma Natha, sternly addressed the scholars, saying, "You foolish pundits, can't you see that the Divine Mother Herself is seated on Bhaskararaya's shoulders, providing the answers?"

Pandit Rajamani Tigunait writes: "In the tantric tradition, the Sixty-four Yoginis are the presiding deities that guide and govern the entire fabric of life. Together they constitute all the benevolent forces of nature. They are the presiding deities of the sixty-four arts and sciences, which cover the whole range of human creativity. Tantric texts, such as Rudra Yamala, explain that it is these yoginis who breathe life into matter. Manifesting in the form of prana (life force), they not only hold the body and mind together, they also animate them. Awakening these forces is the essence of spiritual accomplishment. In fact, only when these forces are awakened do we find meaning and purpose in our own worldly achievements. As long as they are dormant, we are weighed down by life's burdens."

238. Manuvidya

She can be worshipped through the method called Manu-vidya.

In the tradition of Sree Vidya, twelve illustrious devotees are revered for their dedication and penance, through which they discovered and worshipped specific mantras. These twelve devotees are:

1. **Manu**: The progenitor of humanity and the foremost among the devotees
2. **Chandra**: The lunar deity
3. **Kubera**: The god of wealth
4. **Lopamudra**: The wise wife of the sage Agastya
5. **Agasthya**: A revered sage
6. **Manmatha**: The god of love
7. **Agni**: The fire deity
8. **Surya**: The sun deity
9. **Indra**: The king of gods
10. **Skanda**: The god of war
11. **Shiva**: The supreme deity
12. **Durvasa**: A sage known for his temper and ascetic powers

Manu is considered the highest among these devotees, and it is believed that Sreedevi, in the form of the Sree Vidya Mantra, was revealed through him. The worship of Sri Vidya by these twelve devotees is significant in the tradition and is mentioned through thirteen names:

1. **Chandra Vidya (239)**
2. **Hari Brahmendra Sevita (297)**
3. **Rajarajachita (305)**
4. **Tapasaradhya (359)**

5. **Kama Poojita (375)**
6. **Shivaradhya (406)**
7. **Kamalaksha Nishevita (558)**
8. **Kama Sevita (586)**
9. **Lopamudrarchita (647)**
10. **Bhagaradhya (715)**
11. **Guhyakaradhya (720)**
12. **Nandi Vidya (733)**
13. **Martanda Bhairavaradhya (785)**

These names correspond to specific aspects of Sri Vidya worship, emphasizing the diverse ways in which the devotees approached and revered the divine form of Sri Vidya. Each name encapsulates a unique aspect of the worship and the spiritual practices undertaken by these devoted individuals.

239. Chandravidya

She who is worshipped by the Moon

240. Chandramaṇḍalamadhyaga

She is seated in the centre of the moon

241. Charuroopa

She is exquisite

242. Charuhasa

She has an exquisite smile

243. Charuchandrakaladhara

She who wears the moon in Her crown

244. Characharajagannatha

She is the ruler of the entire universe

The Universe is filled with with living and non-living objects. She rules over them all.

245. Chakrarajaniketana

She resides in the Srichakra

246. Parvati

She is the daughter of the Himalayas

247. Padma-nayana

She who is lotus-eyed

248. Padmaragasamaprabha

She who shines like a ruby

249. Panchapretasanaseena

She sits on a seat made up of five corpses

The five forms of Shiva are Brahma, Vishnu, Rudra, Esana, and Sadashiva who emanate from Brahman. According to Her command, they are responsible for the five cosmic tasks:

1. **Brahma**: Creation
2. **Vishnu**: Protection
3. **Rudra**: Destruction
4. **Esana**: Concealment
5. **Sadashiva**: Grace

During theMahapralaya, these deities are relieved of their duties and merge back into Her. At this stage, Sadashiva becomes the seat's plank, while the other four become its legs. Deprived of their powers, they are termed as corpses.

250. Panchabrahmaswaroopini

She who has five Brahmans as her form

251. Chinmayi

She is an embodiment of pure consciousness.

252. Paramananda

She enjoys eternal ultimate bliss.

253. Vigyanaghanaroopini

She is wisdom personified

254. Dhyanadhyatrudhyeyaroopa

She is all three form – meditation, the meditator and object of meditation

255. Dharmadharmavivarjita

She is devoid of both virtues and vices

256. Vishwaroopa

She who takes on the form of this universe

257. Jagarini

She is the waking state

Mandukya Upanishad explains the four states of consciousness – Jagrut, Swapna, Taijas, and Turiya.

Jagrut is the waking state where a person is awake and aware of the external environment through the five senses. It is characterized by the perception of the physical world. Swapna is the dream state, where he experiences dreams. In this state, the mind creates a reality that is not dependent on the physical world but rather on mental impressions and subconscious thoughts. Taijas refers to the dream state where the subtle body, or mind, is active. It is the state of experiencing the mental and dream world, distinguished from the waking state. Turiya is the fourth state of pure consciousness or transcendental awareness. In this state, one experiences a sense of unity with the divine or the ultimate reality, beyond the dualities of existence.

During the waking state of a being, She takes on the name Jagarini

258. Swapanti

She is the dreaming state

259. Taijasatmika

She is the form of the dreaming state

260. Supta

She is the state of sleep

261. Pragyatmika

In the deep sleep state, she takes on its form

262. Turiya

She is the form of the fourth state of transcendence

263. Sarvavasthavivarjita

She is beyond all states of existence.

264. Srishtikartri

She is the cause behind creation

The names from 264 to 274 describe Her five primary functions, referred to as the pancha-krityas. She imbues these functions with Her energy, enabling the five Brahmas (Pancha-brahmas) to perform these tasks. This implies two things: a) She manifests through the five Brahmas, and b) She integrates the five elements (panchabhootas) that had previously been absorbed within Her. The merging of these five elements leads to creation, a process known as Panchikarana.

265. Brahmaroopa

She takes on task of creation

266. Goptri

She takes on the task of protection

267. Govindaroopini

She who is the form of Govinda

268. Samharini

She takes on the task of dissolution

269. Rudraroopa

She takes on the form of Rudra.

270. Tirodhanakari

She takes on the task of causing the disappearance of all

271. Eshwari

To perform the task of Tirodhana, She takes on the form of Eshwara, hence She is called Eshwari

272. Sadashiva

She who takes the form of Sadashiva

273. Anugrahada

As Sadashiva, She accomplishes the task of granting grace

274. Panchakrityaparayana

One who is devoted to the five functions

The five functions of creation, preservation, dissolution, annihilation and causing the reappearance of creation are ascribed to Brahma, Vishnu, Rudra, Eshwara and Sadashiva. These five are merely different forms of Her Shakti and these issues the instructions to carry out the five functions with a twinkling of her eyebrows for a micro second (name 281).

275. Bhanu mandala madhyasta

She is in the centre of the solar system

The process of worshipping Her as Bhairavi is detailed from the names 275 to 280.

276. Bhairavi

She is the energy of Bhairava (another form of Shiva)

277. Bhagamalini

She possesses all the qualities of Bhaga

Material prosperity, courage, valour, fame, knowledge and renunciation are all Her traits. These collectively are known as Bhaga. Bhaga is also one of the names for the Sun God. According to ancient scriptures, our solar system has twelve suns: Mitra, Ravi, Surya, Bhanu, Khaga, Poosha, Hiranyagarbha, Maricha, Aditya, Savitra, Arka, and Bhaskara. These suns influence life on earth. Shining brightly with these twelve suns arranged like a garland around Her neck, She is known as Bhagamalini.

278. Padmasana

She is seated in the lotus pose

Padmasana is a cross-legged sitting posture in yoga. It is one of the most recognized and classic poses, used for meditation and pranayama. Padma also refers to prosperity and this nama suggested that She is seated on it.

279. Bhagavati

She is the form of prosperity

280. Padmanabhasahodari

She who is the sister of Vishnu

281. Unmesha nimishotpanna vipanna bhuvanavali

She who makes creation, sustenance and dissolution take place just within the blinking of Her eyelids

Unmesha and nimesha refer to the actions of opening and closing the eyes, respectively. In the brief moment it takes Her to blink, the creation and dissolution of the universe are completed. The term nimisha also signifies a minute. Emperor Nimi requested that time (kala) be named after him, resulting in the term nimit or nimisha, which eventually became 'minute.' Commonly, a nimisha is considered to be 60 seconds, but its true meaning is a 'fraction of a second', the smallest unit of time.

282. Sahasrashirshavadana

She who has a thousand heads

The word Sahasra means infinite or countless.

283. Sahasrakshi

She who has thousands of eyes

284. Sahasrapad

She who has thousands of feet

285. Abrahmakitajanani

She who is mother of all – from Brahma to the smallest worm

286. Varṇashramavidhiyani

She who establishes the social divisions and castes

The four ashramas represent the ideal stages through which an individual progresses during their lifetime. The four ashramas are:

1. Brahmacharya (Student Stage)
2. Grihastha (Householder Stage)
3. Vanaprastha (Hermit Stage)
4. Sannyasa (Renunciate Stage)

These stages provide a structured framework for living a balanced life, emphasizing the importance of fulfilling personal, social, and spiritual responsibilities.

Varnas are part of a broader social framework which aimed to organize society based on individuals' duties and qualities. These varnas are:

1. Brahmins: Priests, scholars, and teachers
2. Kshatriyas: Warriors, rulers, and administrators
3. Vaishyas: Merchants, agriculturists, and businesspeople
4. Shudras: Labourers and service providers

287. Nijagyaroopanigama

She who uses the Vedas to express Her commands

288. Punyapunyaphalaprada

She who delivers the fruits for all the deeds

289. Shruti srimanta sindoori kruta padabjadhoolika

She who has the dust of Her lotus feet forming the vermilion mark on the parting of the hair on the head of the Vedas, personified as women.

This metaphor beautifully illustrates how the Vedas, personified as women, bow at the feet of Devi. The dust from Her feet sticks to the parting in their hair. Since Her feet are adorned with red colour, the dust is red, which marks the parting of their hair and the point where their forehead meets the hairline with a red hue.

It is essential for auspicious women to wear kumkum on their foreheads, at the beginning of the hair parting, which is why they are called Seemanthinee. The term Sruti is also feminine and relates to both the karma kanda (ritualistic section) and jnana kanda (knowledge section). To signify Brahman, the Upanishads are considered.

Even the Upanishads cannot fully explain the true nature of Brahman through direct statements or complete definitions. They describe it as "not this, not this," using the method of negation. The term "dust" signifies this inadequacy. The dust at Devi's lotus feet symbolizes the Vedas' inability to directly define Devi. Instead, they describe her through negation, conveying only a faint idea. Thus, the "dust" represents the limited understanding of Brahman that one can attain by venerating Devi.

According to our texts, men and women perform obeisance to the deity differently. Men must touch their entire body to the ground when bowing, allowing the dust from the deity's feet to touch their forehead. This practice aims to positively influence their destiny (Brahma lipi), which is believed to be written on their forehead. For women, their auspiciousness is carried in the area above the forehead. When women bow, the hair parting above the forehead touches the ground, bringing them auspiciousness.

The Vedas worshipping Her feet shows Her supremacy over them.

290. Sakala gama sandoha shakti samputa mauktika

She who is the pearl within the oyster shell of the Vedas.

291. Purusharta

She bestows the four-fold values of life

The Purusharthas are the four fundamental goals of human life in Hindu philosophy. They provide a framework for a balanced and fulfilling life, guiding people in their personal and spiritual development. The four Purusharthas are Dharma, Artha, Kama, and Moksha.

Dharma refers to righteousness, moral values, and duties. It is the ethical foundation of life, encompassing the responsibilities and duties one has towards oneself, family, society, and the divine. Living according to Dharma ensures harmony and order in life and society, promoting the well-being of all.

Artha signifies wealth, prosperity, and economic values. It encompasses the pursuit of material well-being and financial stability. Achieving Artha is essential for living a comfortable life and fulfilling one's responsibilities. It is considered legitimate as long as it is pursued in alignment with Dharma, ensuring that wealth is acquired and used ethically.

Kama represents desire, pleasure, and emotional fulfillment. It includes the pursuit of love, enjoyment, and sensory pleasures. Kama is essential for personal happiness and satisfaction. Like Artha, the pursuit of Kama should be guided by Dharma to ensure that desires and pleasures are enjoyed responsibly and ethically.

Moksha is the ultimate goal, representing liberation from the cycle of birth and death (samsara) and the realization of one's true self. It is the attainment of spiritual enlightenment and union with the divine. Moksha transcends the material and emotional pursuits of life, offering eternal peace and freedom.

292. Poorna

She is the all-encompassing whole

293. Bhogini

She who enjoys all worldly pleasures

294. Bhuvaneshwari

She is the queen of the 14 worlds

In Hindu cosmology, the universe is divided into fourteen lokas which are arranged in a vertical hierarchy. These worlds are broadly categorized into seven higher worlds and seven lower worlds.

The Seven Higher Worlds (Upper Realms)

1. Satya-loka: The highest realm, also known as the realm of truth. It is the abode of Lord Brahma, the creator, and is a place of ultimate enlightenment and bliss.
2. Tapa-loka: Inhabited by highly advanced sages and ascetics who have mastered extreme austerities (tapas). It is a realm of intense spiritual practice.
3. Jana-loka: The world of enlightened beings and saints who have attained the state of Jana (knowledge).

4. Mahar-loka: The realm of great sages and enlightened beings who have transcended the material world and live in a state of constant meditation.

5. Svarga-loka: The heavenly realm ruled by Indra, the king of gods. It is a place of pleasure, beauty, and enjoyment, where the righteous souls reside after death.

6. Bhuvar-loka: The realm of semi-divine beings, such as celestial spirits and demigods. It serves as the intermediate space between heaven and earth.

7. Bhu-loka: The earthly realm, where humans and other living beings reside. It is the world we experience through our senses and daily life.

The Seven Lower Worlds (Underworlds)

8. Atala: The first of the lower worlds, ruled by Bala, a demon who possesses magical powers. It is a place of indulgence and illusion.

9. Vitala: The second underworld, ruled by the god Hara-Bhava, a form of Shiva. It is associated with material wealth and pleasure.

10. Sutala: The third underworld, ruled by the demon king Bali, who was granted this realm by Lord Vishnu. It is considered a prosperous and happy place.

11. Talatala: The fourth underworld, ruled by the demon architect Maya. It is a realm of illusion and darkness.

12. Mahatala: The fifth underworld, inhabited by serpent beings (Nagas) and other creatures. It is a place of deep caverns and subterranean life.

13. Rasatala: The sixth underworld, home to the Daityas and Danavas, who are fierce and powerful demons. It is a realm of constant conflict and struggle.

14. Patala: The seventh and lowest underworld, ruled by Vasuki, the king of serpents. It is a realm of beautiful jewels and rich treasures but also of deep ignorance and darkness.

295. Ambika

She who is the great mother

296. Anadinidhana

She is without beginning or end

297. Haribrahamendrasevita

The Gods lead by Vishnu, Brahma and Indra worship Her

298. Narayani

She who is related to Narayana as His sister

299. Nadaroopa

She is the form of sound

300. Namaroopavivarjita

She who is beyond name and form

Everything in the universe can be identified in five ways: existence (Asti), knowledge (Pati), bliss (affection – priyam), name (namam), and form (roopam). The first three, existence, knowledge, and bliss, signify the connection of consciousness (Chit) with the material world and are known as Chit Granthi. The latter two, name and form, are illusory and are called Achit Granthi.

1. **Asti** refers to being. The essence of Brahman is reflected in the feeling of "I exist" (self), which drives all actions.
2. **Pati** represents understanding through knowledge. The conscious part of Brahman is the "I." Every object is understood by the mind because it reflects this consciousness.
3. **Priyam** denotes bliss or affection. Every living being has self-affection due to worldly activities. All actions occur because of the love for things that humans are attached to. These three aspects are permanent and the foundation for activities.

4. **Namam** includes not only the names given by others but also the identification of oneself and others, such as "I am a man" or "This is a horse." It applies to all perceivable matters.

5. **Roopam** refers to the individual appearance of a person or thing. Form is crucial for all activities.

Chapter 8

The names from 301 to 400 form the fourth enclosure. The Avarana is Chaturdasara; the Chakra is Sarva soubhagya dayaka (one which grants abundance)

From this point onward, the names delve into a deeper level of understanding. They reveal that She embodies the essence of mantras, serves as the foundation of creation, and represents both the seed bijakshara and its inherent Shakti. The Lalita Sahasranama highlights that She transcends even the subtlest form of existence, the causal body (karana shareera), and is recognized as the ultimate cause behind all causes (sarva karana karanam).

301. Hreemkari

Hreem is both Her name and form

The mantra Hreem (alternatively spelled Hrim) holds profound significance and is a powerful bija mantra. Hreem is seen as embodying the energy of the sun and the heart, representing illumination, creativity, and divine grace. It is believed to balance and harmonize the energies within the practitioner, fostering spiritual awakening and higher consciousness. The mantra is associated with the concept of Maya, the cosmic illusion, and is used to transcend material illusions to realize the ultimate truth. In meditation and spiritual rituals, chanting Hreem helps to purify the mind, attract positive vibrations, and connect the individual with the universal feminine energy, facilitating personal transformation and spiritual growth. The most important Sri Vidya mantra, the Panchadashakshari, has three divisions and Hreem acts as a connector between its different segments. The hidden meaning here is that this sacred syllable links the individual soul to the Supreme Being just as it links together the three segments of the Panchadasi mantra. Guru Karunamaya says that when we need to clear our surrounding of negative energies, we can chant Hreem which has the power to potentially clear and purify the environment.

302. Hreemati

She who is very modest

The Durga Saptashati extols the virtue of modesty embodied by Her in the verse:

Ya devi sarvabhutesu lajja rupena samsthita

303. Hridya

She who abides in the heart

304. Heyopadeyavarjita

She who is beyond acceptance and rejection

305. Rajarajarchita

She who is worshipped by all the emperors

The presiding deities of various mantras, starting from Manu, Moon, etc., worship Her.

306. Rajnee

She is the empress of this entire universe

As the consort of Rajarajeshwara or Mahakameshwara, she takes on the title of Rajnee.

307. Ramya

She who is beautiful

308. Rajeevalochana

Her eyes are like lotus petals

309. Ranjani

She who delights Her devotees

310. Ramani

She who rejoices with Her devotees

311. Rasya

She is the supreme essence

312. Raṇatkinkinimekhala

She who wears a waist band with tinkling bells

313. Rama

She is a form of Lakshmi

The eight names starting from Rama until Ramanalampata are linked to the bijakshara Sri. They are powerful mantras known as 'Apad kala mantras', which are chanted to alleviate problems and difficulties.

314. Rakenduvadana

She whose face resembles the full moon

315. Ratiroopa

She who is the form of Rati (Manmatha's consort)

316. Ratipriya

She who is loved by Manmatha

317. Rakshakari

She who protects

318. Rakshasagni

She is the slayer of demons

319. Rama

She who gives limitless joy

320. Ramanalampata

She who is devoted to Her husband

321. Kamya

She who is most liked by the learned

322. Kamakalaroopa

She who exists as desires and arts

Both desires and arts (kama and kala) are aspects of Shakti. As a composite form of all intentions, She takes on the name Kamakalaroopa.

323. Kadambakusumapriya

She who is fond of the flowers of the Kadamba tree

The Kadamba tree is described in nama 60.

324. Kalyani

She who is an embodiment of auspiciousness

325. Jagatikanda

She who is the root cause of the universe

326. Karunarasasagara

She who is the ocean of compassion

327. Kalavati

She who is an embodiment of the sixty-four arts

The various arts are outlined in the 236th name Chatushastikalamayi.

328. Kalalapa

She who has arts as Her conversation

329. Kanta

She who is exceptionally beautiful

330. Kadambaripriya

She who loves the nectar of Kadamba flowers

331. Varada

She who grants boons

332. Vamanayana

She who has beautiful eyes

333. Varunimadavihvala

She who is the intoxication caused by spiritual knowledge

334. Vishwadika

She who transcends the whole world

335. Vedavedya

She who can be realized through Vedas.

The Vedas constitute the oldest layer of Sanskrit literature and the oldest scriptures of Hinduism. Composed between 1500 and 500 BCE, they were transmitted orally for centuries before being written down. The Vedas are divided into four main collections: Rigveda, Samaveda, Yajurveda, and Atharvaveda. Each collection (Samhita) consists of hymns (mantras), ritual instructions (Brahmanas), and philosophical and speculative texts (Aranyakas and Upanishads). The Rigveda is the oldest and consists of hymns praising various deities. The Samaveda primarily focuses on melodies and chants for rituals. The Yajurveda contains prose mantras for rituals, while the Atharvaveda includes spells, incantations, and hymns for domestic rituals. Together, these texts form the foundation of Vedic tradition, providing insights into ancient Indian spirituality, cosmology, and society. The Vedas are revered as Shruti ("heard"), signifying their divine origin and authority, and they have profoundly influenced Hindu thought, philosophy, and practice throughout history. Their intricate blend of poetry, philosophy, and ritual has rendered them an enduring and central aspect of Hindu spiritual heritage.

336. Vindhyachalanivasini

She who resides in the Vindhya Mountains

337. Vidhatri

She who bestows everything needed for sustenance

338. Vedajanani

She is the creator of Vedas

339. Vishnumaya

She creates the illusion of Vishnu Maya

Vishnu Maya is described as the supreme and all-encompassing illusion that pervades everything in its path. This illusion envelops the entire creation, placing every being under its influence. It causes beings to believe they are merely their physical bodies and that the material world they perceive is true and permanent. This divine illusion consists of all the gunas (qualities or traits). In his incarnation as Krishna, the Supreme Lord fully manifested this illusion, Vishnu Maya. It is only by Her grace that one can transcend this illusion. Those who surrender at Her divine feet and seek refuge can cross to the other side.

Lord Krishna elaborates on this concept in the Bhagavad Gita: "This divine illusion, composed of gunas is extremely difficult to overcome. I am the creator of this illusion. Whoever surrenders to me, turning away from the world, succeeds in crossing the formidable Maya."

340. Vilasini

She who is playful

The illusion of Vishnu Maya is Her creation for Her amusement. She playfully laughs at those who attempt to transcend this illusion without surrendering to Her and seeking Her assistance, as such efforts are in vain.

341. Kshetra swaroopa

She manifests in the form of the physical body

Till now the names explored the path of devotion (bhakti). The names that follow are the foundations for the Jnana khanda (branch of knowledge) of Lalita Sahasranama where devotion and knowledge are inter-twined.

342. Kshtreshee

She is the empress who governs the gross body

343. Kshetrakshetragnapalini

She who rules over both the body and the being that resides within

344. Kshayavriddhhivinirmukta

She who is free from decay and growth

345. Kshetrapalasamarchita

She is worshipped by Shiva, who is known as Kshetrapala

Kshetrapala is revered as the guardian of a specific area or territory, often a temple or a sacred precinct. The term Kshetrapala is derived from kshetra which means area, and pala which means guardian. Kshetrapala is believed to protect the land and its inhabitants from negative influences, malevolent spirits, and other dangers. Kshetrapala is typically depicted as a fierce and vigilant guardian, holding weapons and standing at the entrance of temples. Usually Kshetrapala is considered a form of Shiva or Bhairava.

346. Vijaya

She who is eternally victorious

347. Vimala

She who is absolutely pure

348. Vandya

She who is adorable

349. Vandarujanavatsala

She who is fond of Her worshippers

350. Vagvadini

She who enables speech

351. Vamakeshi

She who has beautiful hair

352. Vahnimandalavashini

She who resides in the circle of fire

Vahni stands for both fire and the number three. The three visible gods of the Hindu pantheon are Sun, Moon and Fire and our scriptures state that they need to be worshipped everyday. Arghya is offered to the Sun, Tarpana to Moon and Pooja to Agni as a form of worship.

This nama also refers to the Tretagni, the three types of fire described in the Vedas.

Garhapatya Agni is the domestic fire kept in the household hearth. It is considered perpetual and is central to household rituals and offerings. Ahavaniya Agni is the fire into which offerings are made during rituals. It is lit from the Garhapatya fire and is used primarily for conducting yajnas. Dakshina Agni is the southern fire used for specific rituals and sacrifices, particularly those involving ancestors.

The nama could also carry a reference to the three chakras where Sun, Moon and Fire are said to exist, namely the Muladhara, Anahata and Sahasrara respectively.

353. Bhaktimatkalpalatika

She who helps fulfil every desire of Her devotees

Kalpaka is a creeper that grants all the desires of those who sit under it. In the same way, She is a wish-fulfilling climber who gives Her devotees whatever they seek.

354. Pashupasha vimochani

She releases the ignorant from bondage

355. Samhruta shesha pashanda

She who destroys the heretics averse to spiritual values

356. Sadachara pravartika

She who inspires right action

357. Tapatrayagni santapta samahladana chandrika

She who, like the Moon, gives out cooling rays for those suffering distress

The term tapatraya refers to the threefold miseries categorized as follows:

- **Adhyatmika** are internal sufferings originating from one's own body and mind. They include physical ailments like diseases and disabilities, as well as mental anguish caused by worries, anxieties, and negative emotions such as attachment and aversion
- **Adhibhautika are** sufferings are caused by external factors, such as other living beings and physical forces. Examples include attacks by animals, human enemies, and natural calamities like floods and earthquakes
- **Adhidaivika:** These miseries are believed to be caused by divine or supernatural forces. They include suffering due to natural phenomena like seasonal changes and disasters, as well as those attributed to fate, karmic influences, and displeased deities.

Just as moonlight brings comfort and coolness, the Supreme Mother provides relief and solace to devotees who are overwhelmed by distress and burdened by afflictions.

358. Taruni

She who is eternally young.

359. Tapasaradhya

She who is worshipped by ascetics

360. Tanumadhya

She who has a slender waist

361. Tamopaha

She who is the remover of darkness

362. Chiti

She who is the form of knowledge

In this form of illumination, She is all pervading. This is Her true form. Illumination implies that She is a form of complete knowledge. In the Durga Saptashati, She is worshipped as:

Chiti rupena ya kritsnam yetadhyapya sthitha jagat Namastasyai namastasyai namastasyai namo namah

Our salutations to Her who pervades this universe and abides within all beings in the form of consciousness

363. Tatpadalakshyartha

She who is the meaning of the word "tat" in the Mahavakya Tat Tvam Asi

Tat Tvam Asi, a phrase found in the Chandogya Upanishad, is one of the four Mahavakyas of Advaita Vedanta. Translated as "Thou Art That". This profound statement encapsulates the essence of non-dualistic philosophy by asserting the unity of the individual soul with the ultimate reality. Through self-realization and the removal of ignorance, one can experience their true identity with Brahman.

In the spiritual journey, "Tat Tvam Asi" serves as a guiding light for seekers of truth. It is a mantra for meditation, contemplation, and self-inquiry. By internalizing it, practitioners strive to transcend the ego and realize their oneness with the cosmos. The phrase has also been discussed in the context of different Upanishads, each offering unique insights. For instance, in the Brihadaranyaka Upanishad, the concept of self-realization is expanded upon through dialogues that reveal the interconnectedness of all existence.

364. Chidekarasarupini

She who is the highest knowledge

365. Svatmananda laveebhoota brahmadyananda santati

Even the bliss enjoyed by Brahma fades in front of the bliss enjoyed by Her

366. Para

She who exists in the form of the transcendent word

Language is a magnificent tool that allows us to express our thoughts, feelings, and ideas. However, within the vast landscape of linguistic theory, there exist deeper layers beyond mere words – layers that encompass the essence of communication itself. One such profound concept is that of Vak, which in Sanskrit means "speech" or "word." Vak is not just the spoken word; it represents the entire process of communication, from its subtlest form to its manifestation in the physical world.

Everything we know in this world is by Vak, the medium of word and the corresponding idea; So everything in this world can be objectified as Vak. This idea is later developed in the primordial sound of Aum.

The power of speech is hugely glorified in Hindu philosophy. Not only is Devi Saraswati revered as Vak Shakti, the letters (aksharas) and vak are worshiped as the akshara devatas and Vashinyadi Vag Devatas. Vak shakti is elaborated even in the most ancient Rig Veda.

Sound is classified into four distinct categories: sphota, nada, anahata, and ahata. Sphota represents an eternal, indivisible, and creative burst. In Tantra philosophy, sphota originates from the term "sphut," signifying the bursting into bud. It's depicted as the moment when a bud unfurls, emitting a sound that reveals the essence of the word. Letters themselves lack inherent meaning until they are associated with an object or concept. Sphota occurs when the meaning of the word is understood. Before unfolding, sphota merely exists as sound, residing within Sabda Brahman—the transcendental realm of sound. When sphota differentiates, it divides into two components: Sabda (sound) and artha (meaning).

Nada, existing within Sabda Brahman, embodies sound, with Bindu (dot) acting as the force facilitating its manifestation. Anahata, meaning unstruck or unbeaten, is likened to the steady rhythm of the heartbeat and the silent resonance of sound. Ahata signifies an offering and encompasses the musical sounds found in nature. Vak, meaning word, shares linguistic roots with the Latin term Vox, both originating from the Sanskrit Vak.

The connection between Sabda and Vak lies in their shared significance within the realm of language and sound. Sabda refers to sound or speech in its fundamental essence, often associated with the concept of Sabda Brahman, the transcendental source of all sound. It encompasses the inherent vibration and meaning inherent in linguistic expressions.

On the other hand, Vak specifically refers to the spoken word or speech. It represents the external manifestation of Sabda, the actualization of sound through vocalization. Vak is the audible form of Sabda, through which meaning is conveyed and communication takes place.

In essence, Sabda represents the abstract, metaphysical aspect of sound, while Vak represents its concrete, audible manifestation. The connection between the two lies in the transition from the formless to the formed, from the potentiality of sound to its actualization through speech.

In Vedanta and Tantra, Vak is classified into four distinct stages: Para, Pashyanti, Madhyama, and Vaikhari. Each stage represents a level of subtlety and manifestation, offering insight into the nature of language and consciousness.

1. Para: At the pinnacle of the Vak hierarchy lies Para, the transcendent level of speech. It is the unmanifested, pure potentiality of sound. In Para Vak, language exists in its undifferentiated form, devoid of individual words or meanings. It is the realm of pure consciousness where the distinction between speaker, speech, and the object of speech dissolves. Para represents the divine source of all creation, where the Word emerges from the silence of the Absolute.

2. Pashyanti: As the journey of expression begins, Vak moves from the unmanifested to the semi-manifested state known as Pashyanti. Here, language takes on a subtle, visual form, akin to a mental image or a seed. Pashyanti Vak is the realm of intuitive knowledge, where words are perceived as abstract symbols pregnant with meaning. It is the stage where thought crystallizes into language, yet remains unified with the subtle vibrations of consciousness.

3. Madhyama: Progressing further into the realm of manifestation, we encounter Madhyama Vak – the intermediate stage of speech. In Madhyama, language transitions from the subtle to the more concrete level of expression. It is the stage where thoughts begin to take shape as words, residing in the realm of the mind. Madhyama Vak represents the bridge between the inner world of thought and the outer world of sound. Here, language gains clarity and form, preparing for its eventual manifestation.

4. Vaikhari: Finally, Vak culminates in its fully manifest form as Vaikhari – the level of gross speech. Vaikhari Vak is the spoken word, audible to the ears and perceivable by others. It is the stage where language finds its expression in sound waves, articulating thoughts and ideas into coherent sentences. Vaikhari represents the externalization of internal thoughts, allowing for communication and interaction with the world.

- Para is the the unchanging substratum
- Pashyanti is the formation of a slight desire – iccha shakti – to speak
- Madhyama is the construction of a more concrete content through jnana shakti in the mind
- Vaikhari is the final sound that comes out in the mouth using kriya shakti

In essence, the journey of Vak from Para to Vaikhari illustrates the process of creation itself – from the unmanifested to the manifested, from the subtle to the gross. It reflects the dynamic interplay between consciousness and language, highlighting the profound connection between sound, thought, and reality.

367. Pratyakchitirupa

She is the intelligence that exists within every being

368. Pashayanti

She who manifests as speech in its inaudible stage

369. Paradevata

She who takes on the name of Paradevata at the Pashyanti stage of speech

370. Madhyama

She who manifests as speech in the middle stage of its external expression

371. Vaikhariroopa

She who manifests as the uttered word

372. Bhaktamanasahamsika

She who is the swan swimming in the mind the devotees

373. Kameshwaraprananadi

She who is the life force of Her consort Kameshwara

374. Krutagya

She who is all knowing

375. Kamapoojita

She who is adored by the god of love

376. Shringara rasa sampoorna

She who is filled with the essence of love

377. Jaya

She who grants victory

378. Jalandharastitha

She resides within those yogis who perform the bandha.

In yoga, bandhas are specific body locks used to control and direct energy flow (prana) within the body. These locks help to stabilize and support the body's core, enhance the practice of pranayama (breath control), and deepen meditation. There are three main bandhas, and a fourth one that combines all three:

- **Mula Bandha (Root Lock)**: This involves the contraction of the perineum muscles. It is located at the base of the spine, engaging the pelvic floor muscles. The primary purpose of Mula Bandha is to stimulate the root chakra (Muladhara) and control the energy flow from the lower regions upward, promoting stability and grounding.

- **Uddiyana Bandha (Upward Abdominal Lock)**: This bandha is performed by pulling the abdominal muscles in and up, creating a vacuum effect in the thoracic cavity. It is often practiced at the end of an exhale and held while the breath is out. Uddiyana Bandha activates the solar plexus chakra (Manipura), stimulates digestive fire (agni), and directs prana upwards through the central channel (Sushumna Nadi).

- **Jalandhara Bandha (Chin Lock)**: This lock is achieved by tucking the chin down towards the chest while lifting the sternum. Jalandhara Bandha is usually performed in conjunction with pranayama and helps to retain the breath, regulate the flow of blood and energy to the heart, and stimulate the throat chakra (Vishuddha).

- **Maha Bandha (The Great Lock)**: This is the combination of all three bandhas performed simultaneously. It is practiced by first engaging Mula Bandha, followed by Uddiyana Bandha, and finally

Jalandhara Bandha. Maha Bandha is said to balance the entire energy system, harmonizing the flow of prana through the body's chakras and nadis.

379. Odyanapeetha nilaya

She resides in those who perform the abdominal lock

This is explained above as Uddiyana Bandha

380. Bindu mandala vasini

She who resides in the bindu

Bindu is the central dot in the Sri Chakra.

381. Rahoyaga kramaradhya

She who is worshipped through the secret rituals

In the Bahya Pooja, several preparatory steps are performed, such as offering prayers to the teacher, entering the pooja room, and making offerings to the seat. These are followed by nyasas and setting up the vessels. Before invoking the presence of Devi in the image, the worshipper must purify themselves of all impurities. This purification process is known as Rahoyagyam and is performed secretly, not necessarily in a hidden place but internally and without others' knowledge.

During Rahoyagyam, ceremonial fire rites are conducted mentally, involving eight pourings into the fire. This internal homa is centered at the Muladhara, where the ever-present kundalini energy resides, described as a thin, glowing fire. The impurities are offered into this inner fire, causing it to burn brighter. These impurities are the eight factors that separate the devotee from Her: good and bad deeds, virtues and sins from those deeds, the resolve and irresolution to perform these deeds, and righteousness and unrighteousness arising from them. By mentally offering these impurities into the kundalini fire and visualizing their destruction, the worshipper eliminates the barriers controlling the soul. Once these are removed, the soul naturally merges with the Supreme.

This nama emphasizes the need for inner purification and mental offerings to achieve a union with the divine.

382. Rahastarpana tarpita

She who is gratified with secret offerings

Tarpana, derived from the Sanskrit root 'tar' meaning to satisfy or to gratify, is a significant ritual in Hinduism, performed to honor and appease ancestors, deities, and sages. The ritual involves offering water, milk, sesame seeds, and other substances to these entities, and it is an integral part of various ceremonies and observances.

The Rigveda contains hymns that emphasize the importance of honoring ancestors through offerings. The Garuda Purana and the Manusmriti also elaborate on the practice of Tarpana, detailing the methods and benefits of performing these rituals. In the Mahabharata, the significance of Tarpana is highlighted in various contexts, especially in the sections dealing with the duties of householders (Grihastha) and the rites of the deceased.

Types of Tarpana

1. **Pitru Tarpana**: This is the most common form of Tarpana, performed to honor one's ancestors. It is usually conducted during the fortnight of Pitru Paksha, which falls in the month of Bhadrapada (September-October). During this period, offerings of water mixed with sesame seeds, barley, and kusa grass are made while chanting specific mantras to invoke the ancestors and seek their blessings.

2. **Deva Tarpana**: This form of Tarpana is performed to honor various deities. It is typically conducted during major Hindu festivals and special occasions. Offerings are made to the gods to seek their favor and protection.

3. **Rishi Tarpana**: This ritual is performed to pay homage to the ancient sages (Rishis) who have contributed to the spiritual

knowledge and wisdom in Hinduism. It acknowledges their contributions and seeks their guidance and blessings.

4. **Tirtha Tarpana**: This Tarpana is performed at sacred rivers, lakes, and pilgrimage sites (Tirthas). The offerings made in these holy places are believed to have amplified spiritual benefits, purifying the soul and bringing blessings.

383. Sadya Prasadini

She who immediately bestows Her grace

384. Vishwasakshini

She who is witness to everything

385. Sakshivarjita

She who has no witness to record Her deeds

386.Shadangadevatayukta

She who is accompanied by the deities of six limbs

The six angas are heart, head, tuft of hair, shoulders, eyes and weapons (defence drawn around the head as explained in the Anganyasa ritual)

387. Shadgunyaparipurita

She who possesses the six good qualities.

The qualities which she possesses are:

1. Prosperity
2. Righteousness
3. Fame
4. Wealth
5. Wisdom
6. Dispassion

388. Nityaklinna

She who is ever compassionate

389. Nirupama

She who is beyond comparison.

390. Nirvanasukhadayani

She who confers the bliss of nirvana

Nirvana is extensively discussed in various scriptures, including the Upanishads, the Bhagavad Gita, and the Yoga Sutras of Patanjali

The Upanishads describe Nirvana as the realization of the self (as identical to Brahman. The Mundaka Upanishad states, "He who knows the Supreme Brahman becomes Brahman indeed." This realization leads to the dissolution of the ego and the perception of unity with the cosmic reality. In the Bhagavad Gita, Krishna explains to Arjuna the nature of the self and the path to liberation. Nirvana is described as a state of eternal peace and bliss, achieved by renouncing the fruits of actions and realizing one's unity with the divine. In Chapter 2, Verse 72, Krishna says, "That is the state of Brahman. Attaining that, none is deluded. Being established therein, even at the end of life, one attains to oneness with Brahman (Nirvana). Patanjali's Yoga Sutras outline the eightfold path (Ashtanga Yoga) to attain liberation. The culmination of this path is Samadhi, a state of meditative absorption where the individual soul realizes its oneness with the universal soul, leading to Nirvana.

391. Nityashodasikaroopa

She who shines in Her 16 forms.

The Moon has 16 phases, corresponding to the 16 days of the lunar fortnight, known as tithis. Each phase represents a distinct form of Devi, who is venerated with a unique name on each day. The first form is called Nitya, while the final form is known as Tripurambika.

392. Srikanthardhasharirini

She is the left half of Shiva

The iconic representation of Ardha-Nareshwara typically depicts the deity split down the middle, with one half representing Shiva and the other half representing Parvati. The masculine side is adorned with matted hair, a trident, and a tiger skin, signifying asceticism and the destroyer aspect of divinity. The feminine side is depicted with elegant garments, jewelry, and a lotus, symbolizing fertility, beauty, and nurturing aspects.

This duality encapsulates several philosophical and spiritual concepts:

1. **Unity of Opposites**: Ardha-Nareshwara illustrates the idea that seemingly opposing forces are actually complementary and interconnected, reflecting the principle of duality in the cosmos – creation and destruction, asceticism and sensuality, form and formlessness.

2. **Balance and Harmony**: It shows the importance of balance between male and female energies. In Tantra, this balance is crucial for spiritual growth and the attainment of ultimate reality.

3. **Equality of Genders**: The image challenges gender roles and highlights the concept of gender fluidity, promoting the view that both masculine and feminine attributes are equally valuable and necessary.

The names from 393 to 404 relate to Prabha Vidya.

Prabha signifies brightness, light, or effulgence, attributes associated with the Sun. Consequently, this knowledge is referred to as Savitri Vidya, which pertains to the Sun. Savita also represents Supreme Knowledge. Light symbolizes knowledge that eradicates the darkness of ignorance. Just as there is a physical Sun in the sky, there is also a Sun within our hearts that guides us with its light and effulgence. We should recognize that these two Suns are essentially the same.

393. Prabhavati

She who shines with infinite effulgence

Saints are depicted with halos in art and religious iconography to symbolize their holiness, divine light, and spiritual purity. The halo represents an aura of sanctity, associated with enlightenment and closeness to the divine. This imagery reflects the idea that saints possess an inner light or effulgence, akin to the Sun's radiance, reflecting their wisdom. The halo, thus, serves as a visual metaphor for their elevated spiritual state and their role as beacons of knowledge and virtue in the world.

394. Prabharoopa

She is the form of illumination

395. Prasiddha

She is well known to all.

396. Parameshwari

She is the supreme ruler

397. Moolaprakruti

She is the primary cause behind creation

Prakruti is the nature of a specific object when observed without any changes. When it undergoes changes, it becomes Vikruti. That Prakruti which has not undergone any changes is called Moolaprakruti. The Mrigendra Samhita says that Kundalini is called Moolaprakruti and hence She is known by that name.

398. Avyakta

Meaning – She is in an un-manifested, invisible state. This is in keeping with the previous nama, Mulaprakruti in which stage she is invisible.

399. Vyaktavyakta swaroopini

She who is in manifested and the un-manifested forms

She comes into existence from the un-manifest and becomes visible. While Vyakta is perishable and individual, Avyakta is imperishable and collective. She has all these characteristics.

400. Vyapini

She is all pervading.

Chapter 9

Names 401 to 534

The names from 401 to 534 form the fifth enclosure. The Avarana is Bahirdasara; the Chakra is Sarvarthasadhaka (the accomplisher of all)

401.Vividhakara

She manifests in multiple forms

402. Vidya vidya swaroopini

She who is in the form of both knowledge and ignorance

In the context of this nama, Vidya means self-realisation through knowledge. Avidya does not mean ignorance due to lack of knowledge, but rather that which arises because of duality (assumption of separateness).

403. Maha kamesha nayana kumudahlada kaumudi

She who gladdens Shiva's eyes as the moon gladdens the water lilies

The deeper meaning of this nama is that She offers bliss to those who have an interest in worldly affairs. This is in contrast to the Vedic requirement of renunciation which is needed to experience liberation.

404. Bhakta harda tamobheda bhanumad bhanu santati

She is the Sun's rays that dispel the darkness of ignorance

With this the Prabha vidya is complete.

The next 24 names from 405 to 428 throw light on the Shivaduti Vidya.

These names lead us towards Shiva, symbolizing auspiciousness. The effects of this practice are akin to performing Gayatri upasana. Those who listen to, visualize, or comprehend the essence of this vidya will receive blessings from Her.

405. Shivaduti

She who has Shiva as her herald

Devi sent Shiva as a messenger before the battle with the demons Shumbha and Nishumbha, urging them to abandon their wicked ways. This act earned Her the name Shivaduti. 'Sending Shiva' signifies 'sending auspiciousness' to the demons, offering them an opportunity to cultivate good traits.

406. Shivaradhya

She who is worshipped by Shiva

407. Shivamurthi

She who has Shiva himself as Her form

408. Shivamkari

She grants auspiciousness

She blesses the devotees who understand the essence behind Shivaduti and Shivamkari.

409. Shivapriya

She is the beloved of Shiva

410. Shivapara

She is replete with auspiciousness

411. Shisteshta

She who is dear to righteous people

The Vashistasutra explains Shistas or virtuous people as those who have control on their organs, speech and body and whose goals are in accordance with the Vedas.

412. Shista poojita

One who is worshipped by righteous and wise people

413. Aprameya

She who is immeasurable

414. Swaprakasha

She is self – illuminated

415. Manovachamagochara

She is beyond the range of mind and speech

She can only be understood through pure knowledge. The mind cannot grasp Her, and words cannot describe Her.

416. Chichakti

She who is the form of energy called Chit

Chitshakti is the power to remove ignorance and therefore is also known as Chaitanya. She is a form of knowledge, hence she is Chichakti.

417. Chetanaroopa

She is the form of consciousness that exists within all creation.

418. Jadashakti

She is the mechanical force that exists within every inanimate object.

Jada here refers to inanimate energy. Even lifeless objects possess some form of energy. Inherently, every object in creation is inanimate. It is Her energy that animates and empowers every object. Chichakti is the opposite of Jadashakti. Every object, animate and inanimate becomes itself because of its own energy.

419. Jadatmika

She is essence of all mechanical forces

420. Gayatri

She is the deity for the 24-syllable Gayatri mantra

The Gayatri Mantra, one of the most revered and ancient mantras holds profound spiritual and philosophical significance. Found in the Rig Veda, it is a hymn dedicated to Savitar, the Sun deity. The mantra is composed of twenty-four syllables, recited as:

Om Bhur Bhuva Svaa

Tat Savitur Varenyam

Bhargo Devasya Dhimahi

Dhiyo Yo Na Prachodayat

This chant is a plea for enlightenment and wisdom, seeking the divine light to illuminate the intellect and dispel ignorance. The term "Gayatri" itself signifies a meter in Sanskrit poetry, but it also refers to the deity of the mantra, Gayatri, who embodies the universal energy of consciousness. The mantra's invocation of Savitar, the life-giving Sun, symbolizes the source of all life and energy, while the repeated request for illumination shows the aspirant's desire for spiritual awakening and intellectual clarity. Reciting the Gayatri Mantra is believed to confer immense spiritual benefits, fostering inner peace, mental clarity, and a deeper connection to the divine.

421. Vyahruti

She who is the form of invocations that precede the Gayatri mantra.

Some special mantras are called Vyahruti. Brahma chanted the pranava mantra Om by joining A, U and M. Then he chanted Bhu, Bhuva, Suvaha and created the world. When the words Mahah, Janah, Tapah, Satyam were chanted, they gave rise to the seven worlds. These seven words (Bhu, Bhuva, Suvaha, Mahah, Janah, Tapah, Satyam) therefore are the seven vyahruti.

422. Sandhya

She is the form of the deity of transitional periods of the day

The term "Sandhya" refers to the transitional periods of the day, considered highly auspicious for performing prayers and rituals. The three Sandhyas are:

- **Pratah Sandhya (Morning Twilight)** which occurs at dawn, just before sunrise. It is a time for morning prayers, meditation, and the chanting of mantras, especially the Gayatri Mantra. This period is considered ideal for spiritual activities as it signifies the transition from night to day, symbolizing the awakening of consciousness.
- **Madhyahna Sandhya (Midday)** occurs at noon when the sun is at its zenith. Although not as widely observed as the morning and evening Sandhyas, midday is still considered a potent time for spiritual practices and prayers. It represents the peak of activity and the fullness of life and energy.
- **Sayam Sandhya (Evening Twilight)** takes place at dusk, just after sunset. It is a time for evening prayers and reflection, marking the transition from day to night. The evening Sandhya symbolizes the

winding down of daily activities and the preparation for rest and introspection.

These three Sandhyas are integral to the daily routine of devout Hindus, serving as moments of connection with the divine and opportunities for spiritual rejuvenation.

423. Dvija vrinda nishevita

She who is worshipped by the twice born

The term Dwija which means twice born refers to those who undergo a significant spiritual rebirth through the sacred thread ceremony of Upanayana. This term primarily applies to the first three varnas – Brahmins, Kshatriyas and Vaishyas

The first birth occurs naturally at birth, when a child is born into the physical world. The second birth is a symbolic rebirth, when one receives a sacred thread (yajnopavita) and is initiated into the study of the Vedas, The concept of being "twice-born" signifies the transition from a purely physical existence to one that includes spiritual and intellectual development. It marks the beginning of the person's formal education in religious duties, ethics, and responsibilities. The sacred thread worn by the twice-born is a constant reminder of their commitment to their spiritual path and duties. For Brahmins, this second birth emphasizes their role in preserving and teaching the sacred knowledge. For Kshatriyas and Vaishyas, it underscores their responsibilities in governance, protection, and commerce, all guided by ethical and spiritual principles.

Dvija in this name also refers to birds. Just as birds, weary from continuous flight, find rest on a tree branch, so do the mind, senses, and intellect, exhausted from a day's activities, find solace at Her feet in worship. She grants the essential rest in the form of sleep, without which beings would endure endless suffering.

424. Tatvasana

She who is seated on the cosmic elements

The concept of the 24 tattvas is an integral part of Sankhya philosophy, one of the six orthodox schools of Hindu philosophy. These tattvas represent the fundamental building blocks of the universe, describing both the material and subtle aspects of reality. Here are the 24 tattvas:

- **Prakriti (Primordial Nature)**: The unmanifested, original source of all matter and energy.
- **Mahat (Universal Intelligence)**: The first evolution of Prakriti, representing cosmic intelligence or the Great Principle.
- **Ahamkara (Ego)**: The principle of individuation, where consciousness begins to identify with individual existence.

From Ahamkara, three types of elements evolve:

- **Sattva (pure, enlightening)**
- **Rajas (active, passionate)**
- **Tamas (dark, obstructive)**

From Sattva evolve the five senses and mind:

Manas (Mind): The coordinating principle that processes sensory information.

Jnanendriyas (Five Sensory Organs):

- Hearing (ears)
- Touch (skin)
- Sight (eyes)
- Taste (tongue)
- Smell (nose)

Karmendriyas (Five Motor Organs):

- Speech (mouth)
- Grasping (hands)
- Walking (feet)
- Excretion (anus)
- Procreation (genitals)

From Tamas evolve the five subtle elements and five gross elements:

Tanmatras (Five Subtle Elements):

- Sound (Shabda)
- Touch (Sparsha)
- Form (Rupa)
- Taste (Rasa)
- Smell (Gandha)

Mahabhutas (Five Gross Elements):

- Space (Akasha)
- Air (Vayu)
- Fire (Agni)
- Water (Apas)
- Earth (Prithvi)

These 24 tattvas together describe the process through which the unmanifested primordial nature (Prakriti) transforms into the manifold universe, encompassing both the physical and the mental aspects of existence.

425. Tat

She who is the form of tat

Tat is translated as "That" and refers to the ultimate reality or supreme consciousness. In the context of the Mahavakyas, Tat signifies the absolute, unchanging reality that is beyond all dualities and distinctions. For instance, in the famous phrase "Tat Tvam Asi" (That Thou Art) from the Chandogya Upanishad, "Tat" represents Brahman, the ultimate reality or universal spirit. It is used to denote the impersonal aspect of the divine, in contrast to personal deities with specific attributes and forms. It represents the formless, infinite, and eternal essence that underlies all existence.

In the namavali, this name is chanted as Om Tasmayi Namah

426. Tvam

She who manifests as the being

Tvam means 'thou' or the individual self.

This name is called Tubhyam namah – Obeisance to you O mother who is residing within me!

427. Ayi

She who is everything

Ayi is the stage at the merger of Tat and Tvam. In the two earlier names, 'tat' referred to a distant object, and 'tvam' referred to the individual self, illustrating that both entities are manifestations of Her. 'Ayi' now highlights that 'You are the Divine Mother'. The phrase Tat tvam ayi signifies the unity with Her, expressing the state of merging with the Divine Mother.'

This name is chanted as Tasyai namah in the namavali form – Obeisance to Her who is everything.

428. Pancha koshantara stitha

She who dwells in the five sheaths

The concept of the Pancha Koshas is described in the Taittiriya Upanishad. It describes the layers that encase the true self each progressively subtler than the previous, and outlines the journey towards self-realization by transcending these layers.

Annamaya Kosha (Food Sheath) is the outermost sheath, composed of the physical body, which is sustained by food. It includes the muscles, bones, and skin. The Annamaya Kosha represents our gross physical existence and is the most tangible and perceptible layer. Understanding this sheath involves recognizing the body's dependence on external nourishment and its transient nature.

Pranamaya Kosha (Vital Sheath) consists of the vital life force (prana) that animates the physical body. It encompasses the breath and the physiological functions that sustain life, such as circulation and digestion. The Pranamaya Kosha is more subtle than the Annamaya Kosha and is crucial for maintaining the body's vitality and health.

Manomaya Kosha (Mental Sheath) is the layer of the mind and emotions. It includes thoughts, feelings, and the cognitive processes that enable perception and interaction with the world. This sheath is responsible for desires, fears, and all mental activities. It is through the Manomaya Kosha that we experience our everyday psychological reality, and it can be a source of both bondage and liberation.

Vijnanamaya Kosha (Wisdom Sheath) is composed of the higher intellect, discernment, and wisdom. It is associated with the faculty of understanding and intuition, allowing for deeper insight into the nature of reality. The Vijnanamaya Kosha transcends ordinary mental activities and is involved in ethical and moral reasoning, guiding one toward higher knowledge and self-awareness.

Anandamaya Kosha (Bliss Sheath) represents the state of bliss and joy that arises from being in close proximity to the Atman. This layer is characterized by a sense of peace, happiness, and contentment that is not dependent on external circumstances. It is the closest to the true self and is experienced during deep meditation or spiritual ecstasy.

The journey of self-realization involves penetrating these layers, moving from the gross physical body to the subtler realms of energy, mind, intellect, and ultimately reaching the blissful essence of the Atman.

The 24 names corresponded to the 24 syllables in the Gayatri Mantra (which is said to represent the 24 cosmic principles).

In the names below, the form of the Divine Mother Gayatri is extolled.

429. Nisseemamahima

She whose glory is boundless

430. Nityayouvana

She who is eternally young

431. Madashalini

She who is in a state of bliss

432. Mada ghoornita raktakshi

Her bliss makes her eyes flicker

433. Mada patala gandabhoo

Her cheeks are rosy in bliss

434. Chandana drava digdhangi

Her body is smeared with sandal paste

435. Champeyakusumapriya

She loves the fragrant flowers

436. Kushala

She who is skilful

437. Komalakara

She who has a soft form

438. Kurukulla

She who resides in Muladhara chakra

439. Kuleshwari

She is the presiding deity of the Muladhara chakra

440. Kulakundalaya

She who abides in the Muladhara chakra

441. Kaula marga tatpara sevita

She who is worshipped by those following the Kaula tradition

The Samaya, Kaula, and Mishra schools represent three distinct approaches to Sri Vidya. The Samaya school of Sri Vidya is characterized by its emphasis on a highly disciplined and systematic approach to worship and meditation. The term "Samaya" translates to "appropriate time" or "method," indicating a focus on precise rituals and spiritual practices. This tradition upholds a strict adherence to ritual purity, detailed procedures, and adherence to scriptural injunctions. It stresses the importance of proper timing, mantra pronunciation, and ritualistic accuracy to achieve spiritual goals.

The Kaula school represents a more eclectic and experiential approach to Sri Vidya, characterized by its inclusivity and emphasis on practical, often unconventional methods of worship. The Mishra school represents a synthesis of both the Samaya and Kaula approaches, combining the rigorous ritualistic aspects of the former with the experiential and flexible elements of the latter.

442. Kumara gananathamba

She is the mother of Subrahmanya and Ganapati

443. Tushti

She who is the form of contentment

Tushti refers to satisfaction or contentment in the context of divine grace or spiritual fulfillment. The concept of Tushti can be categorized into several types

- Bhakti Tushti arises when one experiences contentment and fulfillment through sincere devotion to a deity.
- Jnana Tushti is attained through the pursuit of spiritual knowledge and understanding. It involves the satisfaction and contentment gained from deep philosophical inquiry, self-realization, and the realization of the ultimate truth or Brahman
- Karma Tushti is experienced when one performs their duties and responsibilities in alignment with dharma

- Santosha Tushti refers to a broader sense of contentment and inner peace experienced in everyday life.
- Divya Tushti is a form of satisfaction that comes from experiencing the grace and blessings of the divine.
- Rasa Tushti is experienced through engagement with the arts, literature, and other forms of aesthetic expression that evoke deep emotional responses.
- Aparoksha Tushti is achieved through direct, personal realization of one's true nature or self.

444. Pushti

She who is complete

445. Mati

She who is the form of wisdom and intellect

446. Dhriti

She who is in the form of fortitude

447. Shanti

She who is in the form of tranquillity

448. Swastimati

She who is the form of eternal truth

449. Kanti

She is the form of radiance.

450. Nandini

She who bestows delight

451. Vighnanashini

She who removes obstacles

452. Tejovati

She who is the cause of illumination

453. Trinayana

She who is three-eyed

The Sun, Moon and Fire are Her three eyes

454. Lolakshikamaroopini

She is the form of affection in women

455. Malini

She who wears a garland of alphabets

Her garland contains all the alphabets from a to ha. Every word, spoken or written, forms a part of this garland.

456. Hamsini

She is the female swan

In Hinduism and yoga philosophy, the swan is considered a symbol of purity and spiritual knowledge. It is believed that the swan has the ability to separate milk from water, symbolizing the ability to discern and choose the essence of truth from the distractions of the material world. In the context of meditation and mantra, "Hamsa" is used as a syllable or sound.

457. Mata

She who is the form of a Mother

458. Malayachalavasini

She who resides in the Malaya mountains

459. Sumukhi

She who has a beautiful face

460. Nalini

She who is like a lotus flower

461. Subhroo

She who has beautiful eyebrows

462. Shobana

She who is radiant with beauty

463. Suranayika

She who is the leader of the Devatas

464. Kalakanthee

She who has a dark blue neck

During the churning of the ocean, Shiva consumed the Halahala poison that emerged. To prevent the poison from reaching His stomach, Devi placed four fingers on His neck, blocking its entry. The poison stayed in His neck, turning it bluish-black, giving Him the name Neelakantha. She is the consort of this form of Shiva as Kalakanthee.

465. Kantimathi

She who is resplendent

466. Kshobini

She who causes agitation

467. Sukshmaroopini

She who is very subtle

468. Vajreshwari

She who is firm like a diamond

Her location is in the Vishudda chakra.

469. Vamadevi

She who is the consort of Shiva in the form of Vamadeva

Her location is in the Anahata chakra.

470. Vayovasthavivarjita

She who is not prone to growth and old age

Her location is the Manipura chakra.

471. Siddheshwari

She who is the ruler of all accomplished adepts

Her location is the Swadhisthana chakra.

472. Siddhavidya

She who is the authority of the knowledge possessed by Siddhas

Her location is the Muladhara chakra.

473. Siddhamata

She is the mother to all Siddhas

Her location is the Ajna chakra.

474. Yashaswini

She who is most renowned

Her location is the Sahasrara chakra.

The six names, Vajreshwari to Siddhamata, represent the six forms She takes to dwell within the six chakras. The seventh name, Yashaswini, signifies Her ultimate position in the Sahasrara chakra. In this Sahasranama, the description of the Chakras starts from the Vishuddha chakra near the throat, rather than the traditional Muladhara chakra at the base of the spine. This approach is taken because the Vishuddha chakra is the primary contact point for the air being inhaled. The air first touches the Vishuddha chakra before traveling down to the other Chakras. Additionally, the Vishuddha chakra is the central hub for various nadis in the body, which converge at this point.

The namas from 475 to 534 focus on the chakras. It is important to understand the concept of chakras to gain an insight into the workings of kundalini.

In the 60 names, each chakra is governed by a specific deity known as a yogini, and there are seven such yoginis. They are described in 7, 9 or 10 lines with each description beginning with the name of the chakra and ending with the name of the yogini who is the presiding deity of that chakra. There is mention of the number of faces they have, the organ or dhatu which they govern, the number of Shaktis that accompany them and their favourite food.

Name	Chakra	Face	Food	Organ/ Dhatu	Shaktis	Bija mantra
Dakini	Vishuddha	One	Payasanna	Skin	16	Ham
Rakini	Anahata	Two	Snigdhaudhana	Blood	12	Yam
Lakini	Manipura	Three	Gudanna	Muscle	10	Ram
Kakini	Swadistana	Four	Dadhyanna	Fat	6	Vam
Sakini	Muladhara	Five	Mudgaudana	Bone	4	Lam
Hakini	Ajna	Six	Haridranna	Bone marrow	2	Om
Yakini	Sahasrara	Infinite	All types	Semen/ Ovum	None	None

It is important to understand that these namas are not direct references to Devi. However, since She is viewed as the embodiment of the kundalini energy, which must ascend through the chakras Muladhara to the Sahasrara, the Vag Devis have incorporated the worship of the deities that preside over these chakras. The description does not follow a linear method of ascent (from Muladhara upwards) or descent (from Sahasrara downwards) but instead starts at the Vishudda chakra where Vak is enabled in the spoken form and then proceeds downwards through the Anahata,

Manipura, Swadisthana, Muladhara and then up to the Ajna and finally reaching the Sahasrara chakra.

Manblunder explains the two possible reasons for this non-linear approach in his blog on the Yoginis: The order in which they are mentioned in this Sahasranama is based on two concepts. Each of these yoginis has many faces. The yogini at vishuddhi chakra has one face and the yogini at sahasrara has many faces. Probably Vag Devis could have prioritized these yogini-s based on the number their faces. Alternatively, Vag Devis could have chosen this order based on the type of bodily element, each of these yoginis represent.

The seven dhatus, or bodily tissues, develop in a specific sequence in an embryo according to Ayurveda. These dhatus represent different levels of nourishment and structure within the body, and they are believed to form in the following order:

- **Rasa (Plasma/Lymph)**: The first dhatu to form, representing the initial nutritive fluid that nourishes all other tissues. It is closely associated with the essence of digested food and provides the basic nourishment to the developing embryo.
- **Rakta (Blood)**: Following the formation of rasa, rakta dhatu, or blood, develops. It provides vital life force and energy, and is responsible for carrying nutrients and oxygen throughout the body.
- **Mamsa (Muscle)**: After rakta, mamsa dhatu, or muscle tissue, forms. This dhatu provides structure, strength, and movement to the body.
- **Meda (Fat)**: Meda dhatu, or fat tissue, develops next. It acts as a reserve of energy and provides lubrication and insulation to the body.
- **Asthi (Bone)**: Asthi dhatu, or bone tissue, is formed after meda. It gives the body its shape, structure, and protection to vital organs.
- **Majja (Bone Marrow/Nervous Tissue)**: Following asthi, majja dhatu forms, which includes bone marrow and nervous tissue. It fills the bones and supports the nervous system, contributing

to the production of blood cells and the transmission of nerve impulses.

- **Shukra (Reproductive Tissue/Semen or Ova)**: The last dhatu to develop is shukra, which is the reproductive tissue, including semen in males and ova in females. It represents the essence of all other dhatus and is responsible for reproduction and vitality.

These seven dhatus are considered to be the building blocks of the human body, and their proper formation and balance are essential for overall health and well-being.

Who are the yoginis?

Yoginis are depicted as attendants or aspects of the Goddess in her various forms, and they play a central role in certain tantric rituals. They are associated with power, protection, and spiritual transformation. Some texts that describe these include the "Yogini Tantra" and various Puranas. Temples associated with them are usually circular or semi-circular in structure, representing the cosmic energy or the mandala. While the names and attributes of the Yoginis can vary depending on the tradition and region, some of the commonly mentioned Yoginis include:

- **Matrika Yoginis**: Linked to the Matrikas, a group of mother goddesses
- **Vidyadhari Yoginis**: Bearers of wisdom.
- **Shivaduti**: Yoginis who serve as messengers of Shiva.
- **Bhairavi Yoginis**: Associated with Bhairava, a fierce aspect of Shiva.

The worship of theis most prominently seen in temples such as the Hirapur Yogini Temple in Odisha, the Ranipur-Jharial Temple in Odisha, and the Chausath Yogini Temple in Madhya Pradesh.

The first ten namas describe Dakini, who resides in the Vishuddha Chakra.

475. Vishuddhichakranilaya

She who resides in the Vishuddha chakra

476. Araktavarna

She who is rosy hued

477. Trilochana

She who has 3 eyes.

478. Khatvangadipraharana

She who is armed with a club

479. Vadanaika samanvita

She who has one face.

480. Payasannapriya

She who loves milk and rice pudding

481. Tvakstha

She is the presiding deity of skin

The first dhatu to form is rasa, representing the initial nutritive fluid that contains and nourishes all other tissues.

482. Pashulokabhayankari

She causes fear in the ignorant

483. Amritadimahashaktisamvrita

She is surrounded by sixteen Shaktis

Amruta, Akarshini, Indrani, Eshani, Uma, Urdvakeshi, Ruddhida, Rookara, Lukara, Lookara, Ekapada, Aishwarya, Omkari, Aushadhi, Ambika and Akshara are the Maha Shaktis who reside at this Vishuddha chakra. They should be visualized at the Vishuddha chakra and should be offered worship.

484. Dakineshwari

She who is the ruler of Vishuddha chakra.

The namas 485 to 494 describe Rakini, who resides in Anahata Chakra.

485. Anahatabja nilaya

She who resides in the Anahata Chakra.

486. Shyamabha

She who has a bluish-black complexion

487. Vadanadvaya

She who has two faces.

The sound that originates at Anahata is connected to the fire element. Fire is known by the name Dwisheersha (two faced).

488. Damshtrojvala

She who has shining tusks

This nama alludes to Her form as Varahi, who uses Her tusks to push a devotee towards acquiring the divine knowledge.

489. Aksha maladidhara

She who wears a rosary

490. Rudhira samsthita

She who resides in the blood

The second dhatu to form is blood which provides vital life force and energy, and is responsible for carrying nutrients and oxygen throughout the body.

491. Kala ratrya dishaktyouhavruta

She who is surrounded by Kalaratri and other Shakti Devis

The twelve Devis that reside with her in the Anahata Chakra are Kalaratri, Kanteeta, Gayatri, Ghantakarshini, Gnarna, Chanda, Chaya, Jaya, Jangarini, Jnanaroopa, Tankahasta, Thankakarini.

492. Snigdhaudana priya

She who loves rice mixed with ghee

493. Mahaveerendra varada

She who grants boons to the warrior chiefs

494. Rakinyamba swaroopini

She who is the presiding deity of Anahata chakra.

The namas 495 to 503 describe the Lakini who resides in the Manipura Chakra.

495. Manipurabja nilaya

She who resides in the Manipura chakra

496. Vadanatraya samyuta

She who is in a form with 3 faces.

The Manipura chakra is located in the abdomen and since this is the place of water, she has three faces to depict the three tatvas of ether, air and water.

497. Vajradika yudhopeta

She who is equipped with the 4 weapons

In the Manipura Chakra, she has in Her four hands a thunderbolt, Shakti, a long stick and the Abhaya mudra

498. Damaryadi bhiravruta

She who is surrounded by Damari and other Maha shaktis

Manipura is 10 petal chakra. The ten energies who accompany Her in this chakra are Damari, Dhankarini, Narna, Tamasi, Sthanvi, Dakshayini, Dhatri, Nari, Parvati and Phatkarini

499. Raktavarna

She who is crimson colour.

500. Mamsanishta

She who is fond of meat

After rakta, the third dhatu – mamsa or muscle tissue, forms. This dhatu provides structure, strength, and movement to the body.

501. Gudanna preeta manasa

She who is pleased rice cooked with jaggery is offered to Her.

502. Samasta bhakta sukhada

She who blesses all devotees with happiness.

In the Bhagavad Gita, Krishna describes four groups of devotees who worship Him:

- Artho – those who are grieved
- Jignyasu – those who seek divine knowledge
- Artharthi – those who desire material comforts
- Gnyani – the wise

She caters to the needs of all types of devotees. She rescues those in distress who seek help, fulfills the desires of those seeking material comforts and bestows knowledge on those who aspire for it.

503. Lakinyamba swaroopini

She who is the presiding deity of Manipura chakra

The names 504 to 513 refer to Kakini who is seated in the Swadhishthana Chakra.

504. Swadisthanambujagata

She who resides in the Swadhisthana chakra.

505. Chaturvaktra manohara

She who is fascinating with Her four faces.

Swadhisthana is the place of fire so the four faces represent ether, air, water and fire.

506. Shuladyudha sampanna

She who has a trident and other weapons

At the Swadhisthana chakra She possesses four weapons – trident, noose, skull and goad.

507. Peetavarna

She who is yellow in colour

508. Atigarvita

She is very proud of Her beauty

509. Medonishta

She who resides in the fatty tissues of the body

The fifth tissue to develop is Medha or fat tissue, develops next. It acts as a reserve of energy and provides lubrication and insulation to the body.

510. Madhupreeta

She who loves honey

511. Bandhinyadi samanvita

She who is surrounded by Bandini and other Maha shaktis

The 6 deities here are Bandini, Bhadrakali, Mahamaya, Yashaswini, Rakta and Lamboshtika.

512. Dadhyanna sakta hrudaya

She who is fond of curd rice

513. Kakini roopa dharini

She who takes on the name of Kakini in the Swadistana Chakra.

The names 514 to 520 describe Sakini, who resides in the Muladhara Chakra.

514. Muladharambujaroodha

She who resides in the Muladhara Chakra.

515. Panchavaktra

She who takes on five faces.

The Muladhara is the place of the earth tatva. She has five faces indicating ether, air, water, fire and earth in this chakra.

516. Asti samsthita

She who presides over the bones in living beings

The sixth dhatu to develop is Asti or bone tissue which gives the body its shape, structure, and protection to vital organs.

At this stage, She assumes the form of Rahu. It is believed that Rahu and Ketu reside in the Muladhara. Rahu is closely associated with the bones in the body. For bone-related issues, an oil lamp is lit during the rahu kala.

517. Ankushadi praharana

She who is armed with goad and other weapons

In this chakra, she has in Her four hands a goad, a lotus, a book and Jnana Mudra

518. Varadadi nishevita

She who is surrounded by Varada and other Maha Shaktis

Here the Maha Shaktis who reside with Her are Varada, Shree, Shanda and Saraswati

519. Mudgaudana sakta chitta

She who is fond of rice cooked with green gram lentil.

520. Sakinyamba swaroopini

She who takes the form of Sakini in the Muladhara Chakra

The names 521 to 527 describe the Divine Mother who is seated in the Ajna Chakra as Hakini Devi.

521. Agnachakrabja nilaya

She who resides in the Ajna Chakra

522. Shukla varna

She who is white complexioned

523. Shadanana

She who has six faces

Ajna Chakra is the place of the mind and to exhibit the energy of the five elements plus the mind, She now has six faces.

524. Majja samstha

She who exists in the form of the bone marrow

Following asti, the sixth dhatu majja forms, which includes bone marrow and nervous tissue. It fills the bones and supports the nervous system, contributing to the production of blood cells and the transmission of nerve impulses.

525. Hamsavati mukhya shakti samanvita

She is accompanied by two deities

The Ajna Chakra has two petals depicting the two Maha Shaktis Hamsavati and Kshmavati

526. Haridrannaika rasika

She who loves rice mixed with turmeric.

527. Hakini roopa dharini

She who takes on the name Hakini at the Ajna Chakra

Devi who is seated in the Sahasrara Chakra as Yakini is described in the following 7 names 528 to 534.

528. Sahasradala padmastha

She who is seated within the thousand-petalled lotus

529. Sarva varnopa shobita

She who shines with all colours

530. Sarva yudha dhara

She who is equipped with every kind of weapon

531. Shukla samstitha

She who is the presiding deity of semen

The last dhatu to develop is shukra, which is the reproductive tissue, including semen in males and ova in females. It represents the essence of all other dhatus and is responsible for reproduction and vitality.

532. Sarvatomukhi

She has innumerable faces in every direction.

533. Sarvaudana preetachitta

She who is pleased with all kinds of food

534. Yakinyamba swaroopini

She who appears at the Sahasrara Chakra in the form of Yakini

The most important names of a yagna are now being taught in Lalita Sahasranama.

Chapter 10

Names 535 to 600

The names from 535 to 600 form the sixth enclosure. The avarana is Antardasara; the Chakra is Sarvarakshakara (one that cures all ills)

535. Svaha

She who is the form of the sacred exclamations with which oblations are made in yagna for gods

536. Swadha

She who is the form of the sacred exclamations with which oblations are made in yagna for pitrus

537. Amati

She who is the form of ignorance

Ignorance (avidya) can also be understood as worldly knowledge, which is distinct from spiritual knowledge. She embodies this worldly knowledge. Yagnas are often performed with the desire to achieve greater material prosperity. These acts, driven by such desires, are considered forms of ignorance and can be classified as amati (ignorance).

538. Medha

She who is the form of knowledge

539. Shruti

She who is the form of the Vedas.

540. Smrithi

She appears in the form of the various smrithis

While Shruti is related to heard knowledge, Smrithi refers to recollected knowledge.

541. Anuttama

She who has no superior

Up to this name, all the names pertained to yagna.

542. Punyakirti

She who is famous for Her virtues

543. Punyalabhya

She who can be attained only through virtuous actions

544. Punyashravanakirtana

It is a virtue to hear about Her or to praise Her

545. Pulomajarchita

She who is worshipped by Pulomaja

The story occurs in the Devi Bhagavatam (Book VI). After Indra killed Puloman, he married Sasee Devi, Puloman's daughter. Later, due to a curse from Gautama for his misconduct with Ahalya, Indra had to hide, and Nahusha took over the rule of heaven. Nahusha demanded that Sasee Devi become his wife. To escape this situation, Sasee Devi worshipped with a powerful mantra of Sree Devi, which she obtained from her teacher, Brihaspati. She earnestly worshipped Tripurasundari with offerings of food and flowers. As a result, Indra was freed from Gautama's curse and was restored to his position as the ruler of heaven.

546. Bandhamochani

She who liberates from bondages

547. Barbaralaka

She who has a forehead of black, curly hair

548. Vimarsharoopini

She who is the power of discrimination

Vimarsha and Prakasha are explained in detail in the introduction. Just to refresh your memory – they are fundamental concepts representing two aspects of the divine consciousness. Prakasha refers to the principle of illumination or light. It symbolizes the pure, undifferentiated consciousness and the self-revealing nature of the ultimate reality, identified with Shiva. Prakasha is the aspect of divine consciousness that signifies the light of awareness, the ability to know or perceive. It is the passive, foundational aspect of consciousness that simply illuminates or makes existence possible. Vimarsha, on the other hand, represents the principle of reflection, discernment, or self-awareness. It symbolizes the dynamic aspect of the divine, associated with Shakti, the active, creative power of consciousness. Vimarsha is the self-reflective quality of consciousness that allows it to be aware of itself, to differentiate, and to manifest in various forms. It is the power of consciousness to engage in self-reflection and experience the world, thus leading to the manifestation of the universe.

In the Sri Vidya tradition, Prakasha and Vimarsha are seen as inseparable and complementary aspects of the same divine reality. Prakasha without Vimarsha would be pure light without self-awareness or creativity, while Vimarsha without Prakasha would be dynamic activity without the foundation of pure consciousness. Together, they represent the unity of the static and dynamic, the illuminating and the reflective, the Shiva and Shakti.

This unity is essential for the process of creation, sustenance, and dissolution in the universe, reflecting the interplay of consciousness and its inherent power. She is that aspect of unity.

549. Vidya

She who is the knowledge

550. Viyadadijagatprasu

She who created the sky and then the entire universe

The Taittiriya Upanishad states that Brahman first created space. From this space, other elements such as air, fire, and water were created.

551. Sarvavyadhiprashamani

She who cures all diseases

552. Sarvamrityunivarini

She who dispels all forms of death

553. Agraganya

She who is the first in this entire creation

554. Achintyarupa

She who is inaccessible to the mind.

555. Kalikalmashanashini

She who destroys all sin

556. Katyayanee

She who is the daughter of Sage Kata

557. Kalahantri

She who dissolves time

558. Kamalakshanishevita

She who is worshipped by the lotus eyed Vishnu

559. Tambulapuritamukhi

She who has a mouth full of betel leaves

560. Dadimikusumaprabha

She who has a complexion like a red pomegranate flower.

561. Mrigakshi

She who has like that of a deer.

562. Mohini

She who is enchanting

563. Mukhya

She who is the first

She is the first among all things that came into being. The Taitireeya Upanishad says – I am the first born out of truth (Ahamasmi Prathama Ja Rutasya)

564. Mridani

She who is the consort of Shiva in Mrida form

565. Mitraroopini

She who is in the form of a friend

566. Nityatrupta

She who is always content

567. Bhaktanidhi

She is the treasure house for devotees

568. Niyantri

She who governs the Universe

569. Nikhileshwari

She who is the empress of creation

570. Maitryadivasanalabhya

She who can be attained by a good disposition

The Bhagavat Gita says that good dispositions are of four types – friendship with those who are happy without being envious (maitree), compassion for those who are suffering (karuna), gladness to see the righteous (mudita) and overlooking the sinful (upeksha).

571. Mahapralayasakshini

She who witnesses the final dissolution

A witness is one who does not participate in the action and is unaffected by its outcome. She is such a witness to the great dissolution.

572. Parashakti

She who is the supreme energy

The dhatus, which we have discussed before, refer to the fundamental bodily tissues that support and sustain the physical body.

- **Rasa (Plasma)**: The nutrient fluid that nourishes all the body's tissues, organs, and systems
- **Rakta (Blood)**: The carrier of life energy (prana) and nutrients, vital for sustaining life
- **Mamsa (Muscle Tissue)**: Provides structure, protection, and movement to the body
- **Meda (Fat Tissue)**: Lubricates the body and provides energy reserves
- **Asthi (Bone Tissue)**: Gives structure and support, protects vital organs, and anchors muscles
- **Majja (Bone Marrow and Nerve Tissue)**: Fills the bones and contributes to the nervous system's functioning
- **Shukra (Reproductive Tissue)**: Responsible for reproduction and vitality
- Three additional elements sometimes included in discussions of dhatus are:
- **Ojas (Vital Essence)**: The essence that gives strength, vitality, and immunity. It is considered the finest product of digestion and the essence of all the dhatus
- **Prana (Life Force)**: The vital life force that energizes all bodily functions and is considered the essence of life itself
- Parashakti (Supreme Energy) is considered the 10th dhatu which governs all others

573. Paranishta

She who is steadfast

574. Prajnyana ghana roopini

She who is the form of pure, concentrated knowledge

575. Madhavi panalasa

She who is intoxicated by alcohol

In this context, madhu symbolizes the intoxication and bliss derived from listening to these sacred mantras

576. Matta

She who is in slumber brought about by intoxication

577. Matruka varna roopini

She who is of the form of all the letters of Sanskrit

Sanskrit has 51 aksharas and since they lend colour to words, they are known as Varnas. In the Yogini Nyasa and the Sanatkumara Samhita, we find that the chakras and letters are all attributed different colours.

Chakra	Sanskrit Letter	Colour
Vishuddi	A to A:	Smoky ash
Anahata	Ka to Tha	Reddish Rose
Manipura	Da to Pha	White
Swadhisthana	Ba to La	Reddish Rose
Muladhara	Va to sa	Gold
Ajna	Ha to Ksha	Lightning

578. Mahakailasanilaya

She who resides in Kailasa

579. Mrinalamridudorlata

Her arms are as tender as lotus stalks

580. Mahaniya

She who is the embodiment of worship

581. Dayamurthi

She who is the embodiment of mercy

582. Mahasamrajyashalini

She who has a vast empire

From the nama 583 (Atma-vidya) to 'nama 621 (Divya Vighraha)' the knowledge is known as Brahma-vidya. This is Divine initiation (divya upadesha).

583. Atmavidya

She who is the doctrine to help understand oneself

A mantra whose presiding deity is a female is called Vidya. Atmavidya is that which throws light on the form of the Brahman. The 727th name Shiva jnana pradayini says that She bestows the knowledge of the Brahman.

584. Mahavidya

She who is the great doctrine

This nama is interpreted as a reference to the Dasa Mahavidyas

The Dasa Mahavidya are a group of ten aspects of the Divine Mother representing different facets of feminine power and knowledge. Each Mahavidya is a distinct deity with unique iconography, attributes, and philosophical significance. They embody the entirety of cosmic functions, from creation to destruction, and reflect the multifaceted nature of the divine feminine.

- **Kali**: Representing the ultimate reality of time and death, Kali is the fierce and powerful form of the goddess. She is often depicted with a garland of skulls, standing on the inert body of Shiva, symbolizing the transcendence of time and the destruction of ignorance.
- **Tara**: The savior and protector, Tara is depicted as a blue-skinned goddess similar to Kali but more compassionate. She guides devotees through spiritual and material difficulties, representing the force that helps overcome suffering and reach enlightenment.
- **Tripura Sundari**: The epitome of beauty and the supreme goddess, Tripura Sundari embodies the principle of desire and the bliss of

creation. She is often depicted as a young, beautiful woman seated on a lotus, symbolizing divine grace and perfection.

- **Bhuvaneshvari:** The goddess of the physical world and the cosmos, She represents the all-encompassing nature of the divine, embodying the entire universe within herself.

- **Bhairavi:** The fierce goddess, Bhairavi embodies the power of destruction and transformation. She represents the aspect of the divine that clears obstacles and destroys negative influences, facilitating the path to spiritual growth.

- **Chhinnamasta:** Depicted as a self-decapitated goddess, Chhinnamasta represents the paradox of life and death, creation and destruction. She signifies the sacrifice of the ego and the flow of vital energy, embodying the idea of self-transcendence.

- **Dhumavati:** The widow goddess, Dhumavati is associated with inauspiciousness, decay, and death. She represents the darker aspects of life, embodying the state of dissolution and the reality of suffering and misfortune.

- **Bagalamukhi:** Known for her power to paralyze enemies, Bagalamukhi is the goddess of stillness and silence. She symbolizes the power to stop and reverse negative forces, representing the control of speech and actions.

- **Matangi:** The outcast goddess, Matangi embodies the power of domination and inner knowledge. She is often associated with pollution and the margins of society, symbolizing the transcendence of social norms and the attainment of esoteric wisdom.

- **Kamala:** The goddess of wealth and prosperity, Kamala is akin to Lakshmi. She represents the fruition of spiritual and material abundance, embodying the principle of generosity and the fulfillment of desires.

The Dasa Mahavidya represent the comprehensive nature of the divine feminine, covering a wide spectrum from benevolent and nurturing to fierce and destructive aspects. They offer a holistic understanding of the cosmos, where creation and destruction, beauty and terror, wisdom and ignorance are all integral parts of the divine play (lila). This pantheon provides a framework for devotees to engage with the complexities of life and the universe, understanding that every aspect, even those that seem negative or frightening, has a place in the grand scheme of existence.

In the practice of Tantra, the Mahavidyas are seen as powerful tools for spiritual transformation. Each goddess is associated with specific mantras, rituals, and meditation practices that help the practitioner harness her unique energy and qualities. The worship of the Mahavidyas is considered a path to self-realization and ultimate liberation, revealing the underlying unity of all existence through the diversity of form.

585. Sri Vidya

She who is the form of the great wisdom of Lalita Tripurasundari

586. Kamasevita

She who is served by the god of desire

As mentioned in an earlier nama, Kama is one of the 12 primary worshippers of Devi.

587. Srishodashaksharividya

She who is the 16-syllable mantra

The Panchadasi mantra is suffixed with one bija to get the 16 syllables of the highly secret Shodashi mantra. This can only be initiated by a guru.

588. Trikuta

She who has groups of letters in threes

The 15-syllable Panchadasi mantra is divided into 3 kutas – Vagbhava kuta, Madhya kuta and Shakti kuta.

The hidden meaning of this nama is that those who chant the mantra with three kutas will get Her anugraha.

589. Kamakotika

She who is the form of salvation

590. Katakshakinkari Bhootakalamakotisevita

Her power is such with a mere glance, multitude of goddesses attend and serve Her.

591. Shirasthita

She who resides in the head

Devi is seen as residing in the Brahmarandhra assuming the form of a guru.

592. Chandranibha

She who shines resplendently like the moon.

593. Phalastha

She who resides in the forehead

Devi is seen as residing in the Anna chakra in the form of the binds of the syllable Hreem

594. Indradhanuprabha

She who shines likes a rainbow

595. Hridayastha

She who resides in the heart.

596. Raviprakhya

She who shines like the Sun

597. Trikonantaradeepika

She who is like a light in a triangle

598. Dakshayani

She who is the daughter of Daksha

599. Daityahantri

She is the slayer of demons

600. Daksha yagna vinashini

She who destroyed Daksha's yagna

The story of Daksha's yagna is a significant episode within the Puranas. It involves themes of pride, familial relationships, divine retribution, and the interplay between the gods. Daksha, one of the Prajapatis and a son of Brahma, was a powerful and influential deity. He had several daughters, including Sati, who was deeply devoted to Shiva. Despite Daksha's disapproval, Sati married Shiva, who was considered unconventional and ascetic. This union was not favored by Daksha, who regarded Shiva as unworthy of his daughter.

To assert his power and to perform a grand yagna, Daksha organized a massive sacrificial ceremony, inviting all the gods and celestial beings except Shiva and Sati. Feeling deeply insulted by the exclusion of her husband, Sati decided to attend the yagna despite Shiva's warning. Upon arriving at her father's yagna, Sati was met with disdain and disrespect. Daksha openly insulted Shiva in front of all the assembled guests. Sati, unable to bear the humiliation of her beloved husband and the disrespect shown by her father, declared that she would sever all ties with her father and, in an act of intense resolve, she immolated herself through the power of her yogic abilities.

When Shiva learned of Sati's death, he was overcome with grief and rage. In his fury, he created Virabhadra and Bhadrakali, fierce beings, from a lock of his matted hair. These fearsome warriors, accompanied by Shiva's ganas (attendants), stormed Daksha's yagna, causing widespread destruction. The gods and sages present were powerless against Shiva's wrath. Virabhadra decapitated Daksha and wreaked havoc upon the yagna. However, upon the pleas of the gods and Brahma, Shiva's anger subsided. He revived Daksha, but with a goat's head as a mark of his punishment and transformation. Daksha, humbled and remorseful, realized the greatness of Shiva and the error of his ways.

The story concludes with the rebirth of Sati as Parvati, the daughter of Himavan (the personification of the Himalayas) and his wife, Mena. Parvati, also devoted to Shiva, eventually marries him, thus continuing the divine cycle and re-establishing their union.

Sati's intense devotion to Shiva and her self-sacrifice highlight themes of loyalty and the spiritual power of love and devotion. Shiva's fierce response and the subsequent punishment of Daksha emphasize the theme of divine justice and the protection of dharma.

Chapter 11

Names 601 to 700

The lines 601-700 form the seventh enclosure. The avarana is asthakona; the Chakra is Sarvarogahara chakra 'cures all ills'.

601. Darandolitadeergakshi

She who has wavering wide eyes extending till her ears

602. Darahasojwalanmukhi

She who has a face that is always shining with a smile

603. Gurumurti

She who assumes the form of a Guru

The term Guru is derived from two roots:

- **Gu** – meaning "darkness" or "ignorance"
- **Ru** – meaning "light" or "dispeller"

In a spiritual context, a guru is considered essential for a disciple's journey toward enlightenment and self-realization as he provides instruction, inspiration, and initiation into spiritual practices. Literally, guru can also mean heavy or weighty, symbolizing the significance and profound impact of the guru's teachings on the disciple.

604. Gunanidhi

She is a treasure house of all good traits

605. Gomata

She is the form of Kamadhenu, the mother of all cows

Kamadhenu, the "wish-fulfilling cow," holds a deeply significant place in Indian mythology, religion, and culture. In Hindu tradition, Kamadhenu is considered the mother of all cows and a symbol of abundance, prosperity, and divine grace. She is said to have emerged during the churning of the ocean (Samudra Manthan), a pivotal event in Hindu cosmology that brought forth various divine entities and treasures.

Kamadhenu is depicted as possessing all the deities within her body and is an embodiment of the Vedas. As the mother of all cows, Kamadhenu is revered not only for her miraculous powers but also for her role in sustaining life on earth through the provision of milk, which is considered a complete food in many Indian traditions. The cow is venerated as a sacred animal, and Kamadhenu represents the epitome of this sanctity. She is associated with the goddess Lakshmi, the deity of wealth and prosperity, and is worshipped in rituals seeking material and spiritual wealth. The reverence for cows in India, symbolized by Kamadhenu, reflects a broader ethical and spiritual framework where all living beings are respected and cared for.

606. Guhajanmabhu

She is seated in the cave known as our heart

607. Deveshi

She is the ruler of all the Devatas

608. Dandanitishta

She who administers justice by meting out the necessary punishment

609. Daharakasha roopini

She who resides in the cave of our heart as ether

The vast, all-encompassing external space that we can see with our eyes is known as Chidakasha. The inner space within us is called Daharakasha.

610. Pratipan mukhya rakanta tithi mandala pujita

She who is worshipped for fifteen days from the first day of the full moon

The names of the months in the Indian calendar are derived from the star in which the full moon appears during that month. In the month of Jyeshta, the full moon is in the star Jyeshta. Similarly, in Vaishaka, the full moon is in the star Vishaka. During Ashwayuja Pournima, the moon is in the star Ashwini.

Ashwini is considered the most important as it is the first among the 27 stars. Therefore, the full moon in the month of Ashwayuja is deemed the most significant and is called Mukhya Rakanta. This month, falling around September-October, is also when the Devi Navaratri worship, lasting for 9 nights, takes place. The full moon following the Navaratri celebrations is considered the most important of the year.

611. Kalatmika

She who is the soul of art

She is the atma for all the 16 phases of moon.

In the context of human life, the 16 kalas represent the stages or aspects that an individual passes through. These 16 kalas are associated with the moon, as the moon is said to have 16 phases from new moon to full moon and back. They are listed below:

1. **Amrita**: Immortality or nectar of life, symbolizing the vital essence of existence
2. **Manada**: Bestower of honor, representing the development of self-respect and dignity
3. **Pusha**: Nourishment, symbolizing physical and emotional growth
4. **Tusti**: Satisfaction, representing the fulfillment of basic needs and desires
5. **Pushti**: Thriving or prosperity, indicating flourishing health and well-being
6. **Rati**: Pleasure, representing the experience of joy and sensual gratification
7. **Dhrti**: Steadfastness, symbolizing perseverance and determination
8. **Sasini**: Energy or vigor, representing physical and mental vitality
9. **Kanti**: Radiance, indicating the development of inner and outer beauty
10. **Jyotsna**: Illumination, symbolizing enlightenment and the quest for knowledge
11. **Sri**: Prosperity or wealth, representing material and spiritual abundance
12. **Prabha**: Splendor, indicating the manifestation of one's inner light
13. **Smriti**: Memory, representing the ability to retain and recall knowledge
14. **Medha**: Intelligence, symbolizing wisdom and cognitive abilities
15. **Apyayani**: Integration, representing the synthesis of experiences and knowledge
16. **Vritti**: Existence or livelihood, indicating the full expression of one's life purpose and activities.

These kalas collectively represent the complete and harmonious development of a person encompassing physical, mental, emotional, and spiritual growth. They are seen as essential aspects of the journey toward self-realization and enlightenment.

612. Kalanatha

She is the master of all the phases of existence

613. Kavyalapavinodini

She who delights in poetry

614. Sachamara ramavani savya dakshina sevita

She is attended on either side by Lakshmi and Saraswati

615. Adishakti

She is the primordial energy

616 and 617. Ameyatma

She is immeasurable and in the form of all-pervading soul

618. Parama

She who is the most supreme

619. Pavanakriti

Her form is holy and sanctifying

620. Aneka koti brahmanda janani

She is the mother to infinite universes

621. Divya vigraha

She has a divine body.

With this the Brahma-vidya upadesha, that began at nama 583, ends. Now the initiation into the Balatripurasundari vidya begins.

622. Klim kari

She who is the personification of the bija Kleem

Kleem is the middle portion (madhya kuta) of Balatripurasundari mantra and is known as the Kamaraja bija as it fulfils all desires.

Kleem consists of three syllables – Ka, La, and Eem. Ka symbolizes Paramatma, La represents the earth element, encompassing all individual beings on earth, and thus signifies the Jeevatma, the individual soul. Eem stands for Lakshmi, the embodiment of the wealth of knowledge.

623. Kevala

She who is the absolute

624. Guhya

She who is most secretive in form and meaning

Guhya also implies that She resides in the cave called the heart.

625. Kaivalya padadayini

She who bestows absolute liberation

There are several paths and types of salvation described in various Hindu texts and traditions. Among these, five prominent types of salvation are:

- Kaivalya means "isolation". It is the state of absolute independence and self-realization where the soul is completely free from the influence of prakriti and its three gunas. Predominantly discussed in the Yoga and Samkhya philosophies, Kaivalya is the ultimate goal of Yoga, where the soul realizes its true nature and exists in its pure form.
- Salokya or "dwelling in the same realm" refers to the state of residing in the same realm as the deity worshipped by the devotee. This form of liberation is common in Vaishnavism and Shaivism, where devotees attain the same world as their chosen deity, such as Vaikuntha (Vishnu's abode) or Kailasa (Shiva's abode).

- Samipya means "proximity." It signifies being close to the deity or being in the intimate presence of the deity. This type of liberation emphasizes the devotee's close association with the deity, experiencing divine companionship and favor.
- Sarupya means "similarity in appearance." It refers to attaining a form similar to that of the deity worshipped. In this form of salvation, the devotee takes on the divine qualities and appearance of the deity, signifying spiritual transformation and oneness in form.
- Sayujya means "union" or "complete absorption." It denotes the state of complete union with the deity, where the soul merges with the supreme divine consciousness. This type of liberation is considered the highest form of moksha in many traditions. The soul achieves total oneness with the deity, losing its individual identity and experiencing absolute bliss and unity.

626. Tripura

She who is the creator of all triads

In Hindu philosophy, several important triads (triple sets of concepts) are foundational to understanding its complex and rich traditions. These triads represent various aspects of the cosmos, divinity, human nature, and spiritual practice. Here are some of the most significant triads:

1. Trimurti

- **Brahma**: The Creator
- **Vishnu**: The Preserver
- **Shiva**: The Destroyer

2. Tridevi

- **Saraswati**: Goddess of Knowledge and Arts, consort of Brahma
- **Lakshmi**: Goddess of Wealth and Prosperity, consort of Vishnu
- **Parvati (or Durga/Kali)**: Goddess of Power and Love, consort of Shiva

3. Three Gunas

- **Sattva**: Purity, harmony, and balance
- **Rajas**: Activity, passion, and dynamism
- **Tamas**: Inertia, darkness, and chaos

4. Three Paths to Liberation (Marga)

- **Karma Yoga**: The path of selfless action and duty
- **Bhakti Yoga**: The path of devotion and love for the divine
- **Jnana Yoga**: The path of knowledge and wisdom

5. Three Major Texts (Prasthanatrayi)

- **Bhagavad Gita**: A philosophical dialogue between Krishna and Arjuna on the battlefield of Kurukshetra.
- **Upanishads**: Philosophical treatises that explore the nature of reality and the self.
- **Brahma Sutras**: A set of aphorisms that systematize and interpret the teachings of the Upanishads.

6. Three Aspects of the Self

- **Sthula Sharira**: The gross physical body
- **Sukshma Sharira**: The subtle body, including mind, intellect, and ego
- **Karana Sharira**: The causal body, the seed of existence

7. Three Worlds (Lokas)

- **Bhurloka**: The earthly realm
- **Bhuvarloka**: The intermediate space, including the atmosphere
- **Swarloka**: The heavenly realm

627. Trijagad vandya

She is revered in all the three worlds

628. Trimurti

She who manifests as the trinity of Brahma, Vishnu and Shiva.

629. Tridasheshwari

She is the ruler of the three stages

The 3 states of waking, dream and deep sleep are the tridashas.

630. Tryakshari

She is in the form of three letters

Balatripurasundari mantra is composed of 3 letters – Aim, Kleem and Sauh

631. Divya gandhadhya

She who emits a divine fragrance

632. Sindura tilakanchita

She wears a vermilion mark on the forehead

633. Uma

She who has AUM in her name

634. Shailendra tanaya

She is the daughter of the king of mountains

635. Gowri

She who is of a golden hue

636. Gandharva sevita

All the Gandharvas serve Her

Gandharvas are celestial beings renowned for their extraordinary musical abilities. They are considered the divine musicians who entertain the gods with their melodious music and songs. They serve as messengers between the gods and humans. They are also depicted as courtiers who attend the divine assemblies of deities, particularly in the court of Indra, the king of gods. Gandharvas are sometimes associated with natural elements like water and forests. They are believed to inhabit the heavens and certain natural spots on Earth.

637. Vishwa garbha

She whose womb contains the universe

638. Swarna garbha

Gold and other valuables are held within Her womb.

639. Avarada

She who destroys demons

640. Vagadishwari

She is the ruler of speech

She is the head of the eight Vasinee and other Vag Devis.

641. Dhyanagamya

She who can be attained by meditation

641. Aparichedya

She who is indivisible by anything

642. Gnanavigraha

She who is the form of knowledge

643. Sarva Vedanta samvedya

She who is known through all the Upanishads

644. Satyananda swaroopini

She who is the supreme knowledge and bliss

645. Lopamudrarchhita

She who is worshipped by Lopamudra

Lopamudra is a philosopher and wife of the sage Agastya. She is important in Sri Vidya as she visualized the Hadi Panchadasi mantra of the Srikula Shasta She was one of the prominent Brahmavadinis. The name Lopamudra signifies the loss (lopa) that the animals and plants suffered by giving their distinctive beauties (mudra's) when Agastya created her. Agastya took parts from various creatures possessing beauty such as eyes of the doe, the grace of the panther, the slenderness of the palm trees, the fragrance of the champaka flower, the softness of the feather on a swan's neck, etc., Agastya was taught the hymn of Lalita Sahasranama by Hayagriva only because Lopamudra was his wife.

648. Leela klupta brahmanda mandala

She for whom creation is merely a game

649. Adrushya

She who is invisible

650. Drushyaharita

She who cannot be perceived

651. Vignatri

She who has a special intelligence

652. Vedya varjita

She is a form of complete knowledge.

653. Yogini

She who is seen in the form of yoga

654. Yogada

She who can be reached through yoga

The earliest references to Yoga are found in the Rigveda. The term Yoga is derived from the Sanskrit root yuj, meaning to yoke or to unite.

The Upanishads, composed between 800-400 BCE, delve deeper into the philosophical aspects of Yoga, emphasizing meditation and the pursuit of self-realization. The Bhagavad Gita is a critical text that presents Yoga as a path to divine realization. It outlines various forms of Yoga, including Karma Yoga, Bhakti Yoga, and Jnana Yoga. Written by Patanjali around the 2nd century BCE, the Yoga Sutras systematize Yoga practice into an eight-limbed path (Ashtanga Yoga). The 8 limbs of yoga are described below:

1. Yama (Ethical Disciplines) refers to moral and ethical guidelines for interacting with the external world. They are foundational principles for living a righteous life.

Components:

Ahimsa: Non-violence or compassion

Satya: Truthfulness

Asteya: Non-stealing or honesty

Brahmacharya: Moderation or celibacy

Aparigraha: Non-possessiveness or non-greed

2. Niyama (Self-Discipline) consists of personal observances and practices for self-discipline and spiritual growth.

Components:

Saucha: Purity or cleanliness

Santosha: Contentment or satisfaction

Tapas: Self-discipline or austerity

Svadhyaya: Self-study or study of sacred texts

Ishvara Pranidhana: Surrender to a higher power or devotion

3. Asana (Postures) are physical postures designed to strengthen and purify the body, making it suitable for prolonged meditation.

4. Pranayama (Breath Control) refers to the control and regulation of breath. It involves techniques to expand and regulate the prana (life force) within the body.

5. Pratyahara (Withdrawal of Senses) It helps in calming the mind and turning attention away from external stimuli, facilitating deeper concentration and meditation.

6. Dharana (Concentration) is the practice of concentration on a single point or object. It trains the mind to become more focused essential for achieving deeper meditation and insight.

7. Dhyana (Meditation) is characterized by continuous and uninterrupted flow of concentration.

8. Samadhi (Enlightenment or Bliss) is the final stage of Yoga, where the practitioner experiences a state of profound unity and bliss, merging with the object of meditation.

655. Yogya

Meaning – She can be reached through practices of yoga.

656. Yogananda

She is the bliss enjoyed by yogis

657. Yugandhara

She who supports all the yugas

In Hindu cosmology, time is divided into four distinct epochs known as the Yugas. Each Yuga represents a different phase in the moral and spiritual development of humanity, with a corresponding decline in virtue and righteousness. These Yugas form a cyclical framework, with each age gradually leading to the next in a repeating cycle. Here is an overview of the four Yugas:

1. Satya Yuga is the first and most auspicious of the four Yugas. It is characterized by truth, virtue, and righteousness. During this age, dharma (righteousness) is fully practiced, and there is a high level of spiritual purity.
2. Treta Yuga follows the Satya Yuga and marks a gradual decline in virtue and spirituality. Though still righteous compared to the subsequent Yugas, it is characterized by the beginning of moral and spiritual decline.
3. Dvapara Yuga marks a further decline in virtue and righteousness compared to the previous Yugas. During this age, moral and spiritual decline is more pronounced, and people become more involved in material pursuits.
4. Kali Yuga is the final and most degenerate age in the Yuga cycle. It is characterized by the greatest decline in virtue, spiritual practices, and morality. It is considered the age of darkness and ignorance.

The Yugas follow a cyclical pattern, where the end of Kali Yuga leads to the beginning of a new Satya Yuga, restarting the cycle. This cycle is known as Chaturyuga.

658. Icchashakti Gnanashakti Kriyashakti swarupini

She who is the form of the 3 energies of desire, wisdom and action

Iccha Shakti, Jnana Shakti, and Kriya Shakti represent three fundamental aspects of Shakti. Iccha Shakti is the power of will and desire, driving the impulse to create and act. It embodies the ability to set intentions and pursue goals, fueling creativity and manifestation. Jnana Shakti, on the other hand, is the power of knowledge and wisdom. It grants insight into the nature of reality, enhancing discernment and understanding. This aspect of Shakti provides the intellectual and spiritual clarity needed to guide and inform one's actions and desires. Finally, Kriya Shakti represents the power of action and transformation. It is responsible for the execution of intentions and the physical manifestation of desires. This shakti governs the dynamic process of change, translating ideas into tangible outcomes.

Together, these three Shaktis are interconnected, with Iccha Shakti initiating desires, Jnana Shakti providing the wisdom to guide those desires, and Kriya Shakti realizing them through action. In the Shakta tradition, these aspects are often personified in Devi who embodies these energies in her role as the creator, sustainer, and transformer of the universe.

659. Sarvadhara

She is the support for everything in creation.

660. Suprathistha

She is firmly established

661. Sadasadroopadharini

She who is the form of being and non-being

662. Ashtamurthi

She who is eight formed

The term Ashtamurthi refers to the eight principal manifestations or forms of Shiva. Here is a overview of the Ashtamurthis:

1. Sadyojata is the form of Shiva associated with creation and the manifestation of the universe. He is often depicted as having a serene and youthful appearance
2. Vamadeva represents the nurturing and compassionate aspect of Shiva. This form is linked with preservation and sustenance.
3. Aghora is the fierce and destructive form of Shiva, associated with dissolution and transformation. He is often depicted with a fearsome appearance.
4. Tatpurusha is the aspect of Shiva that is associated with the process of concealment and the ultimate transcendental reality. This form represents the highest and most abstract aspect of Shiva.

5. Ishana is the form of Shiva that embodies the principle of omnipresence and control. He is often depicted as a benevolent and guiding force.
6. Rudra is a form of Shiva associated with storm and wrath.
7. Mahadeva is a generalized form of Shiva representing his supreme and universal nature.
8. Parameshvarais the supreme lord of all deities, representing the ultimate divine authority and supreme consciousness.

663. Ajajetri

She who helps conquer ignorance.

664. Lokayatra vidhayini

She who directs the course of the world's journey

665. Ekakini

She who is all alone

666. Bhooma roopa

She who is the aggregate of all things

667. Nirdvaita

She who is without duality

668. Dvaitavarjita

She who removes feelings of duality

We now step into Savitri-vidya This is the knowledge pertaining to the Sun God and the namas 669 to 700 teach this.

669. Annada

She grants food to all the beings.

In traditional Hindu dietary practices and Ayurvedic principles, the purity of food is considered essential for maintaining health and spiritual well-being. Food can become impure or unsuitable for consumption due to various defects or doshas. Three primary types of defects that can render food impure are:

1. Jati Dosha refers to the inherent defect or impurity related to the type or category of the food itself. This defect arises from the nature of the food item or its origin. Food that is inherently considered impure or inappropriate according to traditional dietary guidelines, such as certain types of meat or alcohol. Food obtained from questionable or unclean sources, or food that is known to have been prepared in unsanitary conditions.

2. Ashraya Dosha refers to defects related to the conditions or circumstances under which the food is prepared, stored, or served. It focuses on the adherence to proper procedures and the cleanliness of the environment. Food prepared in an unclean or contaminated environment, or by individuals who are not following proper hygiene practices. Food that is improperly stored, leading to contamination or spoilage.

3. Nimitta Dosha refers to defects related to the specific circumstances or causes that render the food impure. This includes the intentions or actions of those involved in the food's preparation or offering. Food prepared with malicious intent or offered in a context that involves negative or harmful purposes.

670. Vasuda

She who is the giver of wealth to all

671. Vriddha

She is fully grown and mature in form

672. Brahmatmaikya svaroopini

She who is the form of Brahman unified with the Atman

673. Brihati

Her form is vast

674. Brahmani

She is the wife of Shiva

Shiva is considered as a brahmin while Vishnu is seen as a kshatriya. The Chandogya Upanishad says: Thou art brahmana among the Devas. The Linga Purana also says: The divine Shambhu is Brahmana and the deity of Brahmanas. As wife of Shiva, She is Brahmani.

675. Brahmi

She is the wife of Brahma

676. Brahmananda

She is a form of the supreme bliss

677. Balipriya

She is pleased when sacrifices are offered to Her.

Bali is not to be understood as animal sacrifice. Here, it refers to Pooja and the articles which are offered as part of the worship. She accepts them with delight.

678. Bhasha roopa

She who is the form of languages

679. Brihat sena

She has a mighty army

680. Bhava bhava vivarjita

She is beyond the states of existence and non-existence

681. Sukharadhya

She can be worshipped comfortably

682. Shubhakari

She bestows auspiciousness

683. Shobhana sulabhagati

She leads us on the easy path to salvation

684. Rajarajeshwari

She is the ruler of the king of kings

685. Rajyadayini

She who can gift kingdoms

686. Rajyavallabha

She is a capable ruler

687. Rajatkripa

She is full of compassion

688. Rajapitha niveshita nijashrita

She raises those who worship Her to a royal status

689. Rajyalakshmi

She is the form of the goddess of sovereignty

690. Koshanatha

She is the guardian of the treasure of the empire.

691. Chaturangabaleshwari

She is ruler presiding over four divisions of the army

Armies consist of four divisions – cavalry, elephants, chariots and infantry.

692. Samrajyadayini

She bestows a kingdom

693. Satyasandha

She who has unbroken promises

694. Sagaramekhala

She who has oceans as girdles

695. Deekshita

She who helps others gain knowledge

696. Daityashamani

She destroys all evil forces

697. Sarvalokavashankari

She holds all the worlds under Her sway.

698. Sarvarthadatri

She who bestows the four purusharthas

699. Savitri

She is the cause for the illumination of the Sun

700. Sachidananda rupini

She is the form of existence, knowledge and bliss

Sachidananda combines three words:

- **Sat** refers to pure being or the eternal reality that underlies everything. It represents the aspect of Brahman as the ultimate, unchanging reality that is beyond the transient, impermanent nature of the material world.
- **Chit** represents the aspect of pure consciousness or awareness. It is the understanding that Brahman is not just existent, but also conscious, and that consciousness is fundamental to the nature of reality.
- **Ananda** refers to the ultimate bliss or supreme happiness that comes from the realization of one's true nature and unity with Brahman. It signifies the aspect of Brahman as the source of all joy and contentment.

Chapter 12

Names 701 to 800

The names from 701 to 800 form the eighth enclosure. The The Avarana is Trikona; the Chakra is Sarvasiddhiprada chakra, 'grants all attainments'.

701. Deshakalaparichchinna

She is undivided by space and time.

She is seen as having neither antecedence nor precedence. The Patanjali Yoga Sutra says: He is a teacher even to the ancestors because he is not defined by time. She is such that she is not limited in any way.

702. Sarvaga

She is omnipresent

703. Sarvamohini

She is bewildering

704. Saraswati

She is the form of the presiding deity of knowledge.

The three historical deities who are mentioned in this Sahasranama are Durga (190), Mahalakshmi (210) and Saraswati (704).

705. Shastramayi

She is the embodiment of all knowledge.

The term Shastra is used to denote a body of knowledge that provides guidance on a specific subject. They are classified into various categories depending on the subject matter they address. Some of the most prominent include:

- **Dharmashastra**: Texts that deal with dharma (moral and legal duties). The Manusmriti is the most well-known text in this category.
- **Arthashastra**: Treatises on politics, economics, and statecraft. The Arthashastra by Kautilya is a seminal work in this genre.
- **Kamasutra**: Texts on love, sexuality, and human relationships by Vatsyayana.
- **Natyashastra**: A treatise on drama, dance, and music, attributed to the sage Bharata.
- **Vyakarana**: Grammatical treatises that discuss the rules and structures of the Sanskrit language by Panini
- **Shilpashastra**: Texts on architecture and iconography.

Shastras include the Vedas and Upanishads.

706. Guhamba

She who dwells in a cave

707. Guhyaroopini

She who is the most secret form

Adi Shankaracharya writes in his commentary of Vishnu Sahasranama for the nama Guhya that it is a reference to:

- He who can be understood by secret Upanishads
- He dwells in the cave in the ether of the heart

The same meaning can be attributed to this nama.

708. Sarvopadhivinimukta

She who is devoid of limitations

709. Sadashivapativrata

She is a devoted wife to Shiva

710. Sampradayeshwari

She is the queen of sacred traditions.

711. Sadhu

She who is suitable

712. Ee

She is a form of Ee, the kamakala letter

When E is suffixed to a male name, it denotes the wife, sister or daughter. Subhadra, the daughter of Vasudeva is Vasudevi. Eshwara's cosort is Eshwari, etc., In this Sahasranama, there are three instances: Padmanabasahodari (280), Narayani (298) and Vaishnavi (892).

Ee is the third letter of the Panchadasi mantra in Kadi Vidya.

713. Gurumandalaroopini

She is the unbroken lineage of Gurus

The traditional guru mandala is:

Sadashiva samarambham vyasa shankara madhyamam asmad acharya paryantam vande Guru paramparam

She represents all Gurus starting from Shiva to the entire succession leading up to our guru. The secret is handed down without interruption from teacher to student.

714. Kulottirna

She who transcends the sphere of the senses.

715. Bhagaradhya

She is worshipped by the Sun God

716. Maya

She is the form of illusion

Maya is a fundamental concept that refers to the cosmic illusion that creates the appearance of the phenomenal world. Maya is what causes the perception of multiplicity and diversity in the universe, leading us to believe that the material world is the ultimate reality. It is described as the power that makes the finite world appear real, even though it is ultimately an illusion when viewed from the perspective of the absolute reality. It has two primary functions: Avarana (veiling) and Vikshepa (projecting). It veils the true nature of Brahman and projects the world of names and forms, making it seem real.

717. Madhumati

She who is with honey or alcohol

The word made refers both to honey and alcohol. Both are offered depending on the marga that is followed. In the Vamachara marga, alcohol is one of the five Panchamakaras. In the Dakshinachara marga, honey is used as an offering.

718. Mahi

She is form of earth

719. Ganamba

She is the mother of all ganas

The term Gana refers to groups or assemblies in various contexts. In Shaivism, the ganas are the attendants or followers of Shiva. They are led by Ganesha. In Sanskrit grammar, the term is used to refer to a class or group of roots that share a common pattern of conjugation or declension.

In a broader religious context, the term refers to assemblies of devotees or participants in a ritual. In Vedic astrology, the concept of ganas is used to categorize human temperaments. There are three types:

Deva Gana: People belonging to this category are believed to have a gentle, kind, and refined nature.

Manusha Gana: The human or earthly temperament. Individuals in this category are thought to have a balanced nature, with traits that are neither too aggressive nor too passive.

Rakshasa Gana The demonic or aggressive temperament. Those under this classification are considered to have a fierce, assertive, and sometimes rebellious nature.

720. Guhyakaradhya

She is worshipped through secretive means

721. Komalangi

She who has a delicate and pleasing form

722. Gurupriya

She who has affection towards the teacher

723. Svatantra

She who enjoys freedom

She possesses all the Tantras as her own, including the Shaiva, Vaishnava, and Ganapatya Tantras, which express the pride of Devi and are thus regarded as hers. To worship Ganapati and other deities, they must first be installed in their respective idols or yantras through Pranaprathishta, which infuses them with life energy that is, in essence, Devi herself. Only with her energy can the worship of other gods be performed. One commentator explains that since the Tantras dedicated to other deities are also under her domain, she is therefore known as Svatantra (independent or self-governed).

724. Sarvatantreshi

She is the ruler of all tantras

725. Dakshinamurthiroopini

She is the form of Dakshinamurthi

Dakshinamurti is Shiva depicted seated under a banyan tree, in the yogic posture of Virasana or Padmasana. His right hand is shown in the Jnana Mudra (with the thumb and index finger touching to form a circle, symbolizing the unity of the Jivatma and Paramatma.) The direction south is associated with death and change in Hindu cosmology, but also with the path of liberation. By facing south, Dakshinamurti symbolizes the dispelling of ignorance and the illumination of true knowledge. He is shown with his right foot placed on a small, dwarf-like figure called Apasmara, who represents ignorance or ego. This symbolizes the suppression of ignorance through wisdom.

Dakshinamurti is considered the embodiment of the ultimate teacher who imparts knowledge directly to the disciples, especially through the medium of silence. This silent transmission of wisdom is believed to be the highest form of teaching, transcending words and concepts. Dakshinamurti is said to have taught four great sages – Sanaka,

Sanandana, Sanatana, and Sanatkumara through silence, revealing the truth of Brahman to them. This illustrates the power of silent, experiential knowledge over intellectual discourse.

726. Sanakadi samaradhya

She is worshipped by the four great sages – Sanaka, Sanandana, Sanatana, and Sanatkumara

727. Shivajnana pradayani

She bestows the knowledge of Shiva

With this the initiation into Saraswati vidya, which began with nama 701, is complete. Dakshinamurty is a form of knowledge and hence acquiring the knowledge of Shiva concludes this upasana.

728. Chitkala

She who is the divine consciousness in all beings

729.Anandakalika

She who is in the form of a bud of divine bliss

Kalika is the tender bud that is yet to blossom. This bud blooms into a flower resulting in infinite bliss.

730. Premaroopa

She is an embodiment of love

731. Priyamkari

She who grants what is dear to Her devotees

732. Namaparayanapreeta

She who is pleased with the litany of Her names

733. Nandividya

She manifests the scripture that deals with absorption into Her

The absorption or merging of the mind is referred to as laya. The ultimate aim of persistent nama japa and the performance of music is the dissolution of the mind, which leads to the experience of true bliss. Nandi symbolizes this concept of laya. When Shiva performs tandava, Nandi accompanies him by playing the Mridangam. As the master of this scripture on merging (Laya Shastra), Nandi embodies the essence of this dissolution.

734. Nateshwari

She is the Shiva who is performing tandava

735. Mithyajagadadishtana

She is the cause of and refuge from for this illusory universe

This name is discussed at length in the first chapter.

In the book Lalita Sahasranama Stotram—An Insight, Swami Shantananda Puri shares a memorable incident about a recent Sankaracharya. One day, the Sankaracharya was performing his daily ritual, offering flowers to the Divine Mother while chanting the Lalita Sahasranamavali. Usually, the entire worship would take around one to one and a half hours. However, on this particular day, the ritual extended for more than four hours, continuing until 3 p.m., leaving the devotees eagerly waiting for their meal.

When someone finally approached the Jagadguru, they found him deep in meditation, eyes closed, completely unaware of the time and surroundings. He had been repeatedly chanting the 735th name, "Mithya Jagadadhishtana," for hours. After being gently interrupted and informed of the delay, the Pontiff laughed and quickly concluded the ritual by reciting the final two names, ending with "Om Sri Lalitambikayai Namah." The episode highlights the profound power of a single divine name, capable of elevating one's consciousness to such an extent that the physical world fades away.

736. Muktida

She who is the bestower of salvation

737. Muktiroopini

She who is the form of salvation itself

738. Lasyapriya

She who is fond of dance

739. Layakari

She who is the cause of absorption

740. Lajja

She who is the form of modesty

741. Rambhadivandita

She who is worshipped by Rambha and other celestial damsels

742. Bhavadhavasudhavrushti

She who is the rain of nectar falling on a fire that burns away the jungle of sin

743. Paparanyadhavanala

She is the fire who destroys sins

744. Daurbhagyatulavatula

She is the gale that blows away misfortunes which are like cotton ball.

Dourbhagya refers to misfortune, bad luck, or adversity in life. The concept encompasses several types of misfortunes that may arise due to karmic influences, planetary positions, or other spiritual and material factors. Here are some of the different types of dourbhagya:

1. Artha Dourbhagya (Financial Misfortune)

This type of misfortune affects a person's wealth, finances, and material prosperity.

- **Examples:** Sudden financial losses, debts, poverty, or inability to sustain wealth.

- **Astrological Influences:** Weaknesses or malefic influences on the 2nd house (house of wealth) or the 11th house (house of gains) in a personâ€™s horoscope can lead to artha dourbhagya.

2. Arogya Dourbhagya (Health Misfortune)

This refers to misfortune related to health and well-being.

Examples: Chronic illnesses, accidents, mental health issues, or poor physical condition.

Astrological Influences: Malefic planets affecting the 6th house (house of health), the 8th house (house of longevity and sudden events), or the placement of the Moon and Ascendant (which indicate physical and mental health) can lead to arogya dourbhagya.

3. Vidya Dourbhagya (Educational Misfortune)

This type of misfortune impacts education, learning, and intellectual growth.

- **Examples**: Inability to complete education, poor academic performance, or lack of opportunities for learning.
- **Astrological Influences**: Malefic influences on the 4th house (house of education) and 5th house (house of intellect and higher learning) can contribute to vidya dourbhagya.

4. Santan Dourbhagya (Misfortune Related to Children)

This refers to difficulties or misfortunes related to having or raising children.

- **Examples**: Infertility, complications in childbirth, health issues of children, or problems in the parent-child relationship.
- **Astrological Influences**: Issues in the 5th house (house of children) and its lord, along with malefic planetary influences, can lead to *santan* dourbhagya.

5. Soubhagya Dourbhagya (Marital Misfortune)

This type of misfortune affects marriage and relationships, particularly the happiness and stability of married life.

- **Examples**: Delayed marriage, unhappy marital life, separation, or divorce.
- **Astrological Influences**: Afflictions to the 7th house (house of marriage), its lord, and Venus (the planet governing relationships) can cause soubhagya dourbhagya.

6. Yatra Dourbhagya (Misfortune in Journeys)

This refers to difficulties and misfortunes encountered during travel or in the pursuit of specific ventures.

- **Examples**: Travel-related accidents, delays, cancellations, or unsuccessful ventures.
- **Astrological Influences**: Afflictions to the 3rd house (house of short journeys) and the 9th house (house of long-distance travel) can lead to yatra dourbhagya.

7. Karma Dourbhagya (Professional Misfortune)

This type of misfortune impacts one' s career, professional success, and reputation.

- **Examples**: Job loss, career stagnation, failure in business, or loss of reputation.
- **Astrological Influences**: Malefic influences on the 10th house (house of career and profession) and its lord can result in karma dourbhagya.

8. Bhagya Dourbhagya (General Misfortune)

This encompasses broader misfortunes that may not be categorized specifically under the other types but affect one's overall luck and life path.

- **Examples**: Continuous bad luck, unexpected misfortunes, or life not progressing despite efforts.

- **Astrological Influences**: Afflictions to the 9th house (house of luck and fortune) and its lord can lead to bhagya dourbhagya

745. Jara dhvanta raviprabha

She who dispels the problems of old age with Her effulgence.

746. Bhagyabdi chandrika

She is the moonlight illuminating the ocean of good fortune

747. Bhakta chitta keki ghanaghana

She who is like the cloud that excites peacocks to dance

748. Roga parvata adhambholi

She is the thunderbolt that can dispel diseases which are as large as mountains.

749. Mrityudarukutarika

She is the axe that cuts down the tree of death.

750. Maheshwari

She who is the supreme sovereign

751. Mahakali

She who takes on the form of Kali

752. Mahagrasa

She who is the great devourer

The entire universe is like a big morsel of food when she devours all the 36 tatvas as Parahanta.

753. Mahashana

She consumes the entire universe

754. Aparna

She who is without debt

Parvati performed rigorous sadhana to win Shiva as her husband. At first, she sustained herself only on uncooked food, then for a while, she survived on fallen leaves (parna). Eventually, she gave up eating even leaves, becoming known as Aparna. This name signifies her power to liberate her devotees from all forms of indebtedness.

755. Chandika

She who gets angry

756. Chandamundasura nishoodini

She who destroyed Chanda and Munda

757. Ksharaksharatmika

She is both impermanent and eternal

758. Sarvalokeshi

She is the ruler of all the worlds

759. Vishwadharini

She supports the universe

760. Trivarga dhatri

She bestows the triad of human values

The Tri-vargas are Dharma, Artha and Kama – aspiration to commit meritorious acts, the capacity to act and the means to complete them.

761. Subhaga

She who grants auspiciousness

762. Tryambaka

She who has three eyes

The same meaning as conveyed in Trinaya (453) and Trilochana (477) referring to Sun, Moon and Agni.

763. Trigunatmika

She who is the form of the three gunas

Trigunas are the three fundamental attributes that govern human nature and the material world. They are:

- **Sattva** is the quality of balance, purity, wisdom, and tranquility. It represents clarity, truth, and knowledge, leading to peace and spiritual growth.
- **Rajas** is characterized by activity, desire, passion, and movement. It drives change, ambition, and a pursuit of goals, often associated with restlessness and attachment.
- **Tamas** is the quality of darkness, inertia, ignorance, and lethargy. It represents confusion, delusion, and a lack of clarity, leading to inactivity and destruction.

764. Svargapavargada

She who bestows either heaven or salvation based on merit

765. Shuddha

She who is ever pure.

766. Japapushpa Nibhakriti

She who has complexion like the hibiscus

767. Ojovati

She who is full of vitality

Please refer to the dhatus where Ojas is discussed as the 8th dhatu.

768. Dyutidhara

She who is full of splendour

769. Yajnaroopa

She who embodies sacrifices

There are five types of sacrifices that a human being can be involved in:

- Deva Yagna – praying to Devatas
- Pitru Yagna – praying to ancestors
- Brahma Yagna – chanting of Vedas
- Manushya Yagna – offerings to fellow humans as service to society
- Bhoota Yagna – helping other living beings on the planet

770. Priyavrata

She who is fond of vows

771. Duraradhya

She who is difficult to worship

772. Duradharsha

She who is hard to resist

773. Patalikusumapriya

She who loves the red trumpet flowers

It is said in the Padma Purana that while Shiva loves the Bilwa tree (Crataeva religiosa), Devi's favourite is the Patali flower (Bignonia suaveolens).

774. Mahati

She who is vast

775. Merunilaya

She who dwells in Mount Meru

776. Mandara kusumapriya

She who loves the hibiscus flower

777. Viraradhya

She who is worshipped by the valiant

778. Viradroopa

She who is the form of the cosmic whole

779. Viraja

She who is devoid of rajas guna

780. Vishwatomukhi

She who has faces in all directions

781. Pratyagroopa

She who is visible to those who look within themselves

782. Parakasha

She who is the form of ether

783. Pranada

She bestows life to all

784. Pranaroopini

She who is the form of life

785. Martanda Bhairavaradhya

She who is adored by Shiva in Martandabhairava form

786. Mantrininyastarajyadhoo

She who hands over authority to Shyamala

787. Tripureshi

She who is the ruler of Tripura

Here Tripura refers individual soul, the inner witness and the supreme consciousness. She rules over them all.

788. Jayatsena

She leads a victorious army

789. Nistraigunya

She is devoid of the three gunas

790. Parapara

She who is the form of Brahman called Para (absolute), Para (relative) and Parapara (both absolute and relative)

With this the Mangala-chandi-vidya upasana, which began with the 750th name, concludes. We are now stepping into Kapardini-vidya-upasana.

791. Satyajananadaroopa

She who is the form of truth, wisdom and bliss

792. Samarasya parayana

She who is equal in nature with Shiva

793. Kapardini

She is the wife Shiva in Kapardi form

Kapardi refers to the aspect of Shiva where he is depicted with matted hair (jata) coiled on the top of his head. The term is derived from the Sanskrit word Kaparda, which means "one with matted hair." This form is closely associated with Shiva's ascetic nature, symbolizing his renunciation, control over desires, and connection with nature.

794. Kalamala

She who wears the 64 arts as a garland

795. Kamadhuk

She who is the form of the wish-fulfilling cow

796. Kamaroopini

She who can assume any form at will

797. Kalanidhi

She is a treasure house of arts

798. Kavyakala

She who is the form of poetic art

799. Rasagna

She who knows all the tastes

Rasas refer to the six primary tastes that are recognized in Ayurveda and Indian culinary traditions. These tastes influence not only the physical body but also the mind and emotions. Each Rasa has specific effects on the body and can be used to balance the three doshas (Vata, Pitta, and Kapha) in Ayurveda. The six Rasas in food are:

- **Madhura (Sweet)**:

  Taste: Sweetness

  Examples: Sugar, honey, milk, rice, fruits like mango and banana.

  Effects: Nourishing, cooling, and grounding. It increases strength, promotes longevity, and balances Vata and Pitta doshas while aggravating Kapha.

- **Amla (Sour)**:

  Taste: Sourness

  Examples: Citrus fruits like lemons and oranges, yogurt, tamarind, vinegar.

  Effects: Stimulates appetite and digestion. It balances Vata dosha but can aggravate Pitta and Kapha.

- **Lavana (Salty)**:

  Taste: Saltiness

  Examples: Salt, seaweed, salted foods.

  Effects: Aids digestion, enhances taste, and maintains water balance in the body. It balances Vata but can increase Pitta and Kapha doshas.

- **Katu (Pungent/Spicy)**:

  Taste: Spiciness or heat

  Examples: Chili peppers, black pepper, garlic, ginger, mustard.

  Effects: Stimulates digestion, clears sinuses, and improves circulation. It increases Pitta and Vata while decreasing Kapha.

- **Tikta (Bitter)**:

  Taste: Bitterness

  Examples: Bitter gourd, neem, fenugreek, kale.

  Effects: Detoxifying and purifying, helps in digestion, and reduces fat. It balances Pitta and Kapha but can increase Vata.

- **Kashaya (Astringent)**:

  Taste: Astringency or dryness

  Examples: Unripe bananas, pomegranate, chickpeas, green tea, cranberries.

  Effects: Cooling, drying, and firming. It balances Pitta and Kapha but can aggravate Vata.

800. Rasa sevadhih

She is a never-ending ocean of bliss

Chapter 13

Names 801 to 900

The names 801 to 900 of Lalita Sahasranama now takes us into the final and most important avarana. The avarana is the Bindu and the Chakra is Sarvanandamaya chakra (replete with bliss)

801. Pushta

She who is well nourished

802. Puratana

She who is primordial

803. Poojya

She is worthy of worship.

804. Pushkara

She who gives nourishment to all

805. Pushkareshshana

She who has beautiful eyes like lotus

806. Paramjyoti

She who is the supreme light

807. Paramdhama

She who is the supreme abode

808. Paramanu

She is the sub-atomic particle

809. Paratpara

She who is the most supreme of the supreme

810. Pashahasta

She who holds a noose in her hand

811. Pashahantri

She who liberates from bondage

812. Paramantravibhedini

She who destroys black magic

813. Moorta and 814. Amoorta

She is both with-form and without-form

815. Anityatripta

She who is satisfied even with our meagre offerings

816. Munimanasahamsika

She who swims like a swan in the lake of the minds of saints

817. Satyavrata

She who is vowed to truth

818. Satyaroopa

She who is eternal form of truth

819. Sarvantaryamini

She who is omniscient in the minds of all

820. Sati

She who is a chaste woman

821. Brahmani

She who instills life force in Brahma

822. Brahma

She who is the Brahman

823. Janani

She is the mother of creation

824. Bahuroopa

She who has many forms

825. Budharchita

She who is worshipped by the wise

826. Prasavitri

She who delivers the universe

A mother takes care of her child in five different ways:

- Janani (823) – she gives shape and makes a baby with the father's contribution

- Mata(457) – protects the life in her womb
- Prasavitri – at the appropriate time, she delivers the baby
- Vidhatree (337) – nourishes the baby
- Amba (985) – she protects during a crisis

827. Prachanda

She who is wrathful

The Taitireeya Upanishad says: For fear of Him the wind, fire and Sun so their respective duties. Therefore, anger is seen as a symbol of Brahman.

828. Ajna

She who is the form of order

She orders through the Vedas and Shastras and Her commands have to be followed.

829. Pratishta

She is the foundation of the universe

830. Prakatakriti

She who is visible to all in manifest form

831. Praneshwari

She is the ruler of the life force

The concept of Prana refers to the vital life force or energy that sustains life and governs the physical and mental functions of the body. It is said to manifest in the body in different forms, each responsible for specific functions.

Five Major Pranas (Pancha Pranas):

- **Prana:**

  Location: Chest and head.

  Function: Governs respiration, intake of breath, swallowing, and absorption of energy. It is the primary Prana, responsible for maintaining life by providing oxygen and energy to the body.

- **Apana:**

    Location: Lower abdomen and pelvic region.

    Function: Governs excretion, elimination, and downward-moving forces such as urination, defecation, childbirth, and menstruation.

- **Samana:**

    Location: Navel region.

    Function: Governs digestion and metabolism, balancing and distributing the energy from food. It is responsible for the assimilation of nutrients and the even distribution of Prana throughout the body.

- **Udana:**

    Location: Throat and upper chest.

    Function: Governs speech, self-expression, and the upward-moving energies. It is also associated with the ability to stand, speak, and other movements of the body. It is involved in the release of Prana at the time of death.

- **Vyana:**

    Location: Whole body.

    Function: Governs circulation, the movement of energy throughout the body, and the coordination of different bodily functions. It supports the activities of the other Pranas and ensures the proper circulation of blood and other fluids.

Five Minor Pranas (Upa-Pranas):

- **Naga:**

    Function: Governs burping, belching, and hiccups. It is related to the release of excess gas from the stomach.

- **Kurma:**

    Function: Governs the blinking and movement of the eyelids, as well as vision. It protects the eyes by controlling blinking and the reflex actions of the eyelids.

- **Krikara:**

  Function: Governs sneezing and the hunger and thirst reflexes. It protects the body by expelling irritants from the nasal passages and throat.

- **Devadatta:**

  Function: Governs yawning and sleep. It induces the body to take in extra oxygen during tiredness or boredom.

- **Dhananjaya:**

  Function: Governs the decomposition and preservation of the body. It is believed to remain in the body even after death, causing the body to decompose.

832. Pranadatri

She who bestows life

833. Panchashatpeetharoopini

She is the form of the 51 shakti peethas.

The Shakti Peethas are considered highly auspicious and powerful places of worship for devotees of the Goddess. They are spread across India, Pakistan, Bangladesh, Nepal, and Sri Lanka.

The temples are not only important pilgrimage sites but are also centers for spiritual practices and rituals dedicated to the divine feminine energy.

Each Shakti Peetha has a unique story and a particular deity (Shakti) associated with it, along with a corresponding Bhairava (form of Shiva) who protects the site.

Shakti Peethas in India

- **Kalighat** (West Bengal) – **Body Part:** Right Toes
- **Kamakhya** (Assam) – **Body Part:** Womb and Genitals
- **Kankalitala** (West Bengal) – **Body Part:** Waist

- **Tarapith** (West Bengal) – **Body Part**: Third Eye
- **Nalhateshwari** (West Bengal) – **Body Part**: Nostrils
- **Vibhash** (West Bengal) – **Body Part**: Left Ankle
- **Bakreshwar** (West Bengal) – **Body Part**: Portion Between Eyebrows
- **Kiratkona** (West Bengal) – **Body Part**: Left Ear
- **Sainthia** (West Bengal) – **Body Part**: Head
- **Nainativu** (Tamil Nadu) – **Body Part**: Anklets
- **Vimala** (Odisha) – **Body Part**: Navel
- **Jwalamukhi** (Himachal Pradesh) – **Body Part**: Tongue
- **Shaktipeeth** (Bihar) – **Body Part**: Left Breast
- Nashik (Maharashtra) Body **Part**: Chin
- **Tulja Bhavani** (Maharashtra) – **Body Part**: Right Shoulder
- **Amarnath** (Jammu and Kashmir) – **Body Part**: Throat
- **Vaishno Devi** (Jammu and Kashmir) – **Body Part**: Hand
- **Katyayani** (Gujarat) – **Body Part**: Back
- **Ujjain** (Madhya Pradesh) – **Body Part**: Upper Lip
- **Raja Rajeswari** (Tamil Nadu) – **Body Part**: Stomach
- **Mangla Gauri** (Bihar) – **Body Part**: Breast
- **Tripura Sundari** (Tripura) – **Body Part**: Right Foot
- **Kanya Kumari** (Tamil Nadu) – **Body Part**: Spine
- **Kalmadhav** (Madhya Pradesh) – **Body Part**: Hair
- **Lokhanath** (Odisha) – **Body Part**: Teeth
- **Manikyamba** (Andhra Pradesh) – **Body Part**: Right Shoulder
- **Chintpurni** (Himachal Pradesh) – **Body Part**: Feet
- **Kanchipuram** (Tamil Nadu) – **Body Part**: Backbone
- **Kashmir** (Jammu and Kashmir) – **Body Part**: Hair
- **Chandranath** (West Bengal) – **Body Part**: Right Thigh
- **Sugandha** (Odisha) – **Body Part**: Nose
- **Yamunotri** (Uttarakhand) – **Body Part**: Stomach
- **Mahur** (Maharashtra) – **Body Part**: Elbows
- **Ambaji** (Gujarat) – **Body Part**: Heart
- **Varanasi** (Uttar Pradesh) – **Body Part**: Earring
- **Danteshwari** (Chhattisgarh) – **Body Part**: Teeth

- **Shrishailam** (Andhra Pradesh) – **Body Part**: Neck
- **Shrikhetra** (Odisha) – **Body Part**: Right Toe
- **Saraswati** (Kashmir) – **Body Part**: Tongue
- **Chandika** (Madhya Pradesh) – **Body Part**: Head
- **Shakti Peethas in Bangladesh**
- **Bhairavparvat** (Sylhet) – **Body Part**: Left Anklet
- **Chhattal** (Chattogram) – **Body Part**: Right Arm
- **Jashoreshwari** (Khulna) – **Body Part**: Palms and Soles
- **Shri Shailam** (Sylhet) – **Body Part**: Neck

Shakti Peethas in Pakistan

- **Hinglaj** (Balochistan) – **Body Part**: Brahmarandhra (top of the head)
- **Shakti Peethas in Nepal**
- **Guhyeshwari** (Kathmandu) – **Body Part**: Both Knees

Shakti Peethas in Sri Lanka

- **Indrakshi** (Lankapuri) – **Body Part**: Anklets
- **Shakti Peethas in Tibet**
- **Karnat** (Tibet) – **Body Part**: Right Ear

Shakti Peethas in Myanmar

- **Chandranath** (Myanmar) – **Body Part**: Right Shoulder

Shakti Peethas in China

- **Manasthala** (China) – **Body Part**: Right Hand

Shakti Peethas in Afghanistan

- **Bhadreshwar** (Afghanistan) – **Body Part**: Left Ankle

834. Vishrunkhala

She who is unfettered

835. Viviktastha

She who dwells in secluded places where there are no human beings

836. Veeramata

She who is mother of heroes

837. Viyatprasoo

She who delivered ether

Shruti texts which explain evolution say that air came from ether, fire from air, water from fire and earth from water. Ether, the first element originated from Brahman.

838. Mukunda

She who bestows salvation

839. Muktinilaya

She who is the abode of salvation

840. Moolavigraharoopini

She who is the root for all energies

841. Bhavajna

She who knows our thoughts and intent

842. Bhavarogaghnee

She who cures the diseases of transmigratory existence

843. Bhavachakrapravartini

She who controls the wheel of transmigratory existence

844. Chandahsara

She who is the essence of all the Vedas

845. Shastrasara

She who is the essence of all shastras

846. Mantrasara

She who is the essence of all the mantras.

847. Talodari

She who has a slender waist

848. Udarakirti

Her fame extends everywhere

849. Uddhama Vaibhava

One who has boundless glory

850. Varnaroopini

One who is the form of letters

851. Janmamrityu jaratapta jana vishrantidayini

She who brings rest to humans consumed by the endless cycle of birth, decay and death

The period between death and the next birth is considered to be a temporary rest. This is the opposite of permanent rest which is ensured if there are no more rebirths. She bestows both types of rest on humans.

852. Sarvopanishadudghustha

She who is proclaimed in all the Upanishads

The term "Upanishad" is derived from roots upa (near), ni (down), and asad (to sit), indicating a student sitting down near a teacher to receive esoteric spiritual knowledge. Composed between approximately 800 BCE and 500 BCE, the Upanishads mark a significant shift from the ritualistic practices of the earlier Vedic tradition to a more introspective, philosophical inquiry into the nature of reality, the self, and the ultimate truth.

There are over 200 Upanishads, but traditionally, around 10 to 13 are considered the principal Upanishads due to their profound influence on

Hindu philosophy. These include the Isha, Kena, Katha, Prashna, Mundaka, Mandukya, Aitareya, Taittiriya, Chandogya, and Brihadaranyaka Upanishads. These texts explore deep metaphysical questions, such as the nature of existence, the relationship between the individual soul and the universal soul, the cycle of birth and rebirth, and the law of karma. They introduce key philosophical concepts like Moksha and Maya.

853. Shantyateetakalatmika

She who presides over the form of ether

The kala of ether tatva is known as Shantyateetha.

854. Gambheera

She whose depth cannot be fathomed.

855. Gaganantastha

She who pervades all ether

Ether here is a reference to Daharakasha (that which lies within the heart), Bhootakasha (one of the five primary elements) and Parakasha (the transcendent ether).

856. Garvita

She who has pride

857. Ganalolupa

She who is fond of music

858. Kalpanarahita

She is beyond imagination

859. Kashta

She who is the form mentioned conclusively in the Vedanta

860. Akanta

She who removes sin

861. Kantardhavigraha

She is one half of Shiva's Ardhanareeshwara form

862. Karyakarananirmukta

She is free from cause and effect

863. Kamakelitarangita

Shiva's love games reach Her as waves

864. Kanatkanakatatanka

She who wears gold ear studs

865. Leela Vigrahadharini

She who playfully assumes many forms

866. Aja

She who has no birth. She is eternal

867. Kshayavinirmukta

She who has no death. She is eternal

868. Mugdha

She who is beautiful

869. Kshipraprasadini

She who blesses instantly

870. Antarmukhasamaradhya

She can be reached through inner practices

In Sri Vidya, the body is imagined as the Sri Chakra and all worship is internal.

871. Bahirmukha sudurlabha

She cannot be attained by external worship

872. Trayi

She who is the embodiment of the three Vedas

Trayee or "the three," refers to the original trio of sacred texts: the Rig Veda, the Yajur Veda, and the Sama Veda. These texts formed the foundation of Vedic knowledge and were considered the primary sources of spiritual wisdom, ritual guidance, and hymns dedicated to various deities.

The Rig Veda is the oldest of the Vedas, consisting of hymns and praises to the gods, which were used during rituals. The Yajur Veda contains prose mantras and sacrificial formulas that were recited by the priests during the performance of rituals, while the Sama Veda is essentially a collection of verses mostly borrowed from the Rig Veda, but set to musical patterns for chanting during rituals.

At a much later period, Maharishi Veda Vyasa undertook the monumental task of reclassifying and systematizing the Vedic hymns. Recognizing the vastness and complexity of the Vedic knowledge, he divided the existing material into four distinct branches, thus adding the Atharva Veda to the original three. The Atharva Veda includes hymns, spells, and incantations related to healing, protection, and everyday life, reflecting a broader spectrum of human concerns beyond the strictly ritualistic content of the other three Vedas.

This reclassification by Veda Vyasa not only helped in preserving the Vedic knowledge more effectively but also made it more accessible and manageable for practitioners and scholars. As a result, the Vedas came to be known as the Chaturveda, or "the four Vedas," which continues to be the recognized structure of these ancient scriptures in Hindu tradition.

873. Trivarganilaya

She is the three vargas of Dharma, artha and kama.

Amongst the four-fold aims of life, the fourth – Moksha, has been removed here as it is not a pre-requisite for this worldly life.

874. Trishta

She who resides in all the trinities (the triads of Hinduism)

875. Tripuramalini

She who takes the form of the head of the Nikarpa Yogini Devis

Tripura Malini is the presiding deity for the antardashara chakra (inner group of 10 triangles) of the Srichakra.

876. Niramaya

She who is without disease

877. Niralamba

She who is without support

878. Swatmarama

She rejoices in herself

879. Sudhashruti

She who is a stream of nectar (bliss)

880. Samsarapankanirmagnasamuddharanapandita

She who is skilled in rescuing those drowning in the sorrow of transmigratory life

881. Yajnapriya

She who is fond of sacrifices

882. Yajnakartri

She is the energy that propels us to perform yagna

883. Yajamanasvaroopini

She is the one performing the yagna

884. Dharmadhara

She is the support for righteousness

885. Dhanadhyaksha

She who has authority over wealth

Kubera is he God of wealth, prosperity, and treasures. He is regarded as the king of the Yakshas, a race of nature-spirits associated with wealth and fertility. He is the guardian of the north (one of the Dikpalas). Kubera is depicted as a short, pot-bellied figure, adorned with jewels and carrying a money pot or a purse. He holds a mace, symbolizing his authority and power, and is sometimes shown riding a man, a symbol of his dominion over material wealth.

Kubera is one of Her twelve most devout worshippers and hence She has authority over wealth.

886. Dhanadhanyavivardhini

She increases wealth and grains

887. Viprapriya

She is fond of those who know the Vedas

Vipras are those who have knowledge of the Vedas and who chant them.

888. Vipraroopa

She is the form of the learned

889. Vshwabhramanakarini

She who causes the revolution of the earth

890. Vishwagrasa

She swallows the entire universe.

After dissolution, the universe is absorbed into Her. For this reason, she is addressed as Vishwagrasa

891. Vidrumabha

She who has the lustre of a coral

892. Vaishnavi

She who is the power of Vishnu

893. Vishnuroopini

She who is the form of Vishnu

894. Ayoni

She who has not originated from anything

895. Yoni nilaya

She who houses the origin of the universe

She is the form of Bindu which is at the centre of the Sri Chakra. This is Her abode.

896. Kutastha

She is firm and immobile

897. Kularoopini

She is the form of a sect called Kaulas

Here she is also the form of Muladhara Chakra

898. Viragoshtipriya

She is fond of the society of worshippers

899. Vira

She is valourous

900. Naishkarmya

She who has no relationship to actions

Chapter 14

Names 901 to 1000

Names 901-1000 are a culmination of the union of Shiva and Shakti and here we see the complete Sri Yantra with the four upward pointing triangles and five downward facing triangles.

901. Nadaroopini

She who is in the form of the primal mystical sound

The importance of nada lies in its ability to lead a person to a state of complete merger. Nada exists even before nama and indeed nama arises from nada. The practice of nada-upasana is a highly advanced and superior form of spiritual practice. After reaching the ninth enclosure, it is nada that facilitates the attainment of the merger with the Divine.

902. Vijnanakalana

She who can be reached through the experience that emerges out of knowledge

903. Kalya

She who is skilful in the arts

904. Vidagdha

She who is skilful

Each being is able to draw from that powerhouse, some amount of effulgence based on the strength of his/her individual power house. The strength of the individual powerhouses is determined based on balance of the goods deeds performed (punya).

905. Baindavasana

She who is seated in the bindu of the Sri Chakra

906. Tatvadika

She is beyond the tattvas

907. Tatvamayi

She is in the form of all the principles

908. Tattvamarthasvaroopini

She who is the essence of great statement Tattvamasi

909. Samaganapriya

She who is fond of songs from the Sama veda

The Chandogya Upanishad, which teaches the profound mantra Tattvamasi is part of the Sama Veda and since it contains such an essential teaching it is special to Her.

910. Sowmya

She who has a nature that is cooling like the Moon

911. Sadashivakutumbini

She who is the consort of Shiva

912. Savyapasavyamargastha

She who exists in both Savya and Apasavya paths

Savya and apasavya can be understood in many ways:

- Creation and destruction
- Waxing and waning fortnights (Shukla paksha and Krishna paksha)
- The rituals performed to appease the Gods (Devakarya) and rituals performed to appease the deceased fore-fathers (pitrukaryas)
- When the Sri Chakra is worshipped from Bhupura to Bindu, it is known as Savya and when worshipped from Bindu to Bhupura, it is Apasavya

913. Sarvapadvinivarini

She removes every type of danger

914. Svastha

She who is the head of heaven

915. Swabhavamadhura

She who has a sweet temperament

916. Dheera

She who is courageous

917. Dheerasamarchita

She who is worshipped by the courageous

918. Chaitanyarghya samaradhya

She who is worshipped with the offering of consciousness

Arghya is a ceremonial offering made during rituals and worship practices. It involves offering water, mixed with other sacred substances like flowers, rice, sandalwood, or turmeric, to a deity, the sun, or a respected person. The word is derived from the root "argha," meaning "worthy" indicating that this offering is made with respect and devotion.

To offer Arghya, the devotee cups water in their hands or uses a small vessel, recites specific mantras, and then pours the water into a designated place, such as on the ground, in a river, or in front of the deity's idol. The act of offering Arghya is a symbolic representation of giving back to nature and the divine, acknowledging the cyclical nature of life and the interdependence between humans and the cosmos.

919. Chaitanya kusuma priya

She who loves the offering of the flower of consciousness

The symbolic offerings (flowers) that one should present to the divine in the form of virtues and inner qualities, rather than just physical flowers are:

- **Ahimsa prathamam pushpam:**

  Ahimsa signifies that non-violence, in thought, word, and deed, is the most important offering to the divine

- **Pushpams-indriya-nigrahah:**

  The control of the indriyas (senses) is the second flower. This indicates the importance of self-discipline and restraint over one's senses as an offering to the divine.

- **Kshanti-pushpam:**

  Kshanti (forbearance or patience) is the third flower. Patience, especially in the face of difficulties or provocations, is considered a valuable offering.

- **Daya-pushpam:**

  Daya (compassion) is the fourth flower. Compassion towards all living beings is emphasized as an essential virtue in spiritual practice.

- **Jnana-pushpam param matam:**

  Jnana (knowledge or wisdom) is the fifth flower, regarded as the supreme offering. The pursuit and application of true knowledge and wisdom are seen as critical to spiritual growth.

- **Tapah-pushpam:**

  Tapas (austerity or penance) is the sixth flower. The practice of self-discipline and austerity is valued as a means to purify oneself and offer this purity to the divine.

- **Satya-pushpam:**

  Satya (truthfulness) is the seventh flower. Speaking and living in truth is considered a powerful offering to the divine.

- **Bhava-pushpam athasthamam:**

  Bhava (sincerity or pure intent) is the eighth and final flower. The attitude or intention behind one's actions and offerings is of utmost importance; sincerity is the essence of all offerings.

This nama emphasizes that the true offerings in spiritual practice are not material, but rather the cultivation of these virtues within oneself. Offering these "flowers" to the divine signifies a life led by high moral and ethical standards, self-control, compassion, and truthfulness, all driven by sincere intent. These virtues are seen as the highest forms of worship, more valuable than any physical offering.

920. Sadodita

She who is ever rising by self-illumination

921. Sadatushta

She who is ever contented

922. Tarunadityapatala

She is crimson coloured like the morning sun

923. Dakshinadakshinaradhya

She accepts worship from the educated and ignorant

924. Darasmeramukhambuja

She who has a lotus face with a radiant smile

925. Kaulini Kevala

She resides as the form of Kundalini.

Though everything is Her manifestation; She can be visualized internally in Her Kundalini aspect.

926. Anarghya kaivalya padadayini

She who confers the abode of priceless salvation

927. Stotrapriya

She loves to hear hymns of praise

Praise offered to Gods can be either Vaidika (based on Vedas) or Loukeeka (not based on Vedas)

All stotras need to have six characteristics:

- Invocation or Salutation (namaskar)
- Blessings that accrue (ashirwada)
- Praising the attainments (siddhanta)

- Praising the exploits (parakrama)
- Depicting the glory (vibhooti)
- Prayer for prosperity (prarthana)

In this Sahasranama, all the six characteristics are covered and examples are listed below:

- Invocation (Mahapujya, Trijagad Vandya, Vandaru janavatsala)
- Blessings that accrue (Sadyaprasadini, Bhakta Soubhagyadayini, Samrajyadayani)
- Final postulate (Atma vidya, Mitya jagadadhistana, Brahmatmaikya Swarupini)
- Praise (Chanda Mundasura Nishudhini, Bhandasurendranirmukta shastrapratyastra varshini, Uddama vaibhava)
- Glory (Anarghya Kaivalya Padadayini, Aneka koti brahmanda janani)
- Prayer (Dayamurti, Rakshakari, Dukhahantri)

928. Stutimati

She who has many praises sung about Her

929. Shrutisamstutavaibhava

She whose glory is praised in the Vedas

930. Manasvini

She who has a mind of Her own

931. Manavati

She who is very high minded

932. Maheshi

She who is the consort of Shiva

933. Mangalakruti

She who has an auspicious

In the Devi Mahatmayam, She is praised as:

Sarva mangala mangalye Shive sarvartha sadhike sharanye tryambake Gauri Narayani namostute.

934. Vishwamata

She is mother for the universe

935. Jagaddhatri

She is the ruler of the world

936. Vishalakshi

She who has large eyes

937. Viragini

She who is dispassionate

938. Pragalbha

She who is daring and powerful

939. Paramodara

She is extremely generous in nature

940. Paramoda

She who is supremely famous

941. Manomayi

She who has the mind itself as her form

942. Vyomakeshi

She who has ether as Her hair

943. Vimanastha

She who is not different from the Devas in the celestial chariot of flight

944. Vajrini

She who is the consort of Indra, who possesses the weapon Vajra

945. Vamakeshwari

She who is the form of Vamakeshvaratantra

Manblunder writes in his blog on Vamakeshwari: Nama 945 refers to Vamakeshvara tantra. This tantra is said to be the 65th tantra apart from the 64 discussed in Soundarya Lahari verse 31 and nama 236 of this Sahasranama. Vamakeshvara Tantra is said to be the most important tantra for Sri Vidya worship. This tantra discusses on internal worship of Shakthi. Vamakeshvari is said to be the source of this Universe.

Shakthi asks Shiva in Vamakesvara tantra "Lord, you revealed to me all the 64 tantras. But you have not told me about 16 Vidyas." Shiva answers by saying that this has not been declared yet and that it is hidden so far. Then Shiva begins declaring this tantra to Devi. Everything in this tantra has been revealed in a very subtle manner.

For example, the bija 'hrim' is declared as 'the form of vidya protecting the self is Shiva, Agni, Maya and bindu.' Unless one knows the bijas of these gods/goddesses, it is difficult to make out the hidden bija. Shiva bija is 'ha', Agni bija is 'ra', maya bija (root of 'eem' or kamakala) is 'i' and bindu is the dot. By joining all this, the bija 'hrim' is arrived. Shiva declares a number of uncommon yet powerful bijas in this tantra.

Vamas mean those who worship Her through left hands. She is the Goddess for these left-hand worshippers. She is also known as Vamesvari, which refers to Her divine power which projects the universe out of Shiva (the Brahman without attributes) and produces the reverse (vama) consciousness of difference.

946. Panchayagnapriya

She loves the offerings made through the five sacrifices

947. Pancha preta manchandi shayini

She is seated on the throne made up of five corpses

This nama is an indication that She is greater than the five tasks of shruti, sthiti, laya, tirodhana and anugraha. The deities responsible for these five tasks are said to be the legs and plank of her seat. Brahma, Vishnu, Rudra, Shiva, and Sadashiva together form the seat or cot on which She rests. Shiva serves as the central plank, while the other four deities act as the legs supporting the cot. By themselves, these five deities are inert, like corpses (pretas), but She infuses them with life-consciousness (chaitanya), enabling them to perform the roles and tasks assigned to them.

948. Panchami

This nama can be understood to mean that She is the consort of Shiva in the Panchamaha form or that she is the fifth day of the lunar fortnight which is considered very auspicious or it can be a reference to Her form as Varahi who is the fifth of the Matru Devis.

949. Panchabhooteshi

She has authority over the five elements

950. Panchasankhyopacharini

She is worshipped with five offerings

Sandal, flowers, incense, lamp and food are the five offerings made to her as they are visualised as the five elements – earth, ether, air, fire and water respectively. These objects are offered mentally by uttering their bijas – lam, ham, yam, ram and vam as explained in detail in the Panchopachara Pooja (Chapter 2).

951. Shashwati

She is eternal

952. Shashwataishwarya

She grants eternal prosperity

953. Sharmada

She is the bestower of happiness

954. Shambumohini

She who bewitches Shiva

955. Dhara

She is form of Earth

956. Dharasuta

She is the daughter of Himalayas

957. Dhanya

She who is ever grateful

958. Dharmini

She who is righteous

959. Dharmavardini

She who promotes righteousness

960. Lokateeta

She transcends the worlds

961. Gunateeta

She transcends the three gunas

962. Sarvateeta

She transcends everything

963. Shamatmika

She is ever tranquil

964. Bandhookakusumaprakhya

She is fond of the Bandhooka flower

965. Bala

She who is the form of a young girl

This nama is a reference to her form as Bala Tripurasundari, She is seen as a nine year old girl.

966. Leela

She takes pleasure in the acts of her devotees

967. Sumangali

She grants auspiciousness

968. Sukhakari

She grants happiness

969. Suveshadya

She looks auspicious in every form of attire.

970. Suvasini

She who lives with Her husband

971. Suvasinyarchanapreeta

She is pleased with the worship from married women

This nama can also imply that She is pleased when married women are treated with respect.

972. Ashobhana

She lives in a state of incomparable bliss

973. Shuddhamanasa

She who has a pure mind

974. Bindutarpanasantushta

She who is pleased with Bindu offerings

During the Sri Chakra puja, tarpana is offered at each chakra after completion of the avarana. The offerings made at the Bindu are dear to Her. It can also mean that even the smallest offering (as small as a dot) is enough to please her.

975. Poorvaja

She is the first born

976. Tripurambika

She who is in the form of Tripura Devi

Tripurambika is the name of the deity of the eighth chakra of Sri Yantra.

977. Dashamudra samaradhya

She is worshipped with the 10 mudras that are offered to Her at the end of the worship.

Mudras are symbolic hand gestures or positions used in Hindu rituals, yoga, and meditation practices. The word comes from the root "mud," meaning "delight" and "ra," which means "to give." Mudras are used to channel energy flow within the body, facilitate spiritual progress, and convey specific meanings or intentions.

At the conclusion of Srichakra Puja, She is worshipped using ten specific mudras, beginning with the Samkshobini Mudra and ending with the Trikhanda Mudra. These mudras must be learned through initiation from a Guru.

978. Tripurashreevashankaree

She has attracted Tripurashree to Her

Tripurashree is the presiding deity of the Sarvartha Sadaka Chakra, the fifth chakra of the Sri Yantra.

979. Jnanamudra

She is the symbol of knowledge

The Jnana Mudra is a significant hand gesture in the practices of meditation and yoga. The term "Jnana" means "knowledge" or "wisdom," and this mudra symbolizes the unity of individual consciousness (represented by the index finger) with universal consciousness (represented by the thumb).

In performing the Jnana Mudra, the tip of the index finger is gently brought to touch the tip of the thumb, forming a circle, while the other three fingers are extended outward. This simple yet profound gesture is often used during meditation to facilitate concentration, inner peace, and spiritual insight. The circle formed by the thumb and index finger represents the cycle of life, the continuous flow of energy, and the interconnectedness of all beings. The three extended fingers can symbolize the three Gunas which are to be transcended in the pursuit of spiritual knowledge.

980. Jnanagamya

She can be achieved through knowledge

981. Jnanajneyaswaroopini

She is both form and object of knowledge

982. Yonimudra

She is the form of the Yoni mudra (9th mudra)

983. Trikhandeshi

She is the ruler of the 10th mudra known as the Trikhanda mudra.

984 & 985. Trigunamba

She is the mother of the three gunas

986. Trikonaga

She resides within the innermost triangle of the Sri Yantra

987. Anagha

She is pure and sinless

988. Adbhutacharitra

She who has many amazing stories

989. Vanchitartapradayini

She bestows on Her devotees all that they seek

Even though she does not have a Varada mudra, She bestows all that which is sought for through Her feet.

990. Abhyasatishayajnata

She can be known only through constant practice and worship

991. Shadadhvateeta roopini

She who transcends the six modes of devotion

The six modes of devotion are

- pada (words)
- bhuvana (worlds)
- varna (alphabet)
- tattva (essence)
- kala (aspect)
- mantra (seed letters)

992. Avyaja karuna murti

She who has compassion without bias

993. Ajnanadhvanta deepika

She who dispels the darkness of ignorance

994. Abalagopavidita

She who is known to even small children and cowherds

995. Sarvanullanghya shasana

No one can disobey Her dictates.

996. Srichakrarajanilaya

She resides in the Srichakra which is the king of yantras

997. Srimattripurasundari

She who is the consort of Shiva in Tripura form

Shiva, who embodies three distinct forms within his being, is referred to as Tripura. According to the Kalika Purana, by the will of Pradhana (the primordial matter), Shiva's body transformed into three parts. The upper part became Brahma, characterized by five faces, four arms, and a body the color of a lotus pericarp. The middle part turned into Vishnu, with a blue complexion, one face, four arms, and holding the conch, disc, club, and lotus. The lower part transformed into Rudra, who has five faces, four arms, a complexion like a white cloud, and wears the Moon as his crest jewel. Since these three forms, or Puras, exist within him, Shiva is called Tripura.

998. Sri Shiva

She who is blessed by Shiva

The realization of this name is the fruit of recitation of Lalita Sahasranama.

999. Shivashaktyaikyaroopini

She who is the union of Shiva and Shakti

All the names recited so far merge into this final state of unity.

1000. Lalitambika

Such a beautiful Mother is Goddess Lalita

The Sahasranama begins with Sri Mata and ends with Lalitambika with both alluding the Her as Mother. According to the Padma Purana,

Lalita means the one who shines with a unique and transcendent beauty. Shivashaktyaikyaroopini describes the form of Shakti and Shiva merged into one and the description of the Ultimate Reality as per our scriptures is Satyam Shiva Sundaram and it is on this note that the Lalita Sahasranama ends. Does this mean that She is more powerful than Shiva? Perhaps, the Vag Devis believe it as they would not have placed this nama as the last one if they had any doubt about Her supremacy. In a way, this name is the culmination of the attributes which include Panchapretasanasina and Panchabrahmasvarupini.

Chapter 15

Uttara Bhaga – Phala Shruti

Phala Shruti literally translates to the hearing of the fruits (Phala meaning "fruit" or "result" and Shruti meaning "hearing"). It appears at the conclusion of hymns or sacred texts, outlining the specific spiritual, material, or karmic benefits that accrue to the person who recites, listens to, or devoutly follows the teachings or practices prescribed in the preceding text. These benefits include blessings such as prosperity, health, peace, liberation, protection from evil, or fulfilment of desires. It emphasizes the power and efficacy of divine names reinforcing the belief in the transformative and protective potency of spiritual practices. It serves to motivate practitioners by promising tangible results from their devotional efforts.

In the context of ritual practice, Phala Shruti is recited to invoke divine blessings or to conclude a ritual with an affirmation of its purpose and expected outcomes. It also reflects the cultural and societal values of the time in which the text was composed. The specific benefits mentioned often align with the concerns and aspirations of the audience, such as wealth, progeny, and protection, thus serving to make the religious teachings more accessible and relevant.

The phala shruti of the Lalita Sahasranama is a separate stotra from the Sahasranama unlike in the Vishnu Sahasranama where it is part of the main stotra. This stotra occurs in the Markandeya Purana and is taught by Sage Markandeya to Sage Agasthya.

The benefits and significance of reciting the Lalita Sahasranama are summarised here:

Surpassing Rituals and Pilgrimages: The recitation of Lalita Sahasranama is considered more spiritually beneficial than several revered practices, including:

Taking sacred baths in holy rivers

Installing multiple lingas in Varanasi

Donating gold in Kurukshetra during a solar eclipse to those who are knowledgeable in the entire Vedas.

Performing the Ashwamedha sacrifice on the banks of the Ganga

Absolution of Sins: Reciting even a single name from the thousand names of Lalita Sahasranama absolves a person of their sins, including those arising from the non-performance of duties prescribed by the scriptures.

Special Significance in Sri Matrye Namah Vidya Worship: For those initiated into Sri Vidya worship, reciting the Lalita Sahasranama is considered the only necessary remedial measure. It is emphasized that resorting to other remedial measures may actually lead to further sin.

Healing Powers:

Placing a hand on the head of a person suffering from fever while reciting the Lalita Sahasranama is believed to bring immediate relief from the fever and other ailments.

When sacred ashes are touched and recited over with the Lalita Sahasranama and then applied to a person, their ailments are said to subside.

For those afflicted by the adverse effects of planets, sanctifying water with the recitation of Lalita Sahasranama and then drinking it is believed to neutralize these planetary influences.

Progeny and Protection:

Couples seeking progeny are advised to consume butter sanctified by the recitation of Lalita Sahasranama, which is believed to enhance fertility.

Lord Sarabheswara is said to annihilate the enemies of those who recite Lalita Sahasranama daily, while Pratyangira Devi destroys the sources of evil inflicted upon the devotee.

Divine Protection: Various deities, such as Bhairava, Kshetrapala, etc., are described as offering specific protections to those who regularly recite the Lalita Sahasranama, ranging from blinding those who harbor ill will against the devotee to spoiling the speech of those who engage in unnecessary disputes with them.

Wealth and Eloquence: Reciting the Lalita Sahasranama daily ensures that Lakshmi remains in the devotee's home, while Saraswati is said to infuse the devotee's words with divine eloquence.

Attractiveness and Purity: Continuous recitation over specific periods is believed to enhance personal attraction and purity, absolving not only the devotee's sins but also the sins of those who merely encounter the devotee.

Proper Gifting: Offering gifts to those who understand the meaning of Lalita Sahasranama is highly meritorious, while offering to unworthy recipients accrues sin. It is emphasized that initiation into Sri Vidya and proper understanding of the Lalita Sahasranama is crucial, as improper initiation or misunderstanding leads to negative consequences for both the initiator and the initiate.

Ritualistic Worship: Performing the worship of Sri Chakra with fragrant flowers, as prescribed, especially on auspicious days like the full moon or Mahanavami is believed to yield immense spiritual gains, including the attainment of the form of Lalitambika herself.

Ultimate Liberation: The highest spiritual benefit of reciting the Lalita Sahasranama is liberation from the cycle of birth and death leading to the devotee's ultimate merger with the divine essence.

Spiritual Maturity: It is noted that those who receive initiation into Sri Vidya and recite the Lalita Sahasranama have likely worshipped various deities over multiple lifetimes, signifying a culmination of their spiritual journey.

Revelation and Secrecy: Finally, Hayagriva reveals this sacred knowledge to the sage Agastya under the direct orders of Lalitambika instructing him to recite the Lalita Sahasranam adaily to receive whatever is desired.

Detailed meaning of Phala Shruti

Ityetannama sahasram khaditham te ghatodbhava
Thus this Sahasranama was told to you, Oh Agastya
Rahasyanam rahasyam cha Lalita preethidayakam
Anena sadrusham stotram na bhootham na bhavishyathi

These thousand names are secret of the secrets and are very dear to Lalita. This type of hymn has never existed in the past nor will exist in future.

Sarvarogaprashamanam sarvasampathpravardhanam
Sarvapamruthy shamanam akalamruthyunivaranam

This cures all diseases and gives rise to all types of wealth It can prevent untimely death.

Sarva jwararthishamanam deergayushyapradhayakam
Putrapradhamaputranam purusharthapradhayakam

It is a cure for all types of fever, and gives rise to long life, It blesses with male progeny and the wealth of salvation

Idham visheshachridevya stotram preethi vidhatakam
Japennityam prayatnena lalitopastitatpara

This special prayer must be chanted daily after worshipping of Lalita

Pratha snathwa vidhanena sandhyakarma samapya cha
Poojagruham tato gathva chakrarajam samarchayeth

After taking a bath in the morning, finishing the oblations as per one's traditions, the

prayer room is entered and first worship is offered to the Sri Chakra.
Vidyam japethsahasram va trishtam shatameva va,
Rahasya namasahasramidham paschat patennara

The Sri Vidya mantra is to be chanted either 1000 or 300 or 100 times and then the Sahasranama is to be read. Here the Sri Vidya mantra refers to the Panchadasi or Shodasi mantras.

Janmamadhye sakruchchapi ya yetatpathathesoudhee
Tasya punyaphalam vakshye srunutvam Kumbhasambhava

Oh, Sage born out of the pot, please hear the results of reading this hymn in the middle of their lives by devotees

Gangadhisarvateertheshu ya snayathkotijanmasu
Koti lingaprathishtam cha ya kuryadh avimukthake
Kurukshethre tu yo dadyat kotivaram ravigruhe,
Koti sournabharanam srotreyeshu dwijanmasu
Ya kotim hayamedhanam aharedgangarodhase
Acharethkoopa kotiryo nirjale marubhootale
Durbhikshe ya prathidinam kotibrahmanabhojanam
Sraddhayaparaya kuryat sahasraparivathsaran
Tath punyam kotigunitam labhyetpunya manuthamam
Rahasya namasahasre namnapyekasya keerthanaath

If a devotee chants even one name out of the thousand, he gets crore times the benefits of the actions below:

- Taking bath in sacred rivers like Ganga
- Consecrating one crore lingas in Benares

- Giving one crore measures of gold ornaments to learned Brahmins in Kurukshetra during a solar eclipse
- Performing crore Ashwamedha yagas in the shores of the Ganges
- digging one crore wells with water in the deserts
- feeding one crore Brahmins daily in times of a famine

Rahasyanamasahasre namaikamapi ya patet
Tasya papani nashyanthi mahantyapi na samshaya

Even if one name among the thousand secret names is read, all the sins committed by a devotee will be destroyed, without doubt

Nityakarmanushtananishidakaranadhapi
Yatpapam jayathe pumsam tatsarvam nashyathidruvam

Even the sin brought on by the act of not performing the daily sacred routines will go away and all the sins would be destroyed speedily.

Bahunatrakimuktena srunutvam Kumbhasambhava
Athraika namno yashakthi patakanam nivartane
Tannivarthyam agam kartum nalam lokachchadurdasa

O Sage Agasthya, listen as I explain how people can free themselves from their sins. By chanting according to their ability, they can undoubtedly eliminate the sins committed across the fourteen worlds.

Yastyakthva namasahasram papahanimabheepsati
Sa hi sheethanivrtyartham himashailam nishevate

Those who wish to get rid of their sins but do not like to chant the thousand names, it is like going to the Himalayas to avoid the cold.

Bhakto ya keerthyan nithyam idam namasahasrakam
Tasmai Sri Lalita preetabheeshtam prayachathi

Devotees who sing these thousand names everyday will be blessed by Lalita by fulfilling their wishes.

Akeertayennidam stothram kadambhaktho bhavishyathi
How can one become a devotee of Lalita if he does chant this hymn?

Nityam sankeertanashaktha keertayeth punyavasare
Sankranthou vishuvechaiva swajanmatrithayeyane
Navamyaam vaa chathurdasyam sithaayaam shukravasare,

People who cannot sing it daily should chant it on special occasions, —
first of every month, first day of the new year and the three birthdays
(self, spouse and first-born offspring), nineth and fourteenth days of
waxing moon, Fridays and on Full Moon Day.

Keertyen namasahasram pournamasyam viseshata
Chanting this hymn on the full moon day is very important
Pournamasyam chandra bhimbhe dhyathwa Sri Lalitaambikaam
Panchopacharai sampoojya paden nama sahasrakam
Sarva roga pranasyanthi deergamayuscha vindhathi
Ayam ayushkaro nama prayoga kalpanodita

On the full moon day, face the full moon and meditate on Lalita. Offer
the five sacred oblations and recite the thousand names. By doing so, all
diseases will disappear, and a long life will be bestowed.

Jwarartham shirasisprushtva patennama sahasrakam
Tat kshnaath prashamam yati shirastado jwaropi cha

If someone has fever, the chanter can touch the person's head and chant
the hymn. The fever and headache will go away soon.

Sarvavyadhi nivrutyartham sprushtva bhasma japedidam
Tadbhasmadharanadeva nashyanthi vyadhaya kshanath

To cure diseases, touch the holy ash while chanting the thousand names.
By wearing that ash, all ailments will be instantly healed.

Jalam samantrasya kumbhastham namasahasrathomune
Abhishichedh grahagrasthan graha nashyanthi tatkshanath

O Sage, store water in a pot and chant the thousand names. By anointing
yourself with that water, all problems caused by planetary influences will
be removed.s

Sudha sagara madhyastham dhyathva Sri Lalitambikam
Ya patennamasahasram visham tasya vinashyathi

Meditating on Lalitambika as She is in the ocean of nectar and chanting this hymn will remove effects of poison

Vandhyana putralabhaya namasahasramantritam,
Navaneetam pradadyatu puthralabho bhaveddruvam

To bless a woman who is unable to conceive with a son, chant the thousand names and offer butter to the Divine. By doing this, she will soon be blessed with a child.

Rajakarshana kaamaschedraja vasathadingmukha
Triratram ya patetaSridevi dhyana tathpara
Sa raja paravashyena turangam va mathangajam
Aruhyath nikatam dasavat pranipatyacha
Tasmai rajyam cha koshamcha dadyadeva vasam gata

To attract the favour of a king, face his palace and recite the thousand names while meditating on the Goddess. By doing so, the king will come under your influence, approach you on horseback or elephant, bow before you, serve you, and offer you his kingdom or a portion of it.

Rahasya nama sahasram ya keertyati nityasa,
Tan mukhaloka matrena muhye loka trayam mune

As soon as saints see the face of someone who chants the thousand secret names daily, they immediately offer their salutations.

Yasthvidham nama sahasram sakruth padathi bhakthiman,
Thasya yea sasthravasthesham nihantha Sarabheswara

The enemies of the devotee who recites these thousand names will be struck down by the arrows of Sarabheswara.

Yo vabhicharam kuruthe nama sahasra padake
Nivarthya thath kriyaam hanyatham vai prathyangira swayam

Anyone who attempts black magic against a devotee who recites the thousand names will be destroyed by Prathyangira Devi herself, as she protects the devotee.

Yea Kroora drushtya veekshanthe nama sahasra padakam,
Thaan andhaan kuruthe ksipram swayam marthanda bhirava

Anyone who looks with cruelty upon a person who recites these thousand names will be instantly blinded by Marthanda Bhairava himself.

Dhanam yo harathe chorair nama sahasra japeen,
Yathra kuthra sthiram vaapi Kshethra palo nihanthi thaam

Anyone who steals the wealth of a devotee who recites these thousand names will be killed by Kshetrapala, regardless of where they hide.

Vidhyasu kuruthe vadham yo vidwan nama jaapeena,
Thasya vak sthambhanam sadhya karothi Nakuleshwari

Anyone who engages in arguments with a learned person who recites the thousand names will be rendered mute immediately by Nakuleshwari.

Yo raja kuruthe vairam nama sahasra japeen
Chathuranga balam tasya Dandinee samhareth swayam

The army of a king who attacks the devotee who recites the thousand names as an enemy will be swiftly destroyed by Dandinee herself.

Ya paden nama saahasram shan masam bhakthi samyutha,
Lakshmi chanchalya rahitha sada tishtathi tadgruhe

A person who recites these thousand names daily with devotion for six months will have the usually fickle Goddess of Wealth, Lakshmi reside permanently in their home.

Masamekam prathidinam, thri vaaram ya patennara
Bharati tasya jihvagrerange nruthyathi nithyasa

Anyone who recites it daily for one month, or at least for three weeks, will have Saraswati, the goddess of intelligence, manifesting as eloquence and wisdom in their speech.

Ya patennamasahasramjanmamadhye sakrunnera
Tad drushtigochara sarve muchyanthi sarva kilbishai

The one who reads these thousand names in the middle of his life will be able to see everything and all his sins would be pardoned.

Yo vethi namasahasram tasmai dheyam dwijanmane
Annam vastram dhanam dhanyam nanyebhyasthu kada chana

Food, clothes, wealth and cereals should be given to the Brahmin who has completely understood the hymn.

Srimantrarajam yovethi srichakram ya samarchati
Ya keertayati namani tam satpathram vidhur budha

Anyone who learns the supreme Sri Mantra, offers it to the Sri Chakra, and chants these thousand names will be esteemed as holy by the learned.

Tasmai deyam prayatnena Sri Devi preethimichata
Ya keerthayathi namaani mantra rajam na vetti ya
Pashuthulya sa vijneya tasmai dattam nirartakam

The goddess, with her boundless love, bestows whatever is desired upon anyone who chants these names and masters the supreme mantra.

Pareekshya vidhya vidhusha thasmai dadhya dwichakshana
There is no point in teaching this mantra to the ignorant. It is to be given to those who are learned and wise.
Sri manthra raja sadrusho yatha mantro na vidhyathe,
Devatha Lalitatulyaa yatha nashi ghatodhbhava

There are no chants which are equal to the Sri Vidya mantra and there is no goddess equivalent to Lalita, Oh Agasthya.

Rahasya nama sahasratulya nasti tatha stuthi
Likhithva pusthake vasthu namasahasramuthamam
Samarchayedsada bhakthya tasya tushyathi Sundari
There is no prayer as great as the secret thousand names
And he who writes these names in a book makes Her happy
Nanena sadrusam stotram sarvatantreshu vidyathe Tasmadupasako
nityam keerthyedhida madarat
There is no such prayer anywhere in the literature of Tantraand her
devotees chant it every day with devotion.

Yebhir nama sahastraishtu Sri Chakram yo archayedh sakruth Padmair va
tulaseepushpai, kalharai vaa, kadambakai

Champakair jathikusmai mallika kara veerakai
Uthpalai bilwapathrerva kundakesara patalai
anyai sugandhi kusumai ketaki madhaveemukhai Tasya punya phalam
vaktum na saknothiMahesvara

Even Shiva would not be able to express comprehensively the effect of
worshipping the Sri Chakra using the thousand names, with lotus, Tulasi,
Kalharraa, kadamba flowers,

Jasmine, Champak, Karaveera, Uthpala leaves of Bilwa, Kesara flowers
other scented flowers like Ketaki, Madavee, Mukha, etc.,
Sa vethi Lalita swachakrarchanajam phalam Anye katham vijaaneeyu
Brahmadhya swalpamedhasa

Only Lalita can shed light on the result of worshipping Her chakra,
possibly Lord Brahma may be able to narrate it to certain extent

Prathimasam pournamasyamabhir nama sahasrakai Rathrou ya
chakrarajasthamarchayeth paradevatham

Sa yeva Lalita roopastadroopa Lalita swayam
Na tayo vidhyathe bhedho bedhackruth papakruthbhavedh

On every full moon night, if she is worshipped with her thousand names on the
Sri Chakra, the devotee will embody the form of Lalita. He will be perceived
only as her, and seeing him as anything else would be considered a sin.

Mahanavamyam yo bhakta Sri Devi chakramadhyagam
Archayennamasahasrai tasyamukti karesthita

The devotee who worships her on Mahanavami day with her thousand names on the Sri Chakra, the devotee will attain salvation.

Yastu nama sahasrena Shukravare samarchayeth
Chakrarajemahadevim tasya punyaphalam srunu

If these thousand names are chanted on Friday, with her thousand names on the Sri Chakra, the devotee will get the benefits that follow.

Sarvan kamanavapyeha sarva soubhagya samyuta
Putra pouthradhisamyuktho bhuktva bhogan yadepsithan

All your desires would be fulfilled You will lead a life with all blessings You will be surrounded by sons and grandsons and enjoy all the pleasures of life.

Anthe Lalitadevya sayujyamadhidurlabham
Prarthaneeyam shivadhyaischaprapnothyeva na samshaya

At the end you would get salvation under Lalita, which is difficult to obtain, and get all benefits of praying to Gods like Shiva

Ya sahasram Brahmananamebhirnama sahasrakai,
Samarchaya bhojayedh bhaktya payasapoopashadrasai
Tasmai preenathi Lalita swasamrajyam prayachathi
Natasya durlabham vastu trishulokeshu varddhte

Dedicating these thousand names to thousand Brahmins, feeding them with sweet payasam, vada made out of black gram, and a meal which is blessed with all six tastes, would make one dear to Lalita, and she would bless you with her kingdom and there would be nothing in the three worlds that would be difficult to get for this man.

Nishkama keertayedhyasthu nama Sahasramuthamam
Brahmajnanamavapnothi yenamuchyathebandanath

He who chants these thousand names without any desires or attachments will get the knowledge of Brahman and will be released from the bonds of life.

Dhanarti dhanamapnoti Yasorthichapnuyatyasa
Vidhyarthi chapnuyad vidyam namasahasra keertanat

One who wants money will get money. One who wants fame will get fame. And one who wants knowledge will get knowledge by singing these thousand names.

Nanena sadhrusham stothram Bhogamokshapradhammune
Keerthaneeyamidham thasmad bhoga mokshadhibhir narai

There is no prayer similar to this

Which will give pleasure and salvation, Oh sage, for men, by singing these thousand names will get both pleasure as well as salvation.

Chathurashrama nishtaicha keertaneeyamidham sada
Swadharma samanushtana vaikalya paripoorthaye

In all the four stages of life, singing these thousand names, And also following one's own Dharma, would help reach his goal without any obstacles.

Kaloupapaikabahule dharmanushtanavarjathe
Namasankeerthanam mukthva nrunam nanyat parayanam

In the age of Kali, when all Dharmas are forsaken, men will get salvation by singing these names and no other.

Loukeekadvachan mukhyam Vishnu nama keerthanam
Vishnu nama saharaischa Shiva namaikamuthamam

In family life it is important to sing the names of Vishnu, but better than singing names of Vishnu is singing names of Shiva.

Shiva nama sahasraischa devya namaikamuthamam
Devi Nama sahasrani kotisa shanthi Kumbhaja

Better than the thousand names of Shiva are the names of the Devi, Oh Agasthya, the thousand names of Devi are one crore times better.

Teshu mukhyam dasavidham namasahasramuchyathe
Rahasya namasahasramidham sashtamdashasvapi

There are ten important names out of these thousand names And all these are praise worthy (the names are Ganga, Gayathri, Syamala, Lakshmi, Kali, Bala, Lalita, Rajarajeswari, Saraswathi and Bhavani.)

Tasmat sankeetayennithyam kalidosha nivruthaye,
Mukhyam Srimathunamethi na janathi vimohita

Singing them daily would cure the ill effects of Kali age, and the name Matha is important and should not be forgotten.

Vishnu namapara kechith Shiva nama para pare
Na kaschidapi lokeshu Lalitanama tatpara

Better than the names of Vishnu are the names of Shiva, but in all the worlds there is nothing better than names of Lalita.

Yenanya devathanama keerthitam Janamakotishu
Tasyaiva bhavathishradhaaSridevi nama keertane

Even if the names of other Gods are sung in crores of births, it is equal only to singing of the thousand names with devotion.

Charame janmaniyatha Srividhyaupasakobhaveth
Nama sahasra pataschatatha charame janmani

A person becomes a Sri Vidya sadhaka only in his last birth and in the same way, chanting these thousand names will also only happen in the last birth.

Yataiva virala loke Sri Vidyachara vedina
Tathaiva viralo guhya nama sahasra pataka

In this world it is rare to find Sri Vidya Upasakas and it is also rare to find those who read the secret thousand names.

Mantraraja japaschaiva chakrarajarchanam tatha
Rahasya nama patascha nalpasya tapasa phalam

Chanting the Sri Vidya mantra followed by worship of Sri Chakra and reading the thousand names gets the same result as practising austerity.

Apatannamasahasram preenayedhya Maheswareem
Sa chakshusha vina roopam pashyedeva vimoodadhi

Without reading these thousand names and trying to please Lalita is like a fool trying to see a form without the eyes.

Rahasyanama sahasram tyaktva ya sidhikamuka
Sa Bhojanam vinaanoonam Kshunnivavruttimabheepsati

Forsaking the thousand names and trying to get occult powers, Is like satiating hunger after forsaking all food.

Yo Bhakta Lalita devya sa nityam Keerthayedidam
Nanyatha preeyatha Devi kalpa kotishathairapi

That devotee who sings these names of Lalita, need not sing any other for she will be pleased,only by singing of this even for hundreds of eons.

Tasmadrahasya namani,Sri Mathu prayata padeth
Yithi they kaditham Stotram rahasyam, Kumbha sambhava

These thousand names are to be read for making the mother happy but this prayer which I told is a secret, Oh sage Agasthya.

Na vidhyaavedhine brooyannabhaktaya kadachana
Yathaiva gopyaSri Vidya tatha gopyamidam mune

The learned in Vedas, if they do not recite these names at least once, the Sri Vidya would be kept secret from them, Oh sage.

Pashutulyeshu nabrooyajjaneshu stotramuthamam
Yodadati vimoodatma Sri Vidya rahithayacha
Tasmai kupyanthi yoginya, sonartha sumahan smruth,
Rahasya nama saahasran thsmad sangopyedhidham

This prayer should not be shared with the ignorant.

If this prayer is taught to one without the knowledge of Sri Vidya, the Yogis would be very angry with them for this would lead them to problems, and that is why these secret thousand names are kept as great secret from everyone.

Swatantrena mayanoktam tavapi kalashodbhava,
Lalita prerana naivamayoktham stotramuthamam

O Sage Agasthya, I would not have shared this knowledge to you of my own volition.

Lalita has advised me to give it to you.
Keertaneeyam idam bhaktya Kumbhayone nirantharam
Tena tushta Mahadevi tavabheeshtam pradasyati

Please recite these with devotion, Oh sage Agasthya, And the goddess will be pleased and fulfil your wishes.

Sri Sootha Uvacha:

Ithyukthva Sri Hayagreevo dhyatva Sri Lalitambikaam,

Anandamagna hrudaya sadhya pulakithobhavat

Sootha said:

After telling thus, sage Hayagriva meditated on Lalita and was drowned in happiness and became enraptured.

Ithi Sri Brahmanda purane Uttara Kande

Sri Hayagrivagasthya samvade, Sri Lalita sahasranamastotra

Phala srutheernama uttara Bhaga

Thus ends the narration of fruits oof reciting Lalita Sahasranama which is in Brahmanda Purana in a discussion between Sage Hayagriva and Sage Agastya.

Chapter 16

Namavali

When the thousand names of the Divine are continuously without prefixing them with Om, it is referred to as Sahasranama. If each of the 1000 names are chanted by prefixing with Om and ending with namah, it is called Sahasranamavali. Sahasranamavali is particularly suited for performing an Archana, where flowers, bilva leaves, tulsi leaves are offered at the end of each name during the recitation.

There are two ways of chanting the Lalita Namavali. One is the traditional method of encasing each nama between Om and namah. The other method which is followed by Sri Vidya sadhakas but is lesser known is to prefix each name with two powerful bijas Hreem and Shreem and ending with namah. Hreem represents Kali and Shreem stands for Lakshmi. These two bijas have the power to bestow auspiciousness and abundance. The same method of Archana can be followed for both ways of chanting.

Each namavali has to begin by offering the necessary Nyasa, dhyana and Panchopachara Pooja. For both methods, the first nama will be Om aim hrim shrim Sri Matrye Namah and will end with Om lalitambikayai namah

Shrim hrim aim Om

Om tatsat brahmarpanamastu Iti Srilalitasahasranamavalih sampoornam

*Please note that the necessary changes will need to be made in each word to chant in namavali form. For example Sri Mata becomes Sri Matrye, samanvita becomes samanvitayai and so on for each name.

1	Om om aim hrim srim sri matrye namah
2	Om srimaharajnai namah
3	Om srimatsimhasanesvaryai namah
4	Om chidagnikundasambhutayai namah
5	Om devakaryasamudyatayai namah
6	Om udyadbhanusahasrabhayai namah
7	Om chaturbahusamanvitayai namah
8	Om ragashvarupapasadhyayai namah
9	Om krodhakarankusojjvalayai namah
10	Om manorupekshukodandayai namah
11	Om panchatanmatrasayakayai namah
12	Om nijarunaprabhapuramajjad brahmandamandalayai namah
13	Om champakasokapunnagasaugandhikalasatkachayai namah
14	Om kuruvindamanishrenikanatkotiramanditayai namah
15	Om ashtamichandravibhrajadalikasthalasobhitayai namah
16	Om mukhachandrakalankabhamriganabhivisesakayai namah
17	Om vadanasmaramangalyagrihatoranachillikayai namah
18	Om vaktralaksmiparivahachalanminabhalochanayai namah
19	Om navachampakapushpabhanasadandavirajitayai namah
20	Om tarakantitiraskarinasabharanabhashurayai namah
21	Om kadambamanjarikluptakarnapuramanoharayai namah
22	Om tatankayugalibhutatapanodupamandalayai namah

23	Om padmaragasiladarsaparibhavikapolabhuve namah
24	Om navavidrumabimbasrinyakkariradanachchadayai namah
25	Om shuddhavidyankurakaradvijapanktidvayojjvalayai namah
26	Om karpuravitikamodasamakarsi digantarayai namah
27	Om nijasallapamadhurya vinirbhatsitakachchapyai namah
28	Om mandasmitaprabhapuramajjatkamesamanasayai namah
29	Om anakalitasadrishyachibukasrivirajitayai namah
30	Om kamesabaddhamangalyashutrasobhitakandharayai namah
31	Om kanakangadakeyurakamaniyamujanvitayai namah
32	Om ratnagraiveya chintakalolamuktaphalanvitayai namah
33	Om kameshvarapremaratnamanipratipanastanyai namah
34	Om nabhyalavalaromalilataphalakuchadvayyai namah
35	Om lakshyaromalatadharatasamunneyamadhyamayai namah
36	Om stanabharadalanmadhyapattabandhavalitrayayai namah
37	Om arunarunakaushumbhavastrabhashvatkatitatyai namah
38	Om ratnakinkinikaramyarasanadamabhusitayai namah
39	Om kamesajnatasaubhagyamardavorudvayanvitayai namah
40	Om manikyamukutakarajanudvayavirajitayai namah
41	Om indragopapariksiptasmaratunabhajanghikayai namah
42	Om gudhagulphayai namah

43	Om kurma prsthajayisnuprapadanvitayai namah
44	Om nakhadidhitisanchannanamajjanatamogunayai namah
45	Om padadvayaprabhajalaparakrtasaroruhayai namah
46	Om sinjanamanimanjiramanditasripadambujayai namah
47	Om maralimandagamanayai namah
48	Om mahalavanyasevadhaye namah
49	Om sarvarunayai namah
50	Om anavadyangyai namah
51	Om sarvabharanabhusitayai namah
52	Om shivakamesvarankasthayai namah
53	Om shivayai namah
54	Om svadhinavallabhayai namah
55	Om shumerumadhyasrngasthayai namah
56	Om srimannagaranayikayai namah
57	Om chintamanigrhantasthayai namah
58	Om panchabrahmasanasthitayai namah
59	Om mahapadmatavisamsthayai namah
60	Om kadambavanavasinyai namah
61	Om shudhasagaramadhyasthayai namah
62	Om kamaksyai namah
63	Om kamadayinyai namah
64	Om devarsiganasanghatastuyamanatmavaibhayai namah
65	Om bhandashuravadhodyuktashaktisenasamanvitayai namah
66	Om sampatkarisamarudhasinduravrajasevitayai namah
67	Omashvarudhadhisthitashvakotikotibhiravrtayai namah
68	Om chakrarajaratharudhasarvayudhapariskrtayai namah
69	Om geyachakraratharudhamantriniparisevitayai namah

70	Om kirichakraratharudhadandanathapuraskrtayai namah
71	Om jvalamalinikaksiptavahniprakaramadhyagayai namah
72	Om bhandasainyavadhodyuktashaktivikramaharsitayai namah
73	Om nityaparakramatopaniriksanasamutshukayai namah
74	Om bhandaputravadhodyuktabalavikramananditayai namah
75	Om mantrinyambavirachitavisangavadhatositayai namah
76	Om vishukrapranaharanavarahiviryananditayai namah
77	Om kamesvaramukhalokakalpitasriganesvarayai namah
78	Om mahaganesanirbhinnavighnayantrapraharsitayai namah
79	Om bhandashurendranirmuktasastrapratyastravarsinyai namah
80	Om karangulinakhotpannanarayanadasakrtyai namah
81	Om mahapashupatastragninirdagdhashurasainikayai namah
82	Om kamesvarastranirdagdhasabhandashurashunyakayai namah
83	Om brahmopendramahendradidevasamstutavaibhavayai namah
84	Om haranetragnishandagdhakamasanjivanausadhyai namah
85	Om srimadvagbhavakutaikashvarupamukhapankajayai namah
86	Om kanthadhah katiparyantamadhyakutashvarupinyai namah
87	Om shaktikutaikatapannakatyadhobhagadharinyai namah
88	Ommulamantratmikayai namah
89	Om mulakutatrayakalebarayai namah
90	Om kulamritaikarasikayai namah
91	Om kulasanketapalinyai namah
92	Om kulanganayai namah
93	Om kulantahsthayai namah
94	Om kaulinyai namah
95	Om kulayoginyai namah
96	Om akulayai namah
97	Om samayantasthayai namah

98	Om samayacharatatparayai namah
99	Om muladharaikanilayayai namah
100	Om brahmagranthivibhedinyai namah
101	Om manipurantaruditayai namah
102	Om visnugranthivibhedinyai namah
103	Om ajnachakrantaralasthayai namah
104	Om rudragranthivibhedinyai namah
105	Om sahasrarambujarudhayai namah
106	Om shudhasarabhivarsinyai namah
107	Om tatillatasamaruchyai namah
108	Om shatchakroparisamsthitayai namah
109	Om mahashaktyai namah
110	Om kundalinyai namah
111	Om bisatantutaniyasyai namah
112	Om bhavanyai namah
113	Om bhavanagamyayai namah
114	Om bhavaranyakutharikayai namah
115	Om bhadrapriyayai namah
116	Om bhadramurtyai namah
117	Om bhaktasaubhagyadayinyai namah
118	Om bhaktipriyayai namah
119	Om bhaktigamyayai namah
120	Om bhaktivasyayai namah
121	Om bhayapahayai namah
122	Om sambhavyai namah
123	Om sharadaradhyayai namah
124	Om sarvanyai namah

125	Om sharmadayinyai namah
126	Om shankaryai namah
127	Om srikaryai namah
128	Om sadhvyai namah
129	Om sharatchandranibhananayai namah
130	Om shatodaryai namah
131	Om shantimatyai namah
132	Om niradharayai namah
133	Om niranjanayai namah
134	Om nirlepayai namah
135	Om nirmalayai namah
136	Om nityayai namah
137	Om nirakarayai namah
138	Om nirakulayai namah
139	Om nirgunayai namah
140	Om nishkalayai namah
141	Om shantayai namah
142	Om nishkamayai namah
143	Om nirupaplavayai namah
144	Om nityamuktayai namah
145	Om nirvikarayai namah
146	Om nishprapanchayai namah
147	Om nirashrayayai namah
148	Om nityashuddhayai namah
149	Om nityabuddhayai namah
150	Om niravadyayai namah
151	Om nirantarayai namah

152	Om nishkaranayai namah
153	Om nishkalankayai namah
154	Om nirupadhaye namah
155	Om nirisvarayai namah
156	Om niragayai namah
157	Om ragamathanyai namah
158	Om nirmadayai namah
159	Om madanasinyai namah
160	Om nishchintayai namah
161	Om nirahankarayai namah
162	Om nirmohayai namah
163	Om mohanasinyai namah
164	Om nirmamayai namah
165	Om mamatahantryai namah
166	Om nishpapayai namah
167	Om papanasinyai namah
168	Om nishkrodhayai namah
169	Om krodhasamanyai namah
170	Om nirlobhayai namah
171	Om lobhanasinyai namah
172	Om nihsamsayayai namah
173	Om samsayaghnyai namah
174	Om nirbhavayai namah
175	Om bhavanasinyai namah
176	Om nirvikalpayai namah
177	Om nirabadhayai namah
178	Om nirbhedayai namah

179	Om bhedanasinyai namah
180	Om nirnasayai namah
181	Om mrityumathanyai namah
182	Om nishkriyayai namah
183	Om nishparigrahayai namah
184	Om nishtulayai namah
185	Om nilachikurayai namah
186	Om nirapayayai namah
187	Om niratyayayai namah
188	Om durlabhayai namah
189	Om durgamayai namah
190	Om durgayai namah
191	Om duhkhahantryai namah
192	Om shukhapradayai namah
193	Om dustadurayai namah
194	Om duracharasamanyai namah
195	Om dosavarjitayai namah
196	Om sarvajnayai namah
197	Om sandrakarunayai namah
198	Om samanadhikavarjitayai namah
199	Om sarvashaktimayyai namah
200	Om sarvamangalayai namah
201	Om sadgatipradayai namah
202	Om sarvesvayai namah
203	Om sarvamayyai namah
204	Om sarvamantrashvarupinyai namah

205	Om sarvayantratmikayai namah
206	Om sarvatantrarupayai namah
207	Om manonmanyai namah
208	Om maheshvaryai namah
209	Om mahadevyai namah
210	Om mahalaksmyai namah
211	Om mridapriyayai namah
212	Om maharupayai namah
213	Om mahapujyayai namah
214	Om mahapatakanasinyai namah
215	Om mahamayayai namah
216	Om mahasatvayai namah
217	Om mahasaktyai namah
218	Om maharatyai namah
219	Om mahabhogayai namah
220	Om mahaishvaryayai namah
221	Om mahaviryayai namah
222	Om mahabalayai namah
223	Om mahabuddhyai namah
224	Om mahasiddhyai namah
225	Om mahayogesvaresvaryai namah
226	Om mahatantrayai namah
227	Om mahamantrayai namah
228	Om mahayantrayai namah
229	Om mahasanayai namah
230	Om mahayagakramaradhyayai namah
231	Om mahabhairavapujitayai namah

232	Om mahesvaramahakalpamahatandavasaksinyai namah
233	Om mahakamesamahisyai namah
234	Om mahatripurashundaryai namah
235	Om chatuhsastyupacharadhyayai namah
236	Om chatuhsastikalamayyai namah
237	Om mahachatuhsastikoti yoginiganasevitayai namah
238	Om manuvidyayai namah
239	Om chandravidyayai namah
240	Om chandramandalamadhyagayai namah
241	Om charurupayai namah
242	Om charuhasayai namah
243	Om charuchandrakaladharayai namah
244	Om characharajagannathayai namah
245	Om chakrarajaniketanayai namah
246	Om parvatyai namah
247	Om padmanayanayai namah
248	Om padmaragasamaprabhayai namah
249	Om panchapretasanasinayai namah
250	Om panchabrahmasparupinyai namah
251	Om chinmayyai namah
252	Om paramanandayai namah
253	Om vijnanaghanarupinyai namah
254	Om dhyanadhyatrdhyeyarupayai namah
255	Om dharmadharmavivarjitayai namah
256	Om vishvarupayai namah
257	Om jagarinyai namah
258	Om svapatnyai namah

259	Om taijasatmikayai namah
260	Om suptayai namah
261	Om prajnatmikayai namah
262	Om turyayai namah
263	Om sarvavasthavivarjitayai namah
264	Om sristhikartryai namah
265	Om brahmarupayai namah
266	Om goptryai namah
267	Om govindarupinyai namah
268	Om samharinyai namah
269	Om rudrarupayai namah
270	Om tirodhanakaryai namah
271	Om ishvaryai namah
272	Om sadashivayai namah
273	Om anugrahadayai namah
274	Om panchakrityaparayanayai namah
275	Om bhanumandalamadhyasthayai namah
276	Om bhairavyai namah
277	Om bhagamalinyai namah
278	Om padmasanayai namah
279	Om bhagavatyai namah
280	Om padmanabhasahodaryai namah
281	Om unmeshanimisotpannavipannabhuvanavalyai namah
282	Om sahasrashirshavadanayai namah
283	Om sahasrakshyai namah
284	Om sahasrapade namah
285	Om abrahmakitajananyai namah

286	Om varnasramavidhayinyai namah
287	Om nijajnarupanigamayai namah
288	Om punyapunyaphalapradayai namah
289	Om shrutisrimantasindurikirtapadabjadhulikayai namah
290	Om sakalagamasandohashuktisamputamauktikayai namah
291	Om purusharthapradayai namah
292	Om purnayai namah
293	Om bhoginyai namah
294	Om bhuvanesvharyai namah
295	Om ambikayai namah
296	Om anadinidhanayai namah
297	Om haribrahmendrasevitayai namah
298	Om narayanyai namah
299	Om nadarupayai namah
300	Om namarupavivarjitayai namah
301	Om hrinkaryai namah
302	Om hrimatyai namah
303	Om hridyayai namah
304	Om heyopadeyavarjitayai namah
305	Om rajarajarchitayai namah
306	Om rajnai namah
307	Om ramyayai namah
308	Om rajivalochanayai namah
309	Om ranjanyai namah
310	Om ramanyai namah
311	Om rasyayai namah
312	Om ranatkinkinimekhalayai namah

313	Om ramayai namah
314	Om rakenduvadanayai namah
315	Om ratirupayai namah
316	Om ratipriyayai namah
317	Om raksakaryai namah
318	Om raksasaghnyai namah
319	Om ramayai namah
320	Om ramanalampatayai namah
321	Om kamyayai namah
322	Om kamakalarupayai namah
323	Om kadambakushumapriyayai namah
324	Om kalyanyai namah
325	Omjagatikandayai namah
326	Om karunarasasagarayai namah
327	Om kalavatyai namah
328	Om kalalapayai namah
329	Om kantayai namah
330	Om kadambaripriyayai namah
331	Om varadayai namah
332	Om vamanayanayai namah
333	Om varunimadavihvalayai namah
334	Om visvadhikayai namah
335	Om vedavedyayai namah
336	Om vindhyachalanivasinyai namah
337	Om vidhatryai namah
338	Om vedajananyai namah
339	Om visnumayayai namah

340	Om vilasinyai namah
341	Om ksetrashvarupayai namah
342	Om ksetresyai namah
343	Om ksetraksetrajnapalinyai namah
344	Om ksayavrddhivinirmuktayai namah
345	Om ksetrapalasamarchitayai namah
346	Om vijayayai namah
347	Omvimalayai namah
348	Om vandyayai namah
349	Om vandarujanavatsalayai namah
350	Om vagvadinyai namah
351	Om vamakesyai namah
352	Om vahnimandalavasinyai namah
353	Om bhaktimatkalpalatikayai namah
354	Om pashupasavimochinyai namah
355	Om samhrtasesapasandayai namah
356	Om sadacharapravartikayai namah
357	Om tapatrayagnishantaptasamahladanachandrikayai namah
358	Om tarunyai namah
359	Om tapasaradhyayai namah
360	Om tanumadhyayai namah
361	Om tamopahayai namah
362	Om chityai namah
363	Om tatpadalaksyarthayai namah
364	Om chidekarasarupinyai namah
365	Om svatmanandalavibhuta-brahmadyanandasantatyai namah
366	Om parayai namah
367	Ompratyak chitirupayai namah

368	Om pasyantyai namah
369	Om paradevatayai namah
370	Om madhyamayai namah
371	Om vaikharirupayai namah
372	Om bhaktamanasahamsikayai namah
373	Om kamesvaraprananadyai namah
374	Om krtajnayai namah
375	Om kamapujitayai namah
376	Om shringararasasampurnayai namah
377	Om jayayai namah
378	Om jalandharasthitayai namah
379	Om odyanapithanilayayai namah
380	Om bindumandalavasinyai namah
381	Om rahoyagakramaradhyayai namah
382	Om rahastarpanatarpitayai namah
383	Om sadyah prasadinyai namah
384	Om visvasaksinyai namah
385	Om sakshivarjitayai namah
386	Om sadangadevatayuktayai namah
387	Om sadgunyaparipuritayai namah
388	Om nityaklinnayai namah
389	Omnirupamayai namah
390	Om nirvanashukhadayinyai namah
391	Om nityasodasikarupayai namah
392	Om srikanthardhasaririnyai namah
393	Om prabhavatyai namah
394	Om prabharupayai namah
395	Om prasiddhayai namah
396	Om paramesvaryai namah
397	Om mulaprakrtyai namah

398	Om avyaktayai namah
399	Om vktavyaktashvarupinyai namah
400	Om vyapinyai namah
401	Om vividhakarayai namah
402	Om vidyavidyashvarupinyai namah
403	Om mahakamesanayanakumudahladakaumudyai namah
404	Om bhaktahardatamobhedabhanumadbhanusantatyai namah
405	Om shivadutyai namah
406	Om shivaradhyayai namah
407	Om shivamurtyai namah
408	Om shivankaryai namah
409	Omshivapriyayai namah
410	Om shivaparayai namah
411	Om sistestayai namah
412	Om sistapujitayai namah
413	Om aprameyayai namah
414	Om svaprakasayai namah
415	Om manovachamagocharayai namah
416	Om chichchaktyai namah
417	Om chetanarupayai namah
418	Om jadasaktyai namah
419	Om jadatmikayai namah
420	Om gayatryai namah
421	Om vyahrtyai namah
422	Om sandhyayai namah
423	Om dvijavrndanishevitayai namah
424	Om tattvasanayai namah

425	Om tasmai namah
426	Om tubhyam namah
427	Om ayyai namah
428	Om panchakosantarasthitayai namah
429	Om nihsimamahimne namah
430	Om nityayauvanayai namah
431	Om madasalinyai namah
432	Om madaghurnitaraktaksyai namah
433	Om madapatalagandabhuve namah
434	Om chandanadravadigdhangyai namah
435	Om champeyakushumapriyayai namah
436	Om kusalayai namah
437	Om komalakarayai namah
438	Om kurukullayai namah
439	Om kulesvaryai namah
440	Om kulakundalayayai namah
441	Om kaulamargatatparasevitayai namah
442	Om kumaragananathambayai namah
443	Om tustyai namah
444	Om pustyai namah
445	Om matyai namah
446	Om dhrtyai namah
447	Om santyai namah
448	Om svastimatyai namah
449	Om kantyai namah
450	Om nandinyai namah
451	Om vighnanasinyai namah

452	Om tejovatyai namah
453	Omtrinayanayai namah
454	Om lolaksikamarupinyai namah
455	Om malinyai namah
456	Om hamsinyai namah
457	Om matre namah
458	Om malayachalavasinyai namah
459	Om sumukhyai namah
460	Om nalinyai namah
461	Om shubhruve namah
462	Om shobhanayai namah
463	Om shuranayikayai namah
464	Om kalakanthyai namah
465	Om kantimatyai namah
466	Om ksobhinyai namah
467	Om sukshmarupinyai namah
468	Om vajresvaryai namah
469	Om vamadevyai namah
470	Om vayovasthavivarjitayai namah
471	Om siddhesvaryai namah
472	Om siddhavidyayai namah
473	Om siddhamatre namah
474	Om yashashvinyai namah
475	Om vishuddhichakranilayayai namah
476	Om araktavarnayai namah
477	Om trilochanayai namah
478	Om khatvangadipraharanayai namah

479	Om vadanaikasamanvitayai namah
480	Om payasannapriyayai namah
481	Om tvaksthayai namah
482	Om pashulokabhayankaryai namah
483	Om amritadimahashaktisamvrtayai namah
484	Om dakinishvaryai namah
485	Om anahatabjanilayayai namah
486	Om syamabhayai namah
487	Om vadanadvayayai namah
488	Om damstrojvalayai namah
489	Om aksamaladidharayai namah
490	Om rudhirasamsthitayai namah
491	Om kalaratryadisaktyaughavrtayai namah
492	Om snigdhaudanapriyayai namah
493	Om mahavirendravaradayai namah
494	Om rakinyambashvarupinyai namah
495	Om manipurabjanilayayai namah
496	Omvadanatrayasamyutayai namah
497	Om vajradhikayudhopetayai namah
498	Om damaryadibhiravrtayai namah
499	Om raktavarnayai namah
500	Om mamsanishthayai namah
501	Om gudannapritamanasayai namah
502	Om samastabhaktashukhadayai namah
503	Om lakinyambashvarupinyai namah
504	Om svadhistanambujagatayai namah
505	Om chaturvaktramanoharayai namah

506	Om shuladyayudhasampannayai namah
507	Om pitavarnayai namah
508	Om atigarvitayai namah
509	Om medonishthayai namah
510	Om madhupritayai namah
511	Om bandinyadisamanvitayai namah
512	Om dadhyannasaktahrdayayai namah
513	Om kakinirupadharinyai namah
514	Om muladharambujarudhayai namah
515	Om panchavaktrayai namah
516	Om asthisamsthitayai namah
517	Om ankusadipraharanayai namah
518	Om varadadi nishevitayai namah
519	Om mudgaudanasaktachittayai namah
520	Om sakinyambashvarupinyai namah
521	Om ajnachakrabjanilayai namah
522	Om shuklavarnayai namah
523	Om sadananayai namah
524	Om majjasamsthayai namah
525	Om hamsavatimukhyashaktisamanvitayai namah
526	Om haridrannaikarasikayai namah
527	Om hakinirupadharinyai namah
528	Om sahasradalapadmasthayai namah
529	Om sarvavarnopasobhitayai namah
530	Om sarvayudhadharayai namah
531	Om shuklasamsthitayai namah
532	Om sarvatomukhyai namah

533	Om sarvaudanapritachittayai namah
534	Om yakinyambashvarupinyai namah
535	Om svahayai namah
536	Om svadhayai namah
537	Om amatyai namah
538	Om medhayai namah
539	Om shrutyai namah
540	Om smrityai namah
541	Om anuttamayai namah
542	Om punyakirtyai namah
543	Om punyalabhyayai namah
544	Om punyasravanakirtanayai namah
545	Om pulomajarchitayai namah
546	Om bandhamochanyai namah
547	Om barbaralakayai namah
548	Om vimarsarupinyai namah
549	Om vidyayai namah
550	Om viyadadijagatprashuve namah
551	Om sarva vyadhiprasamanyai namah
552	Om sarva mrityunivarinyai namah
553	Om agraganyayai namah
554	Om achintyarupayai namah
555	Om kalikalmasanasinyai namah
556	Om katyayanyai namah
557	Om kalahantryai namah
558	Om kamalaksanishevitayai namah
559	Om tambulapuritamukhyai namah

560	Om dadimikushumaprabhayai namah
561	Om mrigaksyai namah
562	Om mohinyai namah
563	Om mukhyayai namah
564	Om mridanyai namah
565	Om mitrarupinyai namah
566	Om nityatrptayai namah
567	Om bhaktanidhaye namah
568	Om niyantryai namah
569	Om nikhilesvaryai namah
570	Om maitryadivasanalabhyayai namah
571	Om mahapralayasaksinyai namah
572	Om parasaktyai namah
573	Om paranishthayai namah
574	Om prajnanaghanarupinyai namah
575	Om madhvipanalasayai namah
576	Om mattayai namah
577	Om matrkavarna rupinyai namah
578	Om mahakailasanilayayai namah
579	Om mrinalamridudorlatayai namah
580	Om mahaniyayai namah
581	Om dayamurtyai namah
582	Om mahasamriajyasalinyai namah
583	Om atmavidyayai namah
584	Om mahavidyayai namah
585	Om Sri Vidyayai namah
586	Om kamasevitayai namah

587	Om srishodasaksarividyayai namah
588	Om trikutayai namah
589	Om kamakotikayai namah
590	Om kataksakinkaribhutakamalakotisevitayai namah
591	Om sirahsthitayai namah
592	Om chandranibhayai namah
593	Om bhalasthayai ai namah
594	Om indradhanuhprabhayai namah
595	Om hrdayasthayai namah
596	Om raviprakhyayai namah
597	Om trikonantaradipikayai namah
598	Om daksayanyai namah
599	Om daityahantryai namah
600	Om daksayajnavinasinyai namah
601	Om darandolitadirghaksyai namah
602	Om darahasojjvalanmukhyai namah
603	Om gurumurtyai namah
604	Omgunanidhaye namah
605	Om gomatre namah
606	Om guhajanmabhuve namah
607	Om devesyai namah
608	Om dandanitisthayai namah
609	Om daharakasarupinyai namah
610	Om pratipanmukhyarakantatithimandalapujitayai namah
611	Om kalatmikayai namah
612	Om kalanathayai namah
613	Om kavyalapavimodinyai namah

614	Om sachamararamavanishavyadaksinasevitayai namah
615	Om adisaktayai namah
616	Om ameyayai namah
617	Om atmane namah
618	Om paramayai namah
619	Om pavanakrtaye namah
620	Om anekakotibrahmandajananyai namah
621	Om divyavigrahayai namah
622	Om klinkaryai namah
623	Om kevalayai namah
624	Om guhyayai namah
625	Om kaivalyapadadadayinyai namah
626	Om tripurayai namah
627	Om trijagadvandyayai namah
628	Om trimurtyai namah
629	Om tridasesvaryai namah
630	Om tryaksaryai namah
631	Om divyagandhadhyayai namah
632	Om sinduratilakanchitayai namah
633	Om umayai namah
634	Om sailendratanayayai namah
635	Om gauryai namah
636	Om gandharvasevitayai namah
637	Om vishvagarbhayai namah
638	Om svarnagarbhayai namah
639	Om avaradayai namah
640	Om vagadhisvaryai namah

641	Om dhyanagamyayai namah
642	Om aparichchedyayai namah
643	Om jnanadayai namah
644	Om jnanavigrahayai namah
645	Om sarvavedantasamvedyayai namah
646	Om satyanandashvarupinyai namah
647	Om lopamudrarchitayai namah
648	Om lilaklriptabrahmandamandalayai namah
649	Om adrishyayai namah
650	Om drishyarahitayai namah
651	Om vijnatryai namah
652	Om vedyavarjitayai namah
653	Om yoginyai namah
654	Om yogadayai namah
655	Om yogyayai namah
656	Om yoganandayai namah
657	Om yugandharayai namah
658	Om ichchashaktijnanashaktikriyashaktisvarupinyai namah
659	Om sarvadharayai namah
660	Om supratisthayai namah
661	Om sadasadrupadharinyai namah
662	Om astamurtyai namah
663	Om ajajaitryai namah
664	Om lokayatravidhayinyai namah
665	Om ekakinyai namah
666	Ombhumarupayai namah
667	Om nidvaitayai namah

668	Om dvaitavarjitayai namah
669	Om annadayai namah
670	Om vashudayai namah
671	Om vriddhayai namah
672	Om brahmatmaikyashvarupinyai namah
673	Om brhatyai namah
674	Om brahmanyai namah
675	Om brahmayai namah
676	Om brahmanandayai namah
677	Om balipriyayai namah
678	Om bhasarupayai namah
679	Om brhatsenayai namah
680	Om bhavabhavavirjitayai namah
681	Om shukharadhyayai namah
682	Om shubhakaryai namah
683	Om sobhanashulabhagatyai namah
684	Om rajarajesvaryai namah
685	Om rajyadayinyai namah
686	Om rajyavallabhayai namah
687	Om rajatkrpayai namah
688	Omriajapithanivesitanijasritayai namah
689	Om rajyalaksmyai namah
690	Om kosanathayai namah
691	Om chaturangabalesvaryai namah
692	Om samriajyadayinyai namah
693	Om satyasandhayai namah
694	Om sagaramekhalayai namah

695	Om diksitayai namah
696	Om daityasamanyai namah
697	Om sarvalokavamsakaryai namah
698	Om sarvarthadatryai namah
699	Om savitryai namah
700	Om sachchidanandarupinyai namah
701	Om desakalaparichchinnayai namah
702	Om sarvagayai namah
703	Om sarvamohinyai namah
704	Om sarasvatyai namah
705	Om shastramayyai namah
706	Om guhambayai namah
707	Om guhyarupinyai namah
708	Om sarvopadhivinirmuktayai namah
709	Om sadashivapativratayai namah
710	Om sampradayesvaryai namah
711	Om sadhune namah
712	Om yai namah
713	Om gurumandalarupinyai namah
714	Om kulottirnayai namah
715	Om bhagaradhyayai namah
716	Om mayayai namah
717	Om madhumatyai namah
718	Om mahyai namah
719	Om ganambayai namah
720	Om guhyakaradhyayai namah
721	Om komalangyai namah

722	Om gurupriyayai namah
723	Om svatantrayai namah
724	Om sarvatantresyai namah
725	Om daksinamurtirupinyai namah
726	Om sanakadisamaradhyayai namah
727	Om shivajnanapradayinyai namah
728	Om chitkalayai namah
729	Om anandakalikayai namah
730	Om premarupayai namah
731	Om priyankaryai namah
732	Om namaparayanapritayai namah
733	Om nandividyayai namah
734	Om natesvaryai namah
735	Om mithyajagadadhisthanayai namah
736	Om muktidayai namah
737	Om muktirupinyai namah
738	Om lasyapriyayai namah
739	Om layakaryai namah
740	Om lajjayai namah
741	Om rambhadivanditayai namah
742	Om bhavadavashudhavrstyai namah
743	Om paparanyadavanalayai namah
744	Om daurbhagyatulavatulayai namah
745	Om jaradhvantaraviprabhayai namah
746	Om bhagyabdhichandrikayai namah
747	Om bhaktachittakekighanaghanayai namah
748	Om rogaparvatadambholaye namah

749	Om mrityudarukutharikayai namah
750	Om mahesvaryai namah
751	Om mahakalyai namah
752	Om mahagrasayai namah
753	Om mahasanayai namah
754	Om aparnayai namah
755	Om chandikayai namah
756	Om chandamundashuranishhudinyai namah
757	Om ksharaksaratmikayai namah
758	Om sarvalokesyai namah
759	Om visvhadharinyai namah
760	Om trivargadatryai namah
761	Om shubhagayai namah
762	Om tryambakayai namah
763	Om trigunatmikayai namah
764	Om svargapavargadayai namah
765	Om shuddhayai namah
766	Om japapuspanibhakrtaye namah
767	Om ojovatyai namah
768	Om dyutidharayai namah
769	Om yajnarupayai namah
770	Om priyavratayai namah
771	Om duraradhyayai namah
772	Om duradharsayai namah
773	Om patalikushumapriyayai namah
774	Om mahatyai namah
775	Om merunilayayai namah

776	Om mandarakushumapriyayai namah
777	Omviraradhyayai namah
778	Om viradrupayai namah
779	Om virajase namah
780	Om vishvatmukhyai namah
781	Om pratyagrupayai namah
782	Om parakasayai namah
783	Om pranadayai namah
784	Om pranarupinyai namah
785	Om martandabhairavaradhyayai namah
786	Om mantrininyastarajyadhure namah
787	Om tripuresyai namah
788	Om jayatsenayai namah
789	Om nishtraigunyayai namah
790	Om paraparayai namah
791	Om satyajnananandarupayai namah
792	Om samarasyaparayanayai namah
793	Om kapardinyai namah
794	Om kalamalayai namah
795	Om kamadughe namah
796	Om kamarupinyai namah
797	Om kalanidhaye namah
798	Om kavyakalayai namah
799	Om rasajnayai namah
800	Om rasasevadhaye namah
801	Om pustayai namah
802	Om puratanayai namah

803	Om pujyayai namah
804	Om puskarayai namah
805	Om puskareksanayai namah
806	Om parasmaijyotishe namah
807	Om parasmai dhamne namah
808	Om paramanave namah
809	Om paratparayai namah
810	Om pashahastayai namah
811	Om pashahantryai namah
812	Om paramantravibhedinyai namah
813	Om murtayai namah
814	Om amurtayai namah
815	Om anityatrptayai namah
816	Om munimanasahamsikayai namah
817	Om satyavratayai namah
818	Om satyarupayai namah
819	Om sarvantaryaminyai namah
820	Om satyai namah
821	Om brahmanyai namah
822	Om brahmane namah
823	Om jananyai namah
824	Om bahurupayai namah
825	Om budharchitayai namah
826	Om prasavitryai namah
827	Om prachandayai namah
828	Om ajnayai namah
829	Om pratisthayai namah

830	Om prakatakrtaye namah
831	Om pranesvaryai namah
832	Om pranadatryai namah
833	Om panchasatpitharupinyai namah
834	Om visrrnkhalayai namah
835	Om viviktasthayai namah
836	Om viramatre namah
837	Om viyatprashuve namah
838	Om mukundayai namah
839	Om muktinilayayai namah
840	Om mulavigraharupinyai namah
841	Om bhavajnayai namah
842	Om bhavarogadhnyai namah
843	Om bhavachakrapravartinyai namah
844	Om chandahsarayai namah
845	Om sastrasarayai namah
846	Om mantrasarayai namah
847	Om talodaryai namah
848	Om udarakirtaye namah
849	Om uddamavaibhavayai namah
850	Om varnarupinyai namah
851	Om janmamrityujarataptajanavishrantidayinyai namah
852	Om sarvopanishadudghustayai namah
853	Om santyatitakalatmikayai namah
854	Om gambhirayai namah
855	Om gaganantahsthayai namah
856	Om garvitayai namah

857	Om ganalolupayai namah
858	Om kalpanarahitayai namah
859	Om kasthayai namah
860	Om akantayai namah
861	Om kantardhavigrahayai namah
862	Om karyakarananirmuktayai namah
863	Om kamakelitarangitayai namah
864	Om kanatkanakatatankayai namah
865	Om lilavigrahadharinyai namah
866	Om ajayai namah
867	Om ksayavinirmuktayai namah
868	Om mugdhayai namah
869	Om ksipraprasadinyai namah
870	Om antarmukhasamaradhyayai namah
871	Om bahirmukhashudurlabhayai namah
872	Om trayyai namah
873	Om trivarganilayayai namah
874	Om tristhayai namah
875	Om tripuramalinyai namah
876	Om niramayayai namah
877	Om niralambayai namah
878	Om svatmaramayai namah
879	Om shudhasrtyai namah
880	Om samsarapankanirmagnasamuddharanapanditayai namah
881	Om yajnapriyayai namah
882	Om yajnakartryai namah
883	Om yajamanashvarupinyai namah

884	Om dharmadharayai namah
885	Omdhanadhyaksayai namah
886	Om dhanadhanyavivardhinyai namah
887	Om viprapriyayai namah
888	Om viprarupayai namah
889	Om visvabhramanakarinyai namah
890	Om visvagrasayai namah
891	Om vidrumabhayai namah
892	Om vaisnavyai namah
893	Om visnurupinyai namah
894	Om ayonyai namah var ayonaye
895	Om yoninilayayai namah
896	Om kutasthayai namah
897	Om kularupinyai namah
898	Om viragosthipriyayai namah
899	Om virayai namah
900	Om naiskarmyayai namah
901	Om nadarupinyai namah
902	Om vijnanakalanayai namah
903	Om kalyayai namah
904	Om vidagdhayai namah
905	Om baindavasanayai namah
906	Om tatvadhikayai namah
907	Omtatvamayyai namah
908	Om tatvamarthashvarupinyai namah
909	Om samaganapriyayai namah
910	Om saumyayai namah

911	Om sadashivakutumbinyai namah
912	Om savyapasavyamargasthayai namah
913	Om sarvapadvinivarinyai namah
914	Om svasthayai namah
915	Om svabhavamadhurayai namah
916	Om dhirayai namah
917	Om dhirasamarchitayai namah
918	Om chaitanyarghyasamaradhyayai namah
919	Om chaitanyakushumapriyayai namah
920	Om sadoditayai namah
921	Om sadatusthayai namah
922	Om tarunadityapatalayai namah
923	Om daksinadaksinaradhyayai namah
924	Om darasmeramukhambujayai namah
925	Om kaulinikevalayai namah
926	Om anardhyakaivalyapadadayinyai namah
927	Om stotrapriyayai namah
928	Om stutimatyai namah
929	Omsrutisamstutavaibhavayai namah
930	Om manashvinyai namah
931	Om manavatyai namah
932	Om mahesyai namah
933	Om mangalakrtye namah
934	Om visvamatre namah
935	Om jagaddhatryai namah
936	Om visalaksyai namah
937	Om viraginyai namah

938	Om pragalbhayai namah
939	Om paramodarayai namah
940	Om paramodayai namah
941	Om manOmayyai namah
942	Om vyOmakesyai namah
943	Om vimanasthayai namah
944	Om vajrinyai namah
945	Om vamakesvaryai namah
946	Om panchayajnapriyayai namah
947	Om panchapretamanchadhisayinyai namah
948	Om panchamyai namah
949	Om panchabhutesyai namah
950	Om panchasankhyopacharinyai namah
951	Omsashvatyai namah
952	Om sashvataisvaryayai namah
953	Om sarmadayai namah
954	Om sambhumohinyai namah
955	Om dharayai namah
956	Om dharashutayai namah
957	Om dhanyayai namah
958	Om dharminyai namah
959	Om dharmavardhinyai namah
960	Om lokatitayai namah
961	Om gunatitayai namah
962	Om sarvatitayai namah
963	Om samatmikayai namah
964	Om bandhukakushumaprakhyayai namah

965	Om balayai namah
966	Om lilavinodinyai namah
967	Om shumangalyai namah
968	Om shukhakaryai namah
969	Om shuvesadhyayai namah
970	Om shuvasinyai namah
971	Om shuvasinyarchanapritayai namah
972	Om asobhanayai namah
973	Omshuddhamanasayai nama
974	Om bindutarpanasantustayai namah
975	Om purvajayai namah
976	Om tripurambikayai namah
977	Om dasamudrasamaradhyayai namah
978	Om tripurasrivasankaryai namah
979	Om jnanamudrayai namah
980	Om jnanagamyayai namah
981	Om jnanajneyashvarupinyai namah
982	Om yonimudrayai namah
983	Om trikhandesyai namah
984	Om trigunayai namah
985	Om ambayai namah
986	Om trikonagayai namah
987	Om anaghayai namah
988	Om adbhutacharitrayai namah
989	Om vanchitarthapradayinyai namah
990	Om abhyasatisayajnatayai namah
991	Om sadadhvatitarupinyai namah

992	Om avyajakarunamurtaye namah
993	Om ajnanadhvantadipikayai namah
994	Om abalagopaviditayai namah
995	Om sarvanullanghyasasanayai namah
996	Om srichakrarajanilayayai namah
997	Om srimattripurashundaryai namah
998	Om srishivayai namah
999	Om shivasaktyaikyarupinyai namah
1000	Om sri Lalitambikaye namah

Shrim hrim aim Om

Om tatsat brahmarpanamastu Iti Srilalitasahasranamavali sampoornam

References

1. Lalita Sahasranama with Bhaskararaya's Commentary – Bhaskararaya, Translated by R. Ananthakrishna Sastry
2. Lalita Sahasranama: A Comprehensive Manual Based on Saubhagya Bhaskara – Swami Tapasyananda
3. Lalita Sahasranama: Text, Commentary and Interpretations – Swami Vimalananda
4. Lalita Trishati and Lalita Sahasranama – Swami Sivananda
5. Lalita Sahasranama: The Thousand Names of the Divine Mother – Dr. R. Ananthakrishna Sastry
6. The Thousand Names of the Divine Mother – John Woodroffe (Arthur Avalon)
7. Lalita Sahasranama: The Sacred Thousand Names of Lalita – V. K. Subramanian
8. Sri Vidya: The Ancient Doctrine of the Great Goddess – Vidya Dehejia
9. Kundalini: An Untold Story – Om Swami
10. Tantra: The Path of Ecstasy – Georg Feuerstein
11. Sri Vidya: The Ancient Doctrine of the Great Goddess – Vidya Dehejia
12. The Greatness of Saturn: A Therapeutic Myth – Robert E. Svoboda (Contains insights into the Sri Vidya tradition)
13. Sri Chakra: The Supreme Yantra – Dr. R. K. Mishra
14. Shakti: The World Mother – Arthur Avalon (John Woodroffe)
15. The Secret of Sri Vidya: Insights into the Life and Teachings of Sri Vidyaranya – S. N. Sastri
16. The Ten Great Cosmic Powers: Dasa Mahavidyas – S. Shankaranarayanan
17. Sri Chakra Yantra: Sacred Geometry and Its Symbolism – K. V. Sharma
18. The Garland of Letters – Arthur Avalon (John Woodroffe)
19. Essence of Srividya – Swami Satyasangananda Saraswati

20. Tripura Rahasya: The Secret of the Supreme Goddess – Swami Sri Ramana Maharshi (translated by Swami Nityananda)

21. Sri Lalita Sahasranamam– N. Ramamurthy

22. Sri Lalita Sahasranama Stotram – an insight – Swami Shantananda Puri

23. The Serpent Power: The Secrets of Tantric and Shaktic Yoga – Arthur Avalon (John Woodroffe)

24. The Goddess in India: The Five Faces of the Eternal Feminine – Devdutt Pattanaik

25. Meditation and Mantras – Swami Vishnu-devananda

26. Yantra: The Tantric Symbol of Cosmic Unity – Madhu Khanna

27. Saundarya Lahari: The Ocean of Beauty – Swami Tapasyananda

28. Sri Vidya Tantra – Dr. Rajmani Tigunait

29. Tantric Visions of the Divine Feminine: The Ten Mahavidyas – David R. Kinsley

30. Kundalini Vidya: The Science of Spiritual Transformation – Joan Shivarpita Harrigan

31. The Yoga of the Nine Emotions – Peter Marchand

32. Sri Chakra: The Hidden Truth – L. R. Chawdhri

33. The Serpent Power: The Secrets of Tantric and Shaktic Yoga – Arthur Avalon (John Woodroffe)

34. Tantra: The Path of Ecstasy – Georg Feuerstein

35. Introduction to Tantra: The Transformation of Desire – Lama Thubten Yeshe

36. The Garland of Letters – Arthur Avalon (John Woodroffe)

37. Kundalini: The Arousal of the Inner Energy – Ajit Mookerjee

38. Tantric Visions of the Divine Feminine: The Ten Mahavidyas – David R. Kinsley

39. Shakti and Shakta – Arthur Avalon (John Woodroffe)

40. The Complete Guide to the Tantras – Swami Satyananda Saraswati

41. Tantra: Sex, Secrecy, Politics, and Power in the Study of Religion – Hugh B. Urban

42. Tantric Yoga and the Wisdom Goddesses: Spiritual Secrets of Ayurveda – David Frawley

43. The Hindu Tantric World: An Overview – N. N. Bhattacharyya

44. Tantra Illuminated: The Philosophy, History, and Practice of a Timeless Tradition – Christopher D. Wallis

45. Kali's Child: The Mystical and the Erotic in the Life and Teachings of Ramakrishna – Jeffrey J. Kripal

46. Sacred Sexuality in Ancient India – Alain Daniélou

47. The Power of Tantra: Religion, Sexuality, and the Politics of South Asian Studies – Hugh B. Urban

48. The Essence of Tantra – Swami Sivananda

49. The Roots of Tantra – Edited by Katherine Anne Harper and Robert L. Brown

50. Tantra in Practice – Edited by David Gordon White

51. The Tantric Mysticism of Tibet: A Practical Guide to the Theory, Purpose, and Techniques of Tantric Meditation – John Blofeld

52. Vijnanabhairava or Divine Consciousness: A Treasury of 112 Types of Yoga – Swami Lakshman Joo

53. Tantra Illuminated: The Philosophy, History, and Practice of a Timeless Tradition – Christopher D. Wallis

54. The Garland of Letters – Arthur Avalon (John Woodroffe)

55. Kularnava Tantra – Translated by Sir John Woodroffe

56. The Doctrine of Vibration: An Analysis of the Doctrines and Practices of Kashmiri Shaivism – Mark S. G. Dyczkowski

57. The Heart of the Yogini: The Yoginihrdaya, a Sanskrit Tantric Text – André Padoux

58. Tantric Visions of the Divine Feminine: The Ten Mahavidyas – David R. Kinsley

59. Mantra Yoga and Primal Sound: Secrets of Seed (Bija) Mantras – David Frawley

60. Meditation and Mantras – Swami Vishnu-devananda

61. Mantras: Words of Power – Swami Sivananda Radha

62. The Healing Power of Mantras – Thomas Ashley-Farrand

63. The Heart of Mantra: Inner Secrets of Gayatri Mantra – Shri Anandi Ma and Dileepji Pathak

64. Mantra: Sacred Words of Power – Alanna Kaivalya

65. Japa Yoga: A Comprehensive Treatise on Mantra-Sastra – Swami Sivananda

66. The Science of Mantra Meditation – Om Swami

67. Mantra Meditation: Change Your Karma with the Power of Sacred Sound – Thomas Ashley-Farrand

68. The Book of Mantras: Sacred Words of Power – Stephen Knapp

69. Mantra: The Ancient Power of Sound – Jonathan Goldman

70. The Practice of Nada Yoga: Meditation on the Inner Sacred Sound – Baird Hersey

71. The Shakti Mantras: Tapping into the Great Goddess Energy Within – Thomas Ashley-Farrand

72. The Mantra Handbook: How to Use Sacred Sound – Lillian Too

73. Chanting the Names of Ma: Mantra Meditation in Shambhala, the Tibetan Tradition – Eva Wong

74. Sacred Symbols of the Sri Chakra – Swami Satyasangananda Saraswati

75. The Shambala Guide to Tantra: Transformations of Desire – Harish Johari

76. Sri Chakra Yantra: Sacred Geometry and Its Symbolism – K. V. Sharma

77. Tools for Tantra – Harish Johari

78. Yantra: The Power of Mystical Diagrams – R. Venugopalan

79. The Power of Tantra Meditation: 50 Meditations for Energy, Awareness, and Connection – Hugh B. Urban

80. Yantras: Tattva and Mantra – Swami Niranjanananda Saraswati

81. The Tantric Mysticism of Tibet: A Practical Guide to the Theory, Purpose, and Techniques of Tantric Meditation – John Blofeld

82. Sri Chakra: The Hidden Truth – L. R. Chawdhri

83. Sacred Geometry: Philosophy and Practice – Robert Lawlor

84. Charles Mackenzie: The Devī Gītā: The Song of the Goddess

85. Shankarnarayanan. S: The Ten Great Cosmic Powers: Dasa Mahavidyas

86. Daniélou, Alain:The Myths and Gods of India: The Classic Work on Hindu Polytheism

87. Kinsley, David R: Hindu Goddesses: Vision of the Divine Feminine in the Hindu Religious Tradition

88. J. Gordon Melton; Baumann, Martin: Religions of the World: A Comprehensive Encyclopedia of Beliefs and Practices

89. Sri Amritananda Natha Saraswati's works

90. Dr David Frawley: Tantric Yoga and the Wisdom Goddesses

91. Dr Sonja Lyubomirsky: Gratitude is Best Attitude (Mindforest)

92. P.R. Krishna Kumar: The Sri Chakra as a symbol of the human body

93. Lalithananda Lalita Prasad Jammulamadaka: Sri Vidya and Sri Chakra

94. Bernhard Wimmer: Sri Yantra

95. Sri Yantra Research Centre
96. Gerard Huet: Sri Yantra
97. Gaia: How to harness the power of Sri Yantra
98. Davidji: How to meditate with Sri Yantra
99. Madhu Khanna: Yantra, the tantric symbol of cosmic unity
100. Rohit Arya: Symbolism of the Sri Yantra
101. Dhyana Foundation: Sri Yantra
102. Sreenivasa Rao's blogs: Sri Chakra
103. Prof. S.K. Ramachandra Rao: The Tantra of Sri Chakra Bhavanopanishad
104. Subhash Kak: The great goddess Lalitha and the Sri Chakra
105. Sri Sivapremanandaji – Sri Vidya Sadhana
106. International Journal of Geology, Agriculture and Environmental Sciences, Vol 5 Issue 2
107. Swami Satyanand Saraswati: The Fantastic Science of Yantra
108. Devadatta Kali (Vedanta Society of California): The Mahavidyas
109. Avalon Arthur: Shakti and Shakta
110. S. Sankaranarayanan: Ten Great Cosmic Powers
111. Sri Amrita Ananda: Sri Devi Khadgamala
112. V Ravi: Understanding and Worshipping Sri Chakra
113. Hindupedia
114. Mircea Eliade: The Sacred and the Profane: The Nature of Religion: The Significance of Religious Myth, Symbolism, and Ritual within Life and Culture
115. Antonotea Gotea: Hridaya Yoga
116. From Britannica on topic of Karma
117. Maya Tiwari: The Path of Practice: A Woman's Book of Ayurvedic Healing
118. Dr. David Frawley: Yoga & Ayurveda, Self-Healing and Self-Realization
119. Judith Anodea: Wheels of Life
120. Judith Anodea: Eastern Body, Western Mind: Psychology and the Chakra System As a Path to the Self
121. Caroline Myss: Anatomy of the Spirit: The Seven Stages of Power and Healing
122. Tiffany Luptak: The Chakras: Inner Portals to Harmony
123. Felise Bermen: Swadhisthana the Second Chakra, one's own abode
124. Tantric Master Shri Aghorinath Ji: A Tantric Masters View of Tantra.

125. Michael M Bowden: Gifts from the Goddess: Selected Works of Sri Amritananda Natha Saraswathi
126. Dr. Shashi Tharoor: The Hindu Way: An Introduction to Hinduism

Also by this Author

Sri Chakra Yantra

Manifest anything with the symbol of everything

Discover how a 12,000-year-old mystical symbol holds the key to awakening your deepest inner potential and enhancing your powers of manifestation.

The Sri Chakra Yantra is an ancient symbol depicting the process of creation in a powerful matrix which represents the macrocosm (the Universe) and microcosm (the human body), thus acting as a powerful, cosmic antenna that allows you direct access to communicate with the Universe.

The book delves into some metaphysical aspects which are reflected in the philosophies underlying Shaktism, Tantra, Dasa Mahavidya and Sri Vidya. Once these concepts throw some light on the basis of Sri Chakra worship, the nature of sacred geometry and the significance, structure and meaning of the Sri Chakra Yantra is explained. This is followed by chapters that focus on the relationship of the human body to the Sri Chakra and its connection with the Pineal Gland. There is also a brief note on healing and the Sri Chakra.

The use of sounds in the path to spiritual growth is discussed with a special focus on the sounds (mantras and stotras) associated with the Sri Chakra Yantra. The book describes the role of mudras and contains details about the initial infusion of energy into the yantra, the method of worship, the path to visualisation and meditation on the Sri Chakra.

Chakras

Learn all about the Chakras – mystical energy centres that are integral to the ancient Indian traditions of Yoga and Ayurveda. The Chakras are inner portals of harmony, linking the physical and spiritual planes, offering a deep and time-tested formula for transformation, abundance and the ability to hack into one's power of manifestation.

This book equips you using simple, everyday language to harness the potential of the tremendous internal energy pools that lie dormant in the body and help you channel it and act upon your life purpose by presenting Chakras as a tool for self-development. The book delves into concepts such as Sankhya, Yoga philosophies and the Karma doctrine in order to establish the context of how the Chakra energies work.

The author has kept in mind the sensibilities of the modern spiritual seeker and their needs and interests, presenting the information in a non-dogmatic and practical manner, thereby allowing everyone an opportunity to learn and experience the benefits of awakening the Chakra energies.

Tantra Mantra and Yantra of Sri Vidya

"Sri Vidya begins where the current understanding of quantum physics ends", say modern-day scholars about this little-known, highly esoteric spiritual tradition that has been carefully kept under wraps by its secretive and serious practitioners. The study of Sri Vidya is fascinating as much as it is frustrating because information about its various aspects is tough to find. This book is an endeavour to explore the Sri Vidya tradition and understand it as the unfolding of Shakti, the inherent power which lies at the core of our being and holds the key to our worldly and spiritual success.

Sri Vidya practice comprises tantra (a technique or framework for worship) whose two main elements are mantra (sacred sound) and yantra (sacred geometry). Tantra can be described in simple terms as the utilisation of the mental faculty to pursue the objectives of worship using mantra and yantra. Mantra is the use of sound energy to bring about oneness with the Divine, while yantra is a geometric drawing which serves as a tool to reach the Divine.

The book delves into concepts such as Sankhya, Yoga, Karma and Kundalini in order to establish the context of how Sri Vidya is to be approached, combining elements of knowledge, devotion and ritual.

The author has kept in mind the sensibilities of the modern spiritual seeker and their needs and interests, presenting the information in a non-dogmatic and practical manner, thereby allowing everyone an opportunity to learn and experience the benefits of Sri Vidya.

This is the third book by the author in the Spirituality Series. The first book was about the Sri Chakra Yantra and the second book had Chakras as its subject.

The Sacred Sounds of Sri Vidya

We find the term "anavritti shabdat" in the Vedanta Sutra. This concept can be understood as utilising the power of sound to attain liberation. Mantras, potent sound forms passed on from generations, not only have the power to evoke positivity but can transform the reality of our perception by bringing about a heightened state of awareness. The Sri Vidya tradition is rich in mantras dedicated to defining the glory of Shakti. This book is an endeavour to explore the main mantras used in the Sri Vidya tradition and understand them as the unfolding of Shakti, the inherent power which lies at the core of our being and holds the key to our worldly and spiritual success.

"Sri Vidya begins where the current understanding of quantum physics ends", say modern-day scholars about this little known, highly esoteric spiritual tradition that has been carefully kept under wraps by its practitioners. Sri Vidya practise is a three-fold one, encompassing mantra (sacred sound), yantra (sacred geometry) and tantra (a technique or framework for worship). Learning about the mantras used in the Sri Vidya tradition is fascinating as it spans an array of techniques, texts and philosophical concepts.

Our minds and beliefs can be our strongest allies or our worst enemies. The book delves into concepts such as the importance of building the right narrative about life and the need for ritual in modern-day lifestyle. Samskara, vritti and vasana are described along with a detailed study of tantra and Sri Vidya before a discussion on mantras in general and then focussing on the mantras used in the Sri Vidya tradition. The subjects covered seek to establish the context of mantra sadhana in Sri Vidya is to be approached, combining elements of knowledge, devotion and ritual.

Dasa Mahavidya: The Ten Great Tantric Wisdom Goddesses

In the mystical realms of the ancient Tantra tradition, a hidden path beckons, veiled in unparalleled mystery and brimming with extraordinary power—the path of the Dasa Mahavidya, the Ten Great Tantric Wisdom Goddesses.

The book plunges into the sacred depths of the Dasa Mahavidya, as the wisdom of ages past fuses seamlessly with contemporary insight. Each chapter unveils magnificent tales, revealing the extraordinary essence of a different goddess. Witness the awe-inspiring might of Kali, the relentless destroyer of illusions, as she wields her cosmic blade to sever the bonds of ignorance. Encounter Lalita Tripurasundari, the enchantress supreme, whose grace can manifest unimaginable miracles. And bask in the benevolence of Kamalatmika, the radiant bestower of abundance and prosperity, whose tender touch can transform lives.

Guided by the hallowed whispers of ancient sages and the ethereal echoes of age-old tantric rituals, immerse in the profound teachings that stir dormant energies, unleashing the boundless power of divine feminine energy. It unveils the secrets of tantra, mantra, and yantra of these ten goddesses—the sacred triad that unlocks the portals to transcendent realms.

This book takes you on an expedition through dimensions where darkness and light engage in a mesmerizing dance, where the very limits of human perception crumble like sandcastles, and where the sovereignty of divine femininity reigns supreme. In the hallowed domains of tantric wisdom, the goddesses stand ready to anoint the path with their benevolent blessings, illuminating the path with their divine radiance.